# HOW TO BUILD BRICK AIRPLANES

## DETAILED LEGO® DESIGNS FOR JETS, BOMBERS, AND WARBIRDS

### PETER BLACKERT

motorbooks

Brimming with creative inspiration, how-to projects, and useful information to enrich your everyday life, Quarto Knows is a favourite destination for those pursuing their interests and passions. Visit our site and dig deeper with our books into your area of interest: Quarto Creates, Quarto Cooks, Quarto Homes, Quarto Lives, Quarto Drives, Quarto Explores, Quarto Gifts, or Quarto Kids.

First published in 2018 by Motorbooks, an imprint of The Quarto Group, 401 Second Avenue North, Suite 310, Minneapolis, MN 55401 USA.
T (612) 344-8100 F (612) 344-8692  www.QuartoKnows.com

Motorbooks titles are also available at discount for retail, wholesale, promotional, and bulk purchase. For details, contact the Special Sales Manager by email at specialsales@quarto.com or by mail at The Quarto Group, Attn: Special Sales Manager, 401 Second Avenue North, Suite 310, Minneapolis, MN 55401 USA.

10 9 8 7 6 5 4 3 2 1

ISBN: 978-0-7603-6164-1

Digital edition published in 2018
eISBN: 978-0-7603-6165-8

Library of Congress Cataloging-in-Publication Data
Names: Blackert, Peter, 1972- author.
Title: How to build brick airplanes : detailed LEGO designs for jets, bombers, and warbirds / Peter Blackert.
Description: Minneapolis, MN : Motorbooks, an imprint of The Quarto Group, 2018. | Includes index.
Identifiers: LCCN 2018013337 | ISBN 9780760361641 (hc)
Subjects: LCSH: Airplanes--Models. | Jet planes--Models. | Airplanes, Military--Models. | Bombers--Models. | LEGO toys. | Models and modelmaking. | CYAC: Airplanes. | Jet planes. | Airplanes, Military. | Bombers. | LEGO toys. | Models and modelmaking.
Classification: LCC TL770 .B534 2018 | DDC 629.133/134--dc23
LC record available at https://lccn.loc.gov/2018013337

Acquiring Editor: Jordan Wiklund
Project Manager: Alyssa Lochner
Art Director: James Kegley
Layout: Kim Winscher

Printed in China

# ACKNOWLEDGMENTS

Thanks again to the editorial team at Motorbooks for inviting me to produce a second LEGO® instruction book, this time building aircraft. Thanks to my publisher, Zack Miller, my editor, Jordan Wiklund—I hope you get to build more than just the Spitfire—and project manager Alyssa Lochner. A special thanks to James Kegley for wrangling all the artwork, the thousands of images throughout this book.

Thanks to the Ford Motor Company allowing me to share the love of engineering and vehicle design with a wider audience, and for their support of STEM mentoring through LEGO.

Thanks to the team at 'The Big Brick' for making the brick prints come together.

Thanks to my family: my wife, Jeana, and my children E, L, and M, for supporting me during the book creation process. And young Miles. Now that you are a bit bigger you've had the opportunity to build some of the models instead of them being off-limits.

# CONTENTS

# PREFACE

In my first book, *How To Build Brick Cars*, I had the opportunity to share my love of the subject (cars) and my passion for constructing models of them in the medium of LEGO®. I confess that I don't design real aircraft—that is a field generally reserved for those who have studied aeronautical engineering. They tend to be clever folks, dealing in magic as much as in science (not really—but it can feel that way).

Aircraft are nonetheless fascinating, and they marry two dreams: how mankind can make machines, and how to fly as a bird. The magic comes in the marriage of the two, as engineers grappled with their industrial-revolution-age machines and how to get them in the air. There were, for instance, no flying steam locomotives, though the concept of a flying machine drawn in 1850 might have adopted the principle.

Before we ever created a machine, we dreamed of flying. It is a common dream we have as children, along with invisibility and more wishes. Though most flight now occurs in sealed airliners, early aviators (and those who like to hang-glide) probably had the closest experience to that of birds in flight. Exhilarating and risky!

Looking at birds from a structural point of view reveals the ingredients for powered flight. In the hollow bones of birds we see the construction required to give strength and lightness. The shape of birds helps us understand low aerodynamic drag. In birds of prey, we see a serrated trailing edge of their wings and tail—the principles that guide us to some of the stealth technologies. Though they look unusual compared to the aircraft that have gone before, the B-2 Stealth Bomber and the Boeing X-32 prototypes are planes that do not have vertical stabilisers, like birds, but use different mechanisms for controlling the flow of air across the surface of the aircraft for manoeuvring.

I have produced this book in the hope that I can open the window into how machines can be made that can fly. Aircraft are amazing machines, and aeronautics presents itself as one distinct field of engineering and the wider STEM career pathway, one that may be of interest to pursue for younger readers of this book.

The great thing about a second book is that you can fix most of things that needed improving from the first one. Thanks to the team at Motorbooks, we have worked to make improvements to the book, notably in regards to the parts information for the models, which are now in tables, and have clearer images. Some other feedback from the first book that bears repeating here: start at the beginning of the book and work up to the Intermediate and Advanced models. The book is necessarily condensed to encompass this much material, and even experienced builders will find some of the models presented to be extremely challenging.

Something we have tried to add realism to the models is brick printing—the aircraft insignia and nameplates for aircraft stands. Thanks to the team at The Big Brick, we are able to provide this service to those who want to build the aircraft with the printed parts (see Resources on page 190).

I hope that you enjoy building the models in this book, and use them as a basis to try some aircraft design of your own.

Regards,
Peter

# WHY BUILD BRICK PLANES?

B rick airplanes: perhaps someone will make one eventually, but house bricks do not make a good building material for aircraft. The bricks here are LEGO®, though, and the models—though notionally adhering to the design principles of flight—do not fly.

*How to Build Brick Airplanes* is about creating models of a selection of real aircraft covering more than one hundred years of flight. The earliest plane, the Sopwith Camel, began service in 1917 and was one of the earliest fighting aircraft in WWI. One hundred years later, the Lockheed-Martin F-35B can fly at nearly twice the speed of sound, use stealth technology to approach its target without detection, slow to a hover, and even just about manage a vertical take-off.

The aircraft in this book cover key periods during a century of technological development and achievement. It is perhaps unfortunate that our greatest achievements in flight are often driven by conflict—a need for competitive advantage, born of adversity. The SR-71 Blackbird, the fastest plane ever built, capable of flying close to the edge of space, never dropped a bomb. Instead, it was used as a weapon of intelligence, able to fly to any location on earth, equipped with cameras, to spy on the enemy, safe in the knowledge that it could out-speed any missile.

LEGO bricks provide the medium of creation here. The simple models use fewer than 100 parts; the Lockheed P-38 Lightning in the final chapter uses over 2,000. The larger the model, the finer the fidelity of model-making. This is true of all models. A simple model describes simply the principle; the more complex the model, the more detail it reveals. The B-2 Spirit and all models in the Intermediate and Advanced Sections have moving aerodynamic "control surfaces;" these are also built using modular techniques that represent the assemblies used in real aircraft and describe their function. The Lockheed P-38 Lightning adds LEGO Technic® piston engines and gear-driven undercarriage to display still greater detail.

In *How to Build Brick Airplanes*, the model-making skills applied to aircraft are just an offshoot of the wider STEM toolkit used by engineers to do their job every day. In my work as an automotive engineer for the Ford Motor Company, I used mathematics, mechanics, structures, materials engineering, and importantly, problem solving to create motor vehicles. I have the opportunity as part of Ford's commitment to STEM education in schools to lead LEGO Robotics programs, in which this STEM toolkit is shared with young people who may one day follow a career in these areas. *How to Build Brick Airplanes* is my opportunity to share my interests in the fields of aeronautical engineering and LEGO model creation with a much wider audience.

# HOW TO USE THIS BOOK

Designing LEGO® cars and aircraft is a skill set that has taken me a great many years of building to master. In writing this book on aircraft, I have expanded some of the design techniques seen in *How to Build Brick Cars*, though the instructional methodology follows the same principles through detailed instructions. The book provides material to aid builders, new or experienced alike, with design techniques and solutions that they can use to create their own model aircraft.

A new builder may find some of the advanced designs beyond their Lego parts collection, building experience, or comfort zone. It is strongly recommended to start in the Miniplanes section before moving on to the Intermediate and Advanced designs.

For the experienced builder, I hope that the less complex models are nonetheless a rewarding building exercise at a smaller scale, and that the more complex models reveal an advanced world of model building, one that more closely reflects the challenges and rewards of designing and engineering real aircraft for the real world.

| Build Introduction | Symbol/Nomenclature/ Technique | | What does it mean? What should I do? |
|---|---|---|---|
| Fokker DR.1 | **1** | **29** | The large bold numbers for the instructions start at 1 and number progressively. This helps keep track of the stage that the build is in overall and provides some guidance to the next instruction step when alternative designs can be chosen. |
| Fokker DR.1 | **1** | **4** | The small numbers in the colored box fields show the step level when creating an assembly. An assembly is a collection of parts that create a cohesive structure prior to being joined to the main model. |
| Fokker DR.1 | ↻ | | This symbol indicates that the assembly or model should be rotated to aid the next step, or to see what it looks like from the reverse side. |
| Sopwith Camel | 2× | | A number followed by × indicates that the builder should create that number of common assemblies. |
| Fokker DR.1 | **5** LHS | | This symbol indicates that the following assembly steps show how to build the left-hand side (LHS) of the model. It also indicates that this assembly stage should also be built in a reflected right hand side assembly. **It is recommended to assemble the LHS and RHS assemblies at the same time as mirrors of each other.** |
| Fokker DR.1 | → | | Arrows indicate the position for smaller assemblies to be placed on the main model, where this might be difficult to see clearly. |

The building instructions introduce various symbols and nomenclature progressively through the chapters, allowing for the instruction sets to be condensed in the available pages whilst still maintaining clarity. The following symbols and typography are there to aid the builder in selecting the correct parts at each building stage, preparing intermediate assemblies, and connecting to the base model architecture.

**A note on parts and part numbers.** There are two appendices at the back of this book. The Build Components appendix (page 164) includes a list of parts needed for each plane. These are indicated with part numbers and color numbers. The part number is used in LEGO Digital Designer (LDD) and other software. It is also the part number that you will need to use to order parts from LEGO or a third-party seller (such as Bricklink). The color numbers are used by LEGO to identify specific colors. For example, red is color 21. (There has been a change to the tone on both light and dark grey. To improve part cost and availability, please feel free to use the new and old tones interchangeably.) The second appendix, the Parts Index (page 185), is a visual guide to all the parts used in the book, in part-number order.

| Chapter Introduction | Symbol/Nomenclature/ Technique | What does it mean? What should I do? |
|---|---|---|
| Supermarine Spitfire | LHS + RHS | Mostly used in conjunction with the mirror symbol, this indicates that the assembly includes additional steps, or is the final assembly, for the right-hand or left-hand side only. |
| Albatros D.Va | | This symbol, which is also used in the parts list, indicates the length (in standard bricks) of the LEGO Technic axle to be used at this assembly stage. |
| Supermarine Spitfire | | Many of the plane models have brick-built windows. The instructions to build these can be quite confusing. To aid the process, the parts to be added at each instruction stage are colored pale yellow. |
| SR-71 Blackbird | A | The use of [A] and [B] symbols indicates that a choice of designs can be considered. The [A] or [B] logo will sit in the corner of the finished assembly, and guide the following assembly instructions. |
| Albatros D.Va | 6 | This number, i.e. [6], indicates that the main instruction stage 6 is the assembly that should be attached at the position indicated by the arrow. |

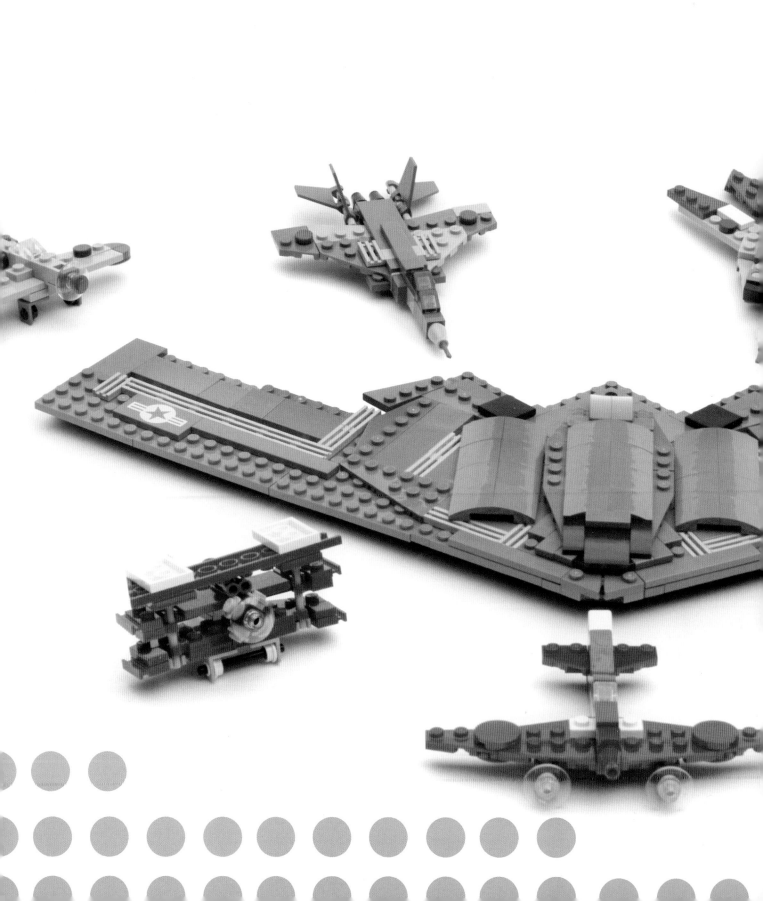

# MINIPLANES

We begin with Miniplanes. Not planes that carry only one person (or none), but models built in a very small scale. All the planes in this section are modelled from 1:90 (Fokker DR.1) through to 1:125 (P-51 Mustang). This scale means it is not possible to include a LEGO® minifig in the aircraft, but they are a good scale to sit on a shelf or be mounted on a stand.

The image at left shows the vast size of the B-2 Spirit bomber—it is close in scale to the other planes present, though the two WWI planes would be even smaller if they were at identical scale! The B-2 is a very challenging build, however, and has as many parts as the models in the Intermediate section.

This chapter follows chronological order, in part to support the increasing size and complexity of the models, but in checking the specification tables, you will also see the rapid development of power and speed between 1914 and 1974. The aircraft are iconic models of their era, but are also typical for their time. The difference between failure and success was often found in small details.

# FOKKER DR.1

scale: 1:90

The Fokker Dr.I derives its name from the German *Dreidecker*, which means "triplane." The aircraft has three wings, stacked vertically. Although seen in a multitude of colors and decorations—a common occurrence in German aircraft in the *Luftstreitkräfte* during World War I—the model shown here is decorated in the colors of Germany's most famous pilot, Baron Manfred von Richthofen—the Red Baron! The Fokker Dr.I was the aircraft in which he achieved his last nineteen victories and in which he was killed on April 21, 1918.

Biplanes and triplanes were common in World War I due to the fledgling nature of aeronautical engineering. The long wings common today were not robust enough to handle the forces seen in flight, so two (or more) wings were a safer option. Nonetheless, aircraft lost their wings all too often, frequently killing their pilots.

Early aircraft also deployed a variety of interesting engines. The Fokker Dr.I used an Oberursel rotary engine with 9 cylinders. Rotary and radial engines are similar in configuration, but rotary engines spin the entire engine array around during operation. The Fokker Dr.I had a mere 110 horsepower (82 kW), allowing a maximum speed of 115 miles per hour (185 km/h).

**COUNTRY OF ORIGIN:** German Empire

**PRODUCTION:** 1918

**RETIRED:** 1918

**NUMBER MADE:** 329

**LENGTH/WINGSPAN:** 18' 11" (5.77 m) / 23' 7" (7.19 m)

**LOADED MASS:** 1,291 lb. (586 kg)

**POWERPLANT:** 1 × Oberursel Ur.II 9-cylinder rotary engine

**THRUST:** 110 hp (82 kW)

**MAXIMUM SPEED:** 115 mph (185 km/h)

**COMBAT RADIUS:** 185 miles (298 km)

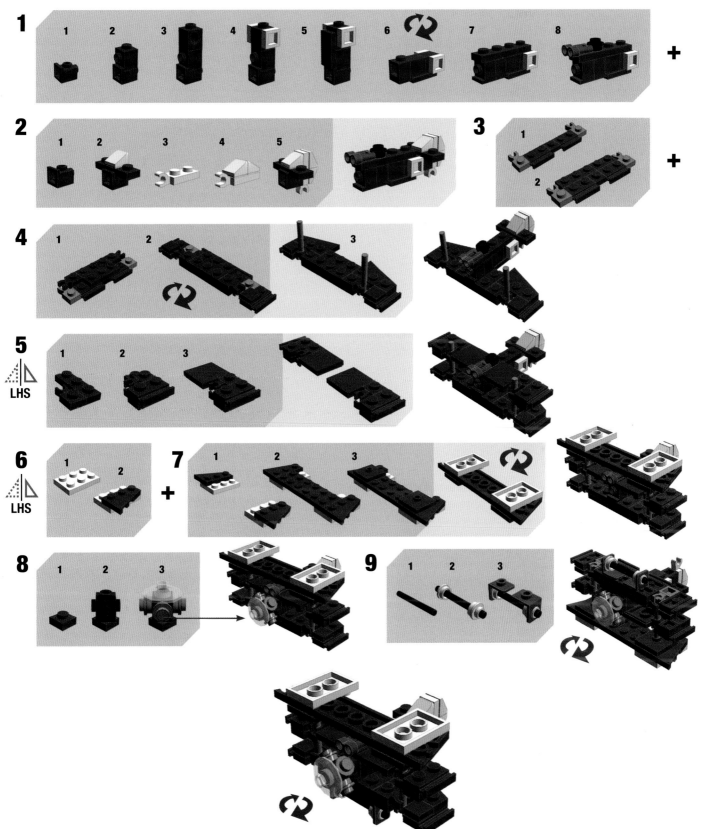

11

SOPWITH AVIATION COMPANY
# SOPWITH CAMEL

scale: 1:105

The Sopwith Camel was one of the most iconic aircraft of World War I. A staggering 5,490 were built and operated by the Allied forces during the last year and a half of the war.

The Sopwith Camel was a biplane design with two sets of wings, one above the other. The Camel's construction was typical for the period: a wooden box-section fuselage (body) with plywood paneling around the pilot for protection, aluminum engine coverings, and fabric coverings for the wings, fuselage, and tail. Minimizing weight was a key goal in the design of early aircraft, and the Camel weighed 930 pounds (420 kg) empty.

Wanted! Skinny pilots only!

The Sopwith was powered by a variety of different engines, mostly the Clerget 9B or the Bentley BR1, both 9-cylinder rotary engines. Various versions had between 110 and 150 horsepower. The engine made up nearly 40 percent of the empty weight of the aircraft.

The Sopwith Camel was known to be a difficult aircraft to fly, but it was extremely maneuverable (desirable in air-to-air combat) due to its tightly packaged engine, fuel tank, and pilot. This reduced the aircraft polar moments (an engineering term referring to the distance of mass from the central rotation point), a key goal in designing fighter aircraft even today.

**COUNTRY OF ORIGIN:** United Kingdom

**PRODUCTION:** 1917–1920

**RETIRED:** 1920

**NUMBER MADE:** 5,490

**LENGTH/WINGSPAN:** 18' 9" (5.72 m) / 28' (8.53 m)

**LOADED MASS:** 1,453 lb. (659 kg)

**POWERPLANT:** 1 × Clerget 9B 9-cylinder rotary engine

**THRUST:** 130 hp (97 kW)

**MAXIMUM SPEED:** 113 mph (182 km/h)

**COMBAT RADIUS:** 150 miles (242 km)

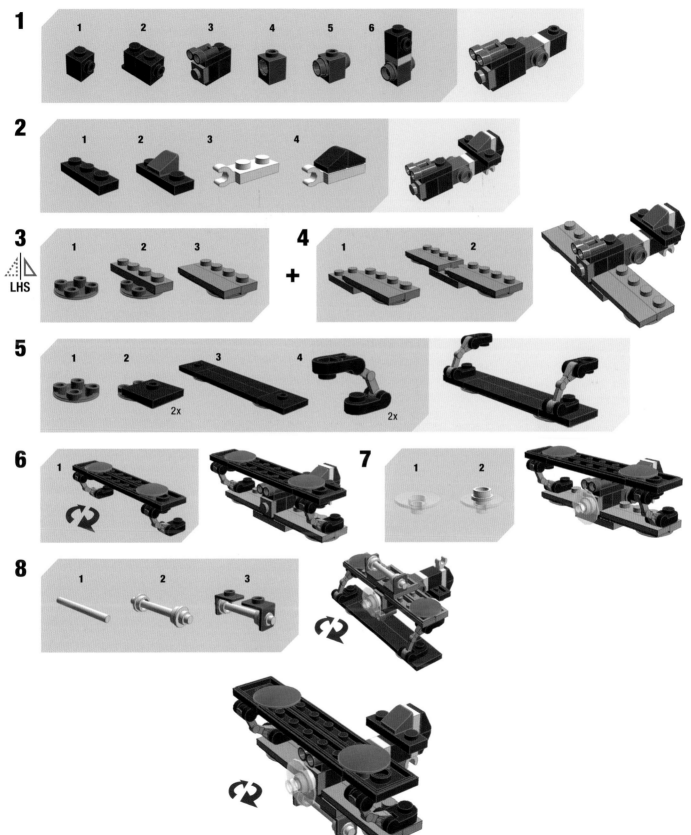

# De HAVILLAND
# DH.88 COMET

scale: 1:110

A mere five de Havilland DH.88 Comets were ever built. Its inclusion here is due to the staggering number of aviation records achieved by the aircraft during its operational history.

Its most famous achievement was the MacRobertson race—"The Great Air Race"—a long-distance multistage journey from the Mildenhall in the United Kingdom to Melbourne, Australia. The race was scheduled for October 1934.

At the time, the United States had taken a lead in aviation, but Geoffrey de Havilland, a British aviation pioneer and founder of the de Havilland aircraft manufacturing firm, was determined that the race be won by a British aircraft.

To create a high-speed aircraft with good range and fuel capacity, a number of innovations were needed. The DH.88 housed two inverted Gipsy Six engines, one under each wing. The front profile was very small, reducing aerodynamic drag. The front of the fuselage, normally reserved for the engine, was used to increase the fuel tank size. Variable-pitch propellers were used to improve liftoff performance and high-speed cruise performance.

The majority of the aircraft was wood; to handle the wing and engine loads, a nautical engineering technique of wood paneling layup was used. The outer sections of the wing were even lighter, with the ply reduced to 0.07 inches (1.75 mm).

Three DH.88 aircraft were entered in the MacRobertson race: the dark 28 G-ACSR, the G-ACSP *Black Magic*, and the winning aircraft, G-ACSS *Grosvenor House*, the model shown here, which completed the race in 71 hours, 18 seconds.

**COUNTRY OF ORIGIN:** United Kingdom

**PRODUCTION:** 1934–1935

**RETIRED:** 1940

**NUMBER MADE:** 5

**LENGTH/WINGSPAN:** 29' 0" (8.84 m) / 44' 0" (13.41 m)

**LOADED MASS:** 5,550 lb. (2523 kg)

**POWERPLANT:** 2 × de Havilland Gipsy Six R six-cylinder air-cooled inverted inline engine

**THRUST:** 230 hp (172 kW)

**MAXIMUM SPEED:** 237 mph (382 km/h)

**COMBAT RADIUS:** 2,925 miles (4,710 km)

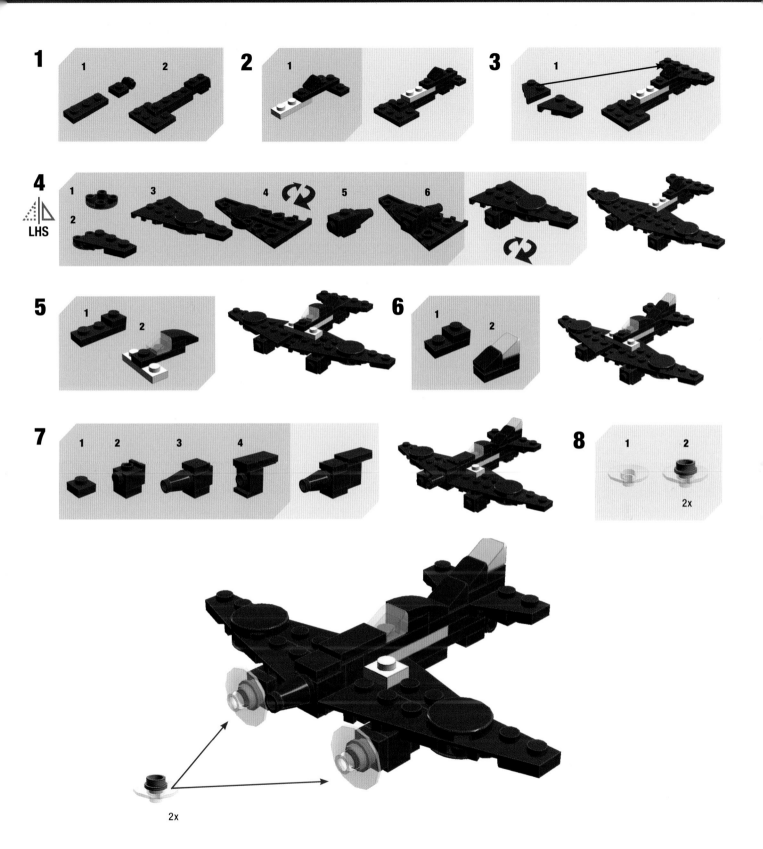

# P-51D MUSTANG

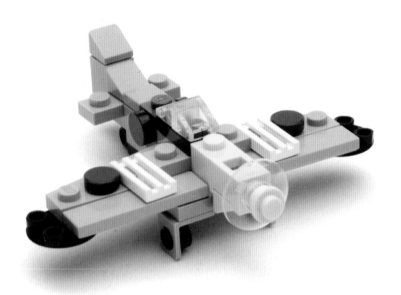

scale: 1:125

**M**USTANG. It was a fitting name for a World War II fighter designed to defend Europe from the advancing German armies and the feared Luftwaffe.

The P-51 Mustang was first developed for the British Royal Air Force, utilizing spare North American production facilities. The Mustang Mk I entered service over France in January 1942.

The original specification used the Allison V-1710 engine, which was also used in the P-38 Lightning. This engine did not perform well at high altitude, so early Mustang action in Europe was confined to ground attack and reconnaissance. An upgrade to the Roll-Royce Merlin V-12 and its US-licensed Packard V-1650-7 version transformed the Mustang into its B/C and D versions, respectively, lifting the game to the advanced Luftwaffe aircraft both figuratively and literally. The Mustang was now able to perform well at altitude and had the range to fly as a bomber escort over Germany.

The P-51 was also used in the Pacific theater in China and, late in the war, as a bomber escort against Japan in 1944.

The two Mustang versions shown here have famous squadron markings. The aircraft with the 21-red tail represents the Tuskegee Airmen, a flying corps of African American airmen known for their bravery. The plane with the yellow nose is the P-51D *Detroit Miss* from the 375th Fighter Squadron. Urban L. Drew flew this plane to great renown in 1944, famously downing six enemy aircraft in a single mission.

| | |
|---|---|
| **COUNTRY OF ORIGIN:** | United States |
| **PRODUCTION:** | 1942 |
| **RETIRED:** | 1984 |
| **NUMBER MADE:** | 15,000+ |
| **LENGTH/WINGSPAN:** | 32' 3" (9.83 m) / 37' 0" (11.28 m) |
| **LOADED MASS:** | 9,200 lb. (4,175 kg) |
| **POWERPLANT:** | 1 × Packard V-1650-7 liquid-cooled V-12 with 2-stage intercooled supercharger |
| **THRUST:** | 1,490 hp (1,111 kW) |
| **MAXIMUM SPEED:** | 440 mph (708 km/h) |
| **COMBAT RADIUS:** | 825 miles (1,377 km) |

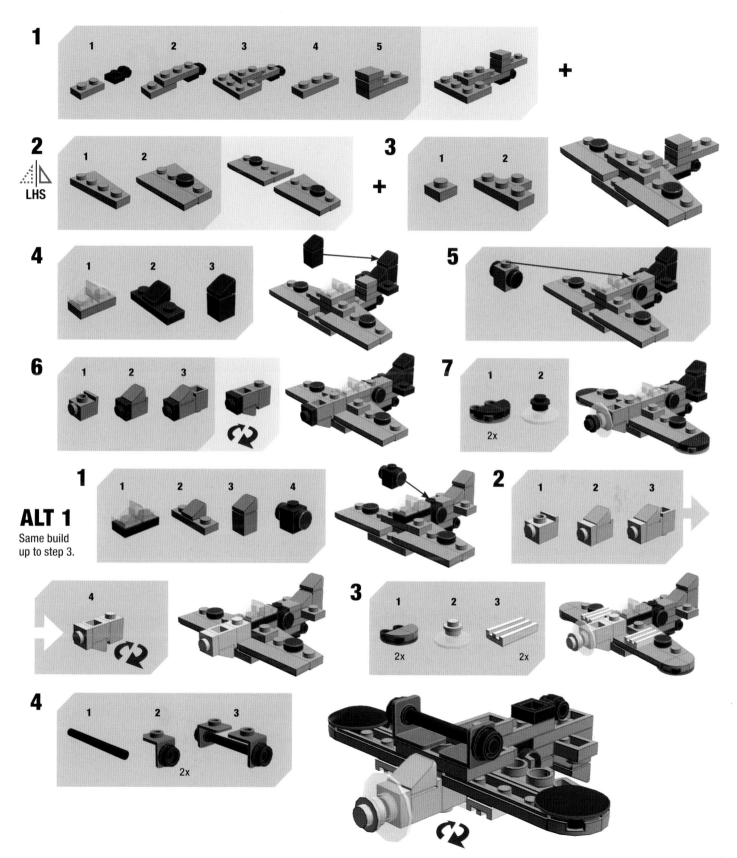

# 1

**1** **2** **3** **4** **5**

+

# 2

LHS

**1** **2**

# 3

**1** **2**

+

# 4

**1** **2** **3**

# 5

# 6

**1** **2** **3**

# 7

**1** **2**

2x

# ALT 1
Same build up to step 3.

**1**

**1** **2** **3** **4**

# 2

**1** **2** **3**

**4**

# 3

**1** **2** **3**

2x 2x

# 4

**1** **2** **3**

2x

## MIKOYAN
# MiG-29

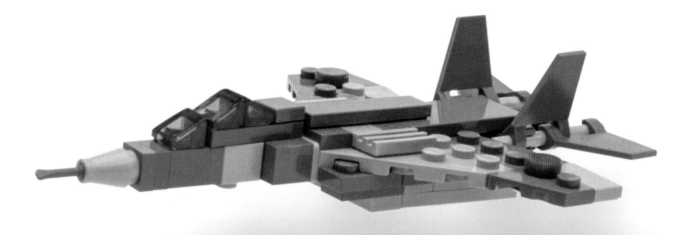

scale: 1:120

The MiG-29 Fulcrum, built by Mikoyan, is a late–Cold War air-superiority jet fighter developed during the 1970s that entered service in 1982. The MiG-29 was developed to counter the new jet fighter aircraft designed for the United States (the F-15 Eagle and F-16 Fighting Falcon) as well as European NATO allies and independent states.

The MiG-29 was a very successful commercial product, and over 1,600 aircraft have been built since its introduction. Many were sold to more than thirty nations, primarily former Eastern Bloc countries, India, and many Russian-allied nations in the Middle East.

Advances in aeronautical engineering and combat aircraft over the past three decades have focused on electronic systems controlling avionics (flight), radar tracking and evasion, and weapons deployment. The MiG-29 has been progressively upgraded in these systems, usually starting with the Soviet and Russian air forces before being sold in later years to customers.

The MiG-29 has a high-speed interceptor capability, achieving Mach 2.25 (2.25 times the speed of sound) at high altitude, dropping to Mach 1.21 at low altitude. The aircraft is powered by two Klimov RD-33 after-burning turbofans (jets) producing 18,342 pounds (81.59 kN) of force each.

The MiG-29 is still in Russian service, though a plan is in place to replace the aircraft with a fifth-generation fighter within the decade.

**COUNTRY OF ORIGIN:** USSR

**PRODUCTION:** 1982

**RETIRED:** In Service

**NUMBER MADE:** 1,600+

**LENGTH/WINGSPAN:** 56' 10" (17.32 m) / 37' 3" (11.36 m)

**LOADED MASS:** 33,370 lb. (14,900 kg)

**POWERPLANT:** 2 × Klimov RD-33 after-burning turbofan

**THRUST:** 18,342 lbf (81.59 kN) each

**MAXIMUM SPEED:** Mach 2.25 (1,490 mph, 2,400 km/h)

**COMBAT RADIUS:** 444 miles (715 km)

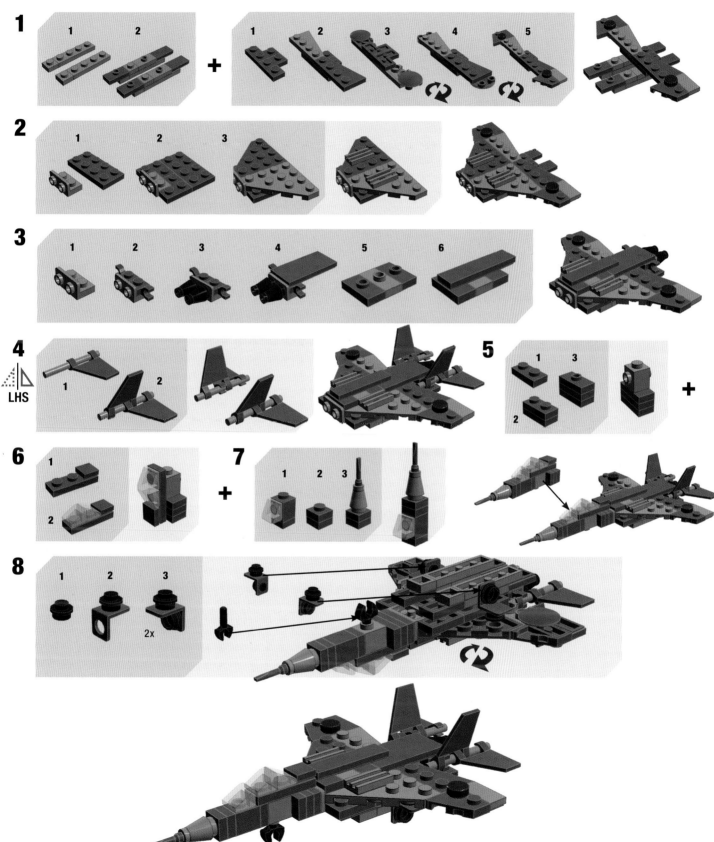

# GRUMMAN
# F-14 TOMCAT

scale: 1:120

The Grumman F-14 Tomcat was introduced in 1974 as the primary naval air-superiority fighter and interceptor, as well as for tactical aerial reconnaissance. The aircraft was developed during the Vietnam War and incorporated many design concepts based on experiences of US aircraft flying against Soviet MiGs during the war.

Naval-based aircraft have been typically designed with unique specifications: two engines (for the sake of reliability), two crew members (one to fly, one to navigate), long range, and the ability to be deployed from aircraft carriers. The F-14's role was to defend naval assets at sea and to project US military strength abroad.

These specifications can be seen in the variable geometry (swing) wings, which allow for enhanced lift at low speed, supersonic flight (Mach 2.4), and a compact footprint when stowed. Though designed primarily for the US Navy, the F-14 was also adept as a ground-attack airframe, a role it played primarily for its sole foreign customer: the Imperial Iranian Air Force. A total of seventy-nine F-14As were delivered to Iran prior to the Revolution. The newly named Islamic Republic of Iran Air Force saw much action during the Iran-Iraq war through the 1980s, though over time, it became more difficult for the country to maintain this fleet. The F-14 is still flown by the Iranian air force.

In the United States, the aircraft was updated and flown until 2006, at which point it was retired and its role passed to F/A-18E/F Super Hornets—a plane designed to similar specifications and layout.

**COUNTRY OF ORIGIN:** United States

**PRODUCTION:** 1974

**RETIRED:** 2006

**NUMBER MADE:** 712

**LENGTH/WINGSPAN:** 62' 9" (19.1 m) / 64' 0" (19.55 m)

**LOADED MASS:** 61,100 lb. (27,700 kg)

**POWERPLANT:** 2 × General Electric F110-GE-400 after-burning turbofans

**THRUST:** 16,610 lbf (73.9 kN) each

**MAXIMUM SPEED:** Mach 2.34 (1,544 mph, 2,486 km/h)

**COMBAT RADIUS:** 575 miles (926 km)

**1**

1 2 3 4 5

6 7 8

**2**

1 2 3 4

5 6

**3**

LHS

1 2 3

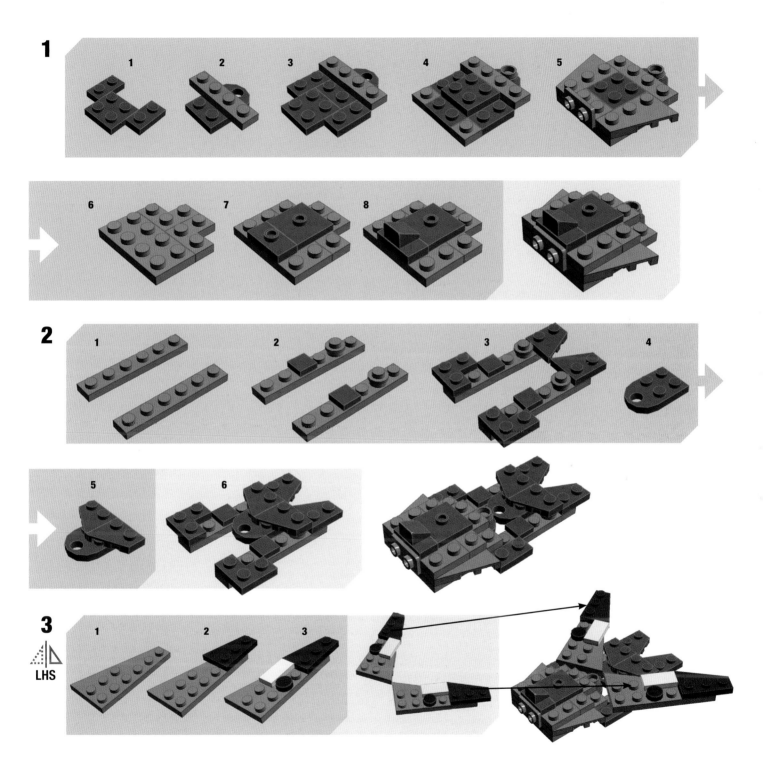

**4**

1  2  3  4  5  6

2x

+

**5**

1  2  3  4  5

4

**6**

LHS

1

2

**7**

1  2

2x

**8**

LHS

1  2  3  4

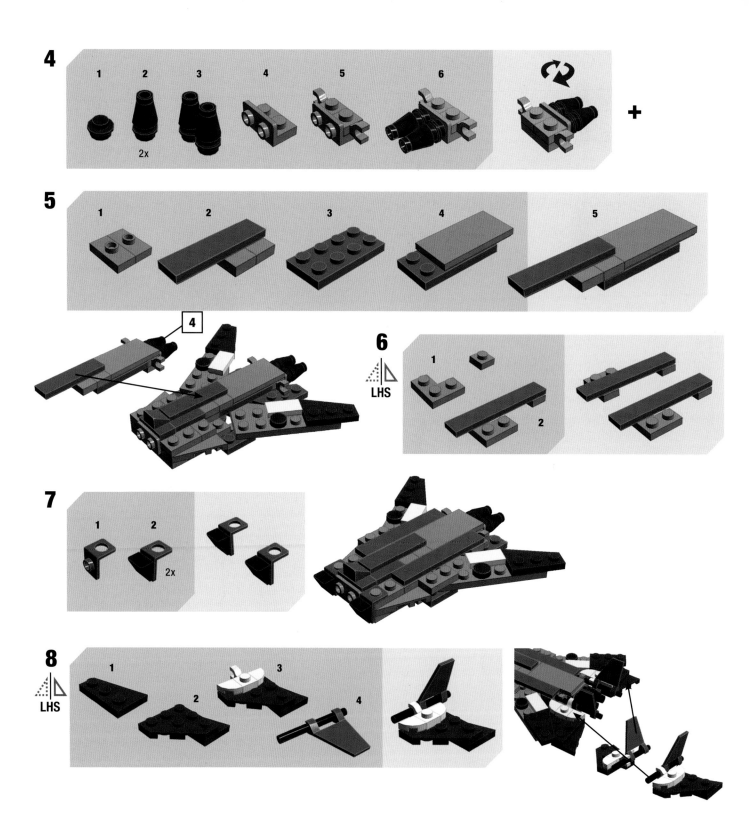

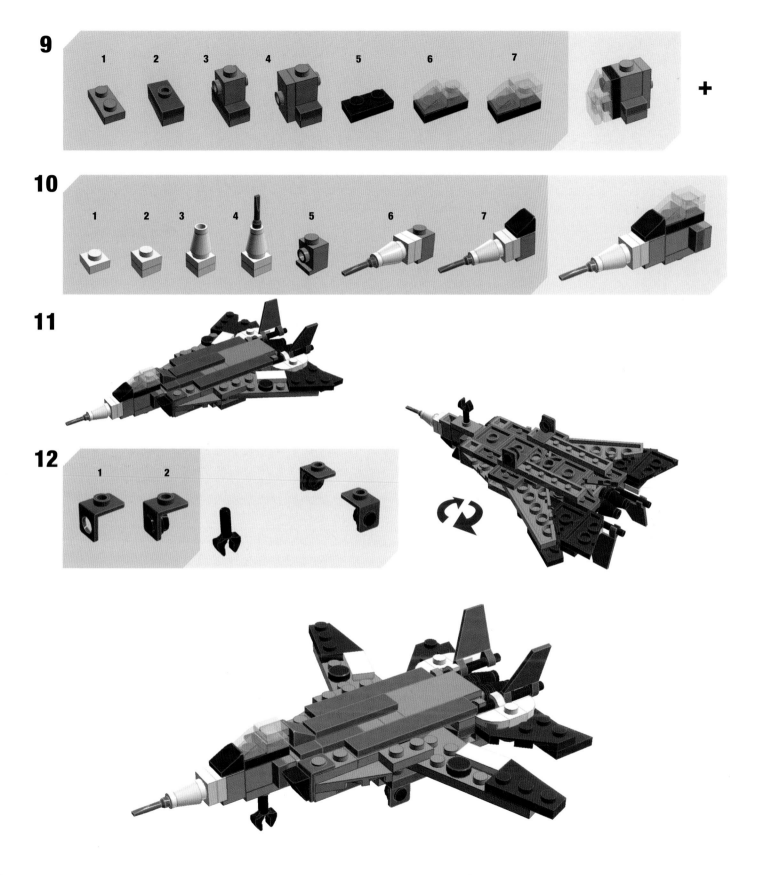

**9**

1 2 3 4 5 6 7 +

**10**

1 2 3 4 5 6 7

**11**

**12**

1 2

# NORTHROP-GRUMMAN
# B-2 SPIRIT

scale: 1:115

Introduced to the US Air Force in 1989 and first deployed in combat using non-nuclear ordinance in the Kosovo War of 1999, the B-2 Spirit stealth bomber saw significant action in the second Iraq War. The original intent of the B-2, however, was as a strategic strike bomber during a large-scale Cold War nuclear conflict.

The B-2 began concept development in the early 1970s under a deep veil of secrecy. Many early proof-of-concept prototypes were operated out of Area 51, and Northrop was selected to carry the project forward in 1981. A design brief change in the mid-1980s saw the aircraft modified from a high-altitude aircraft to a low-altitude, terrain-following one whose design, material, coating, and advanced electronic systems all minimized radar detection by enemy equipment.

Its silhouette disguises how large the plane really is—at 172 feet (52.4 m) across the wings, the B-2 is only slightly narrower than a B-52 bomber. The wing surface appears to be the whole aircraft, as the cabin is little more than a raised bump in the front center. The front edge is a continuous triangular form with a 110-degree included angle. The rear edge of the aircraft has a sawtooth profile with 110-degree voids.

Though the B-2 treads quietly from a radar signature perspective, the aircraft is loud and powerful. Each of the four engines produces 17,300 ft. (77 kN) of force to lift the 336,500-lb. (170,600-kg) maximum-weight aircraft. Despite this power, the non-afterburning engines can only push the B-2 to Mach 0.95 (630 mph/1,010 km/h). The goal of the B-2 is speedy but unobservable penetration, not high-speed intrusion.

| | |
|---|---|
| **COUNTRY OF ORIGIN:** | United States |
| **PRODUCTION:** | 1997 |
| **RETIRED:** | In Service |
| **NUMBER MADE:** | 21 |
| **LENGTH/WINGSPAN:** | 69' 0" (21.0 m) / 172' 0" (52.4 m) |
| **LOADED MASS:** | 336,500 lb. (152,200 kg) |
| **POWERPLANT:** | 4 × General Electric F118-GE-100 non-after-burning turbofans |
| **THRUST:** | 17,300 lbf (77 kN), each |
| **MAXIMUM SPEED:** | Mach 0.95 (630 mph, 1,010 km/h) |
| **COMBAT RADIUS:** | 3,450 miles (5,550 km) |

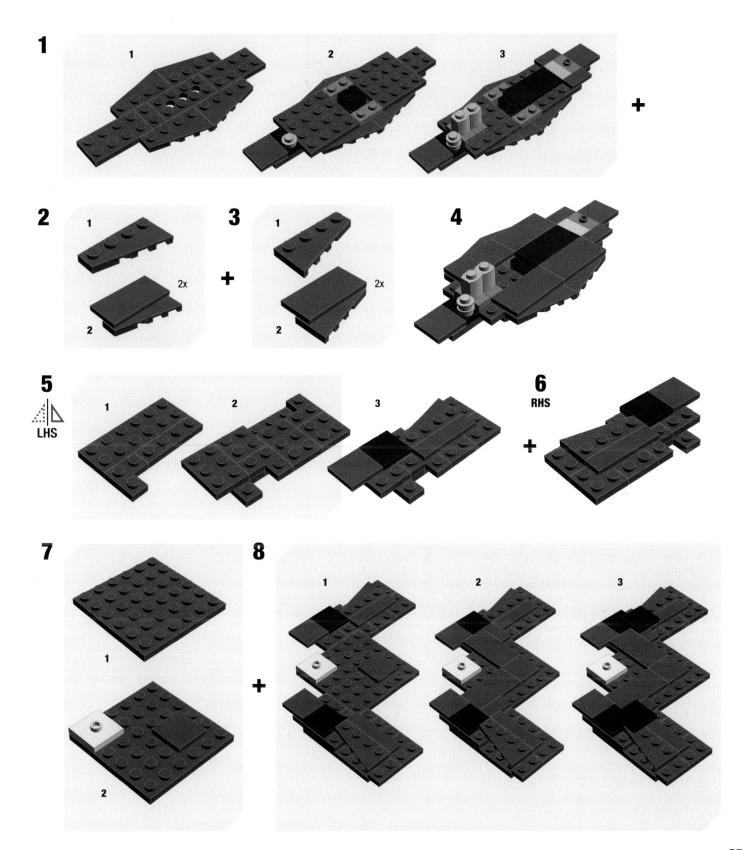

**1**

1    2    3    +

**2**    **3**    **4**

1    1
2x    2x
2    2

**5**    **6**

LHS    RHS

1    2    3    +

**7**    **8**

1    1    2    3

2    +

**9**

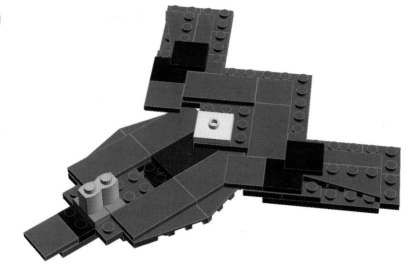

**10**

**11**

**12**

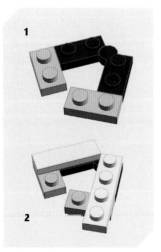

**13**

**14**

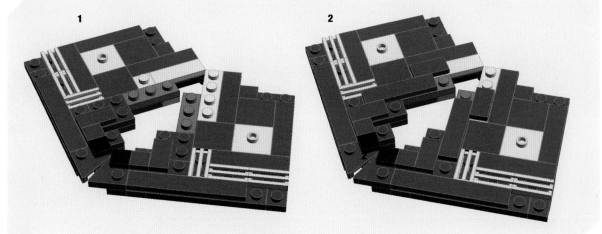

1

2

**15**

4x

**16**

1

2

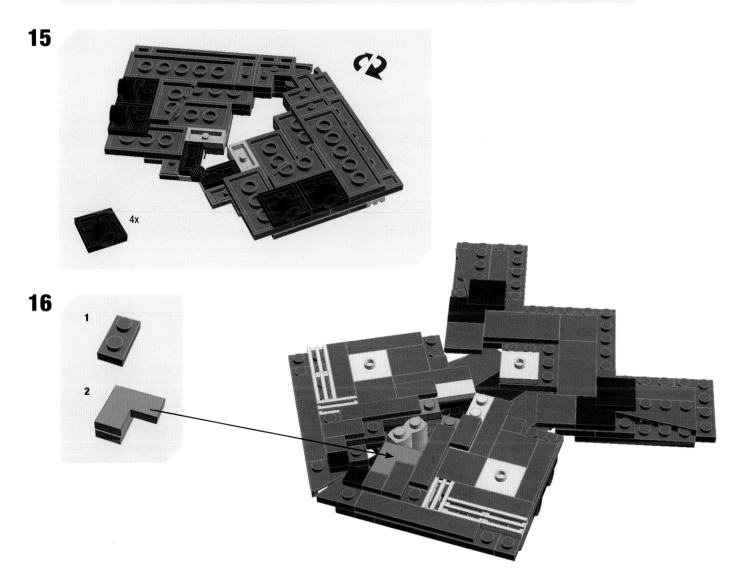

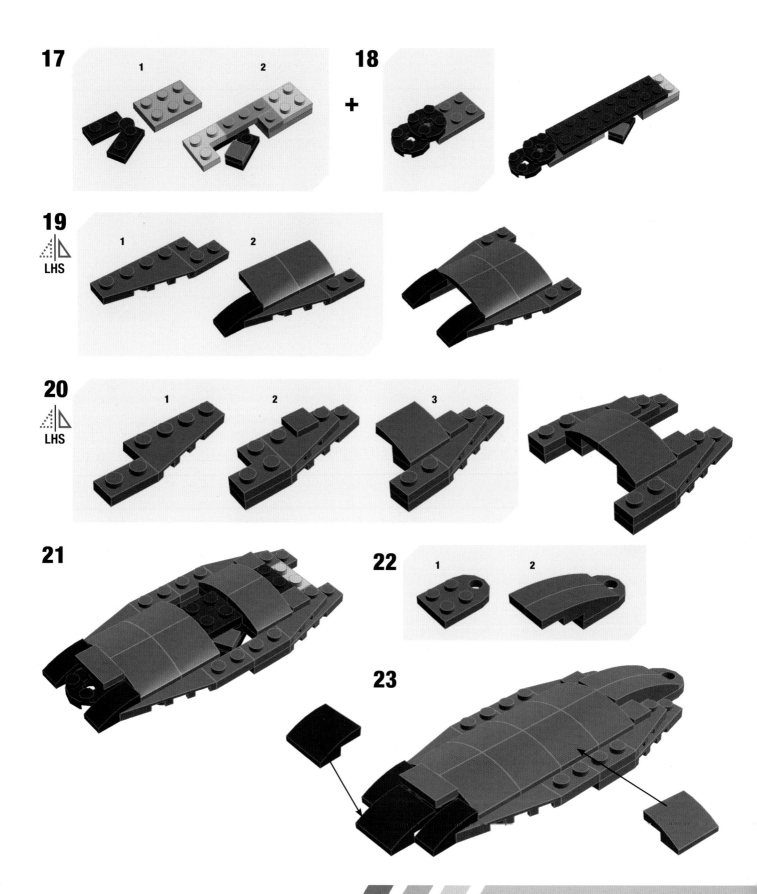

**24**

1    2    3

2x

**25**    **26**

Rotate Engine Covers
approximately 30° to
face straight ahead.

**27**

**28**

LHS

1    2    3

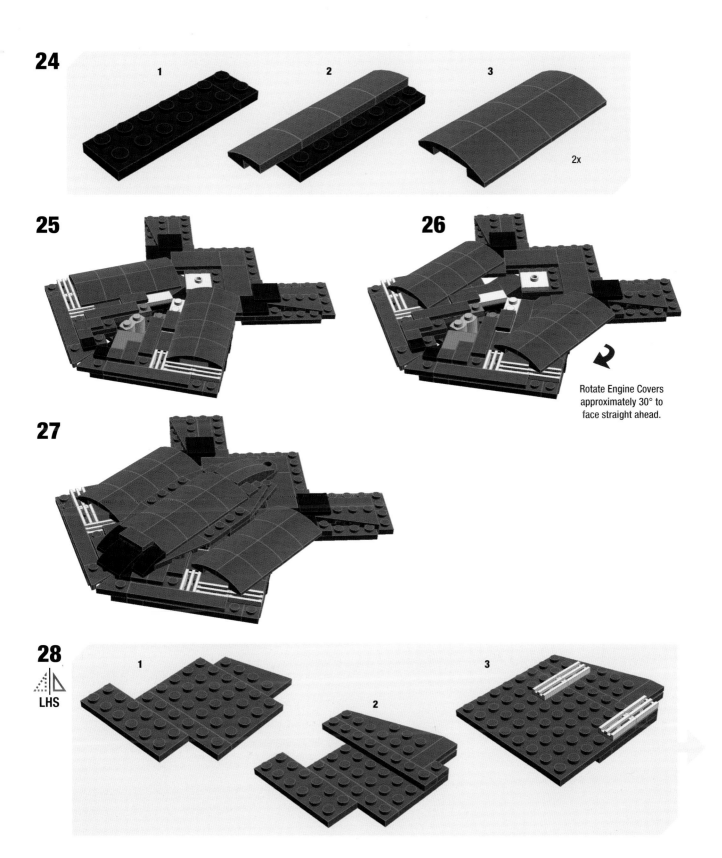

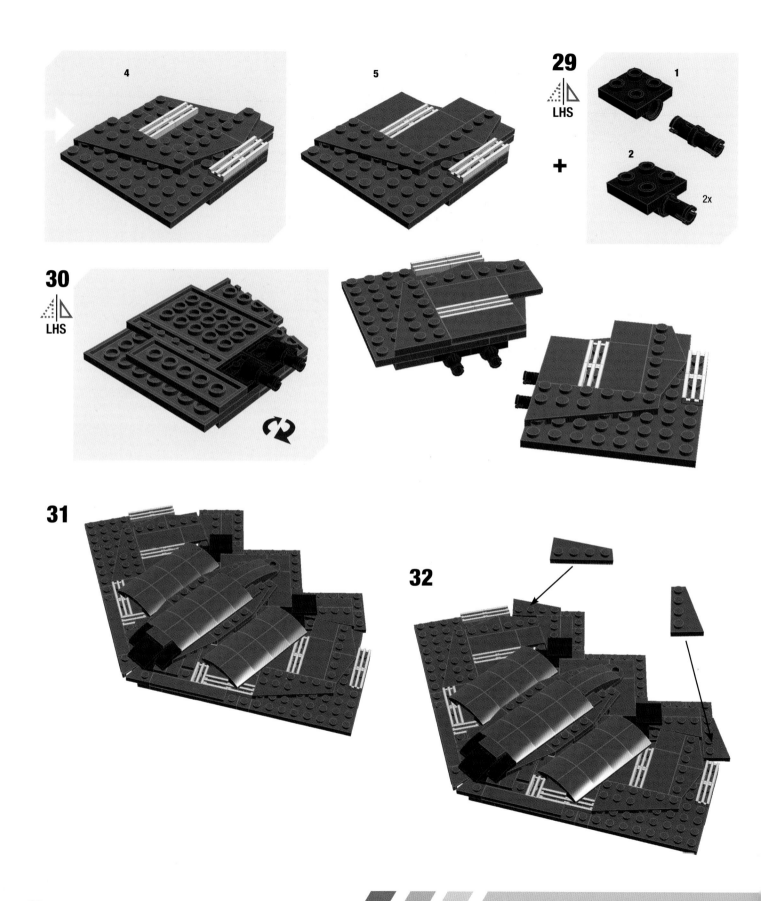

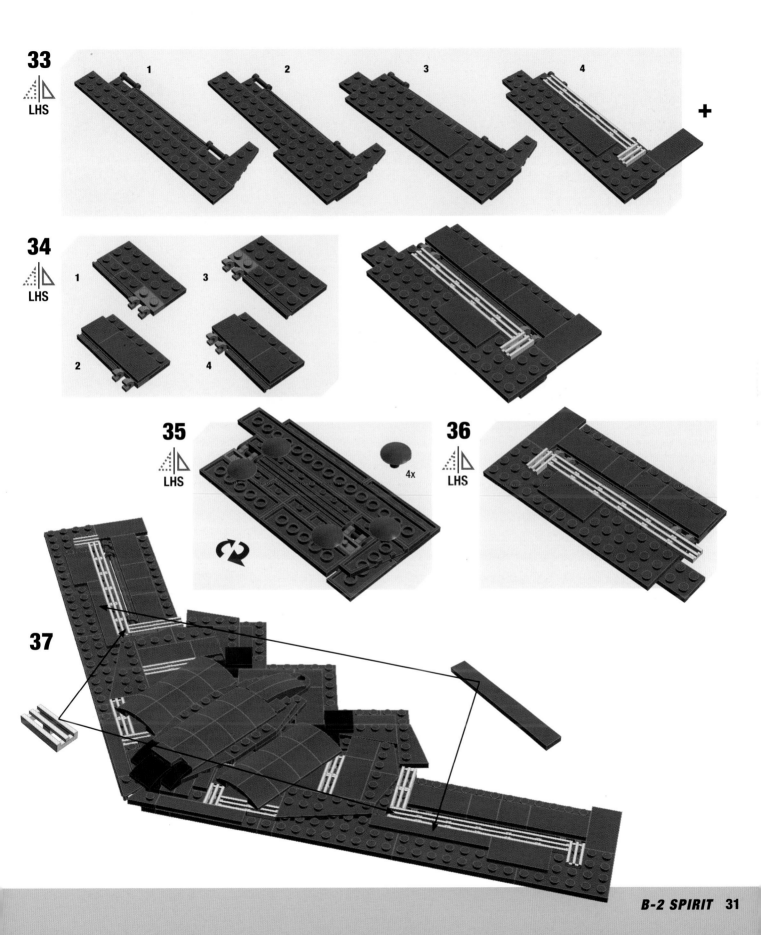

**33**

LHS

1    2    3    4

+

**34**

LHS

1    3

2    4

**35**

LHS

4x

**36**

LHS

**37**

# INTERMEDIATE

There are five aircraft in this section. Three are propeller-driven, modelled in the same 1:32 scale, covering the period between WWI and WWII. Prior to WWII, jet aircraft had been in early development, but both jets and propeller aircraft evolved quickly, and jets did not achieve an advantage until after the war; from then on power and speed increased rapidly.

The two jet aircraft in the book, modelled in 1:48 scale, bookend the jet age. The Dassault Mirage III was flying less than a decade after the war, and was capable of nearly twice the speed of sound. The Lockheed-Martin F-35 is the very latest aircraft designed in the Western hemisphere, though it is barely faster than the Mirage sixty years its junior. Airframe competitiveness has become about much more than sheer speed. Modern electronics and materials engineering deliver stealth capabilities and communications technologies (called avionics).

The models in this section and beyond can carry LEGO® minifigs, and are assembled using a modular construction technique. Again, they are very typical for their era, and the techniques can be used as a template to make similar aircraft. The engines are modeled separately, and can also be mounted alongside the aircraft they are fitted to.

# ALBATROS-FLUGZEUGWERKE
# ALBATROS D.Va

scale: 1:32

The Albatros D.V was the final development of the Albatros D.I family and the final Albatros fighter to see service. A critical shortcoming of earlier models of the series—wing failure—was the primary design flaw to be rectified once and for all in the D.V design. Unfortunately, the new design retained many features contributing to the structural failures, and it remained a bugbear that plagued the Albatros through its short operational history.

In all, nearly 2,500 aircraft were produced to maintain Imperial German air power in World War I. A benefit of the D.V over the earlier series was a new elliptical section fuselage, said to save 71 pounds (32 kg) on an empty 1,515-pound (697-kg aircraft). The D.V used a largely carryover inline 6-cylinder Mercedes D.IIIa engine rated at 170 hp (127 kW). (The D.Va had a slightly more powerful engine to offset an additional 23 kilograms of weight.) The D.Va commenced production in October 1917 and ceased in April 1918, by which time there were 131 D.V and 928 D.Va aircraft in service.

Germany's most famous World War I pilot, Baron Manfred von Richthofen, operated the D.V, and the model shown here is in the style in which his D.V Serial D.4693/17 was painted.

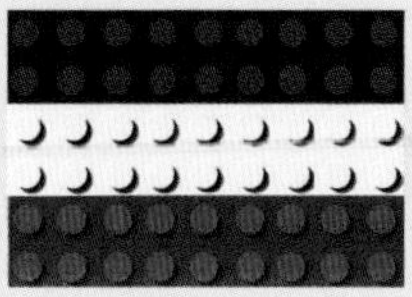

**COUNTRY OF ORIGIN:** German Empire

**PRODUCTION:** 1917

**RETIRED:** 1918

**NUMBER MADE:** ~2,500

**LENGTH/WINGSPAN:** 24' 1" (7.33 m) / 29' 8" (9.05 m)

**LOADED MASS:** 2,066 lb. (937 kg)

**POWERPLANT:** 1 × Mercedes D.IIIau 9-cylinder piston engine

**THRUST:** 200 hp (150 kW)

**MAXIMUM SPEED:** 116 mph (186 km/h)

**COMBAT RADIUS:** 185 miles (150km)

**NOTE:** This build is done in a series of 5 modules.

# MODULE A
FRONT FUSELAGE

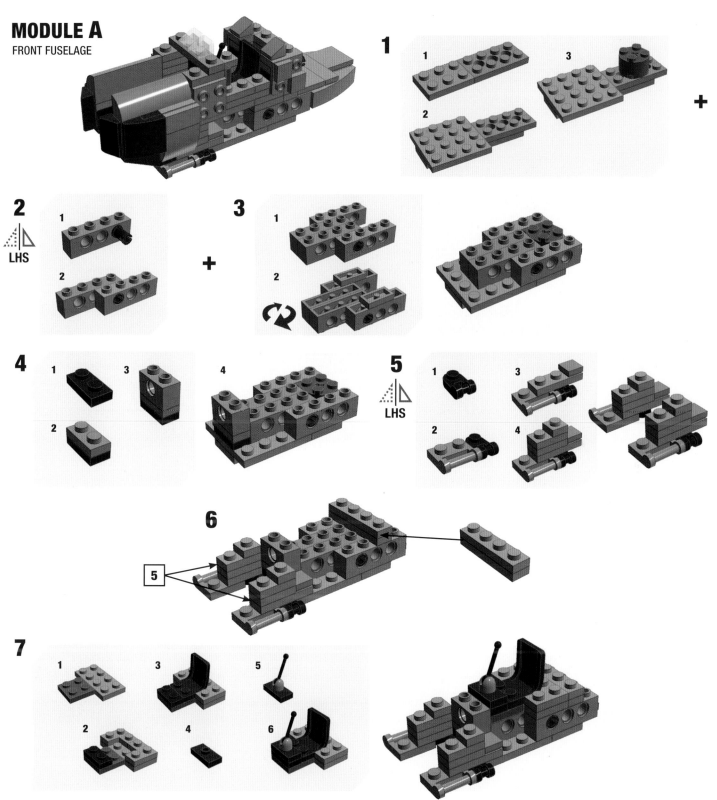

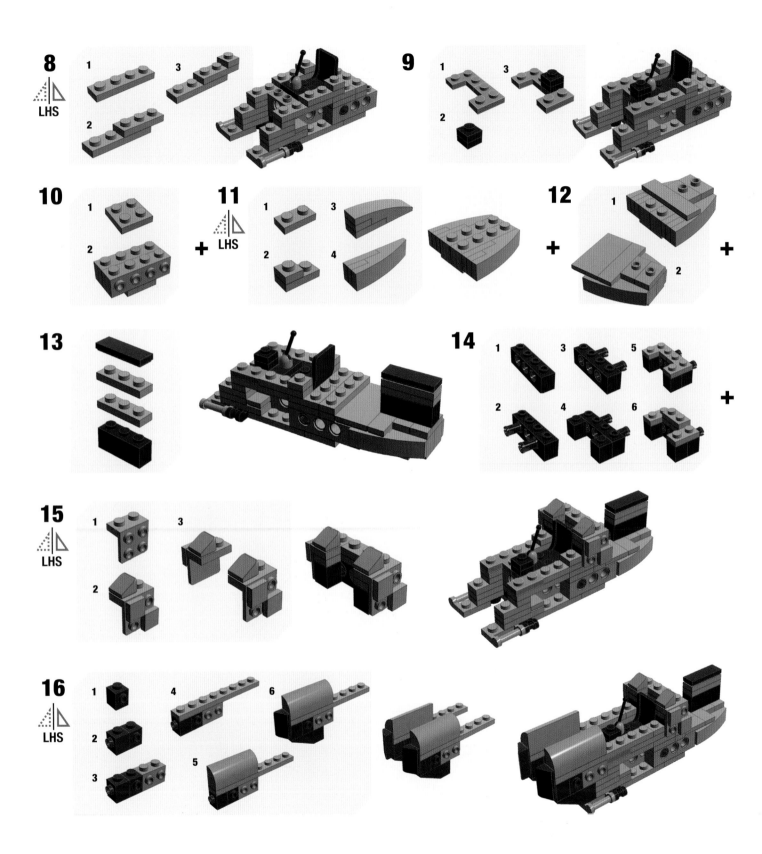

**8**

LHS

**9**

**10**

**11** +

LHS

**12** + +

**13**

**14** +

**15**

LHS

**16**

LHS

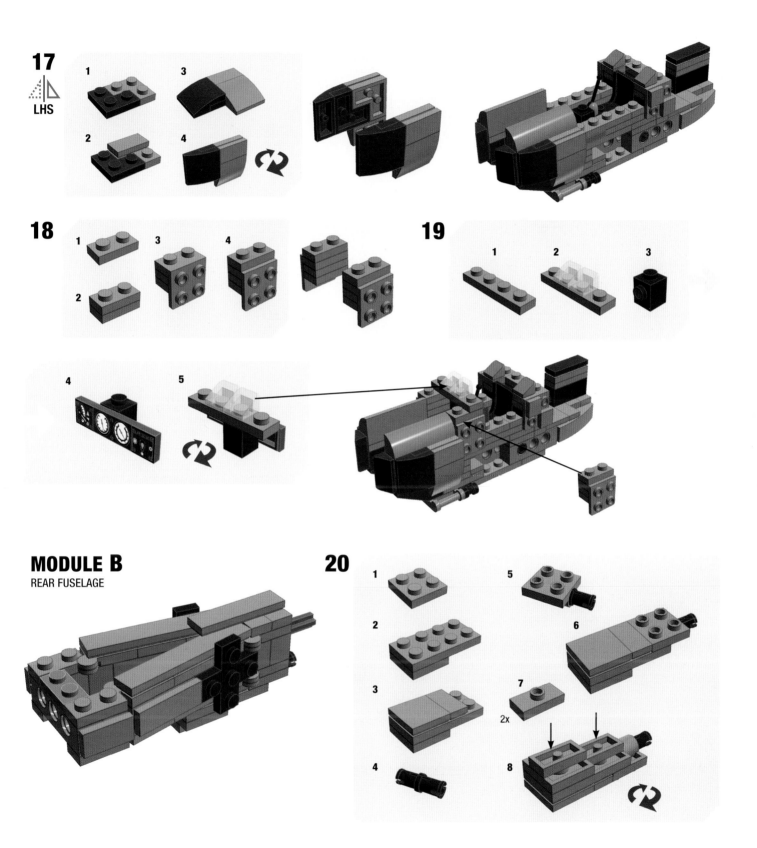

# 17

LHS

# 18

# 19

# MODULE B
REAR FUSELAGE

# 20

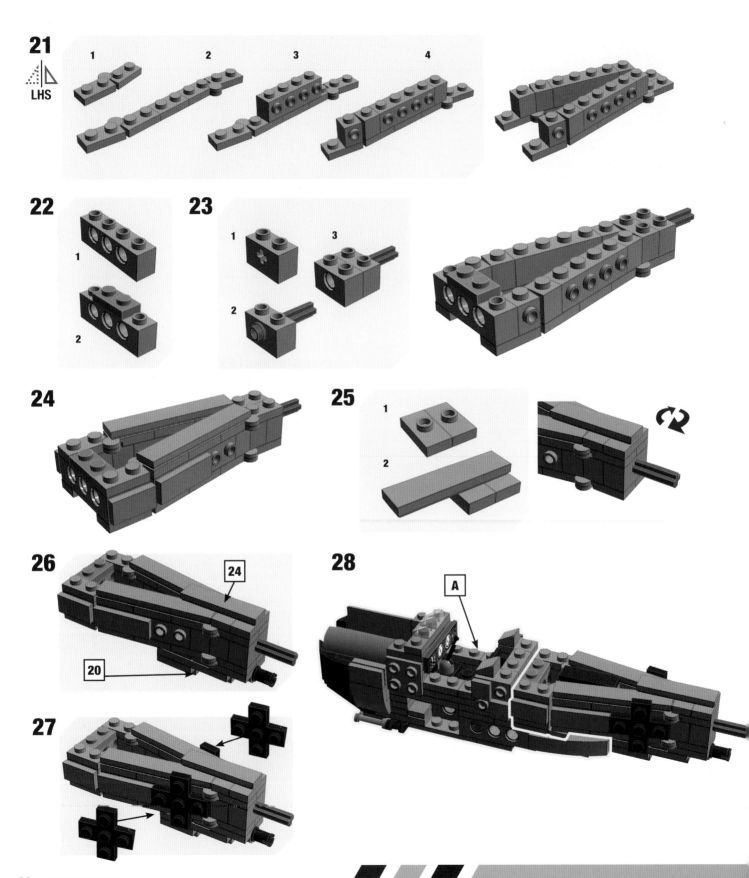

**21**

LHS

1      2      3      4

**22**

1

2

**23**

1      3

2

**24**

**25**

1

2

**26**

24

20

**27**

**28**

A

**29**

1

2

3

**30**

LHS

1

2

**31**

28

**32**

1

2

**33**

**34**

LHS

1

2

3

**+**

1

2

**35**

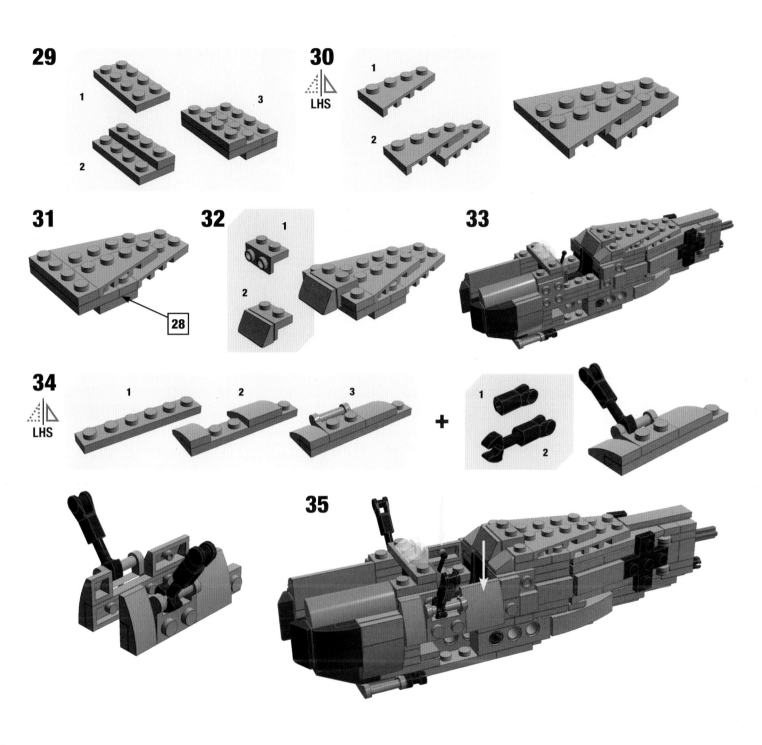

# MODULE C PROPELLER ASSEMBLY

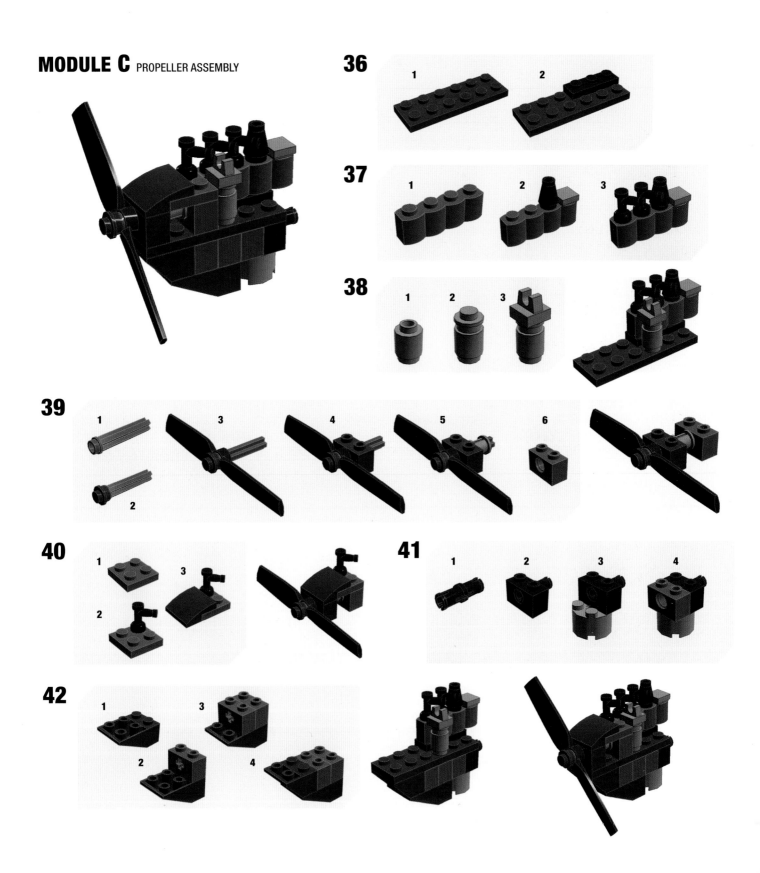

**43**

**44**

C

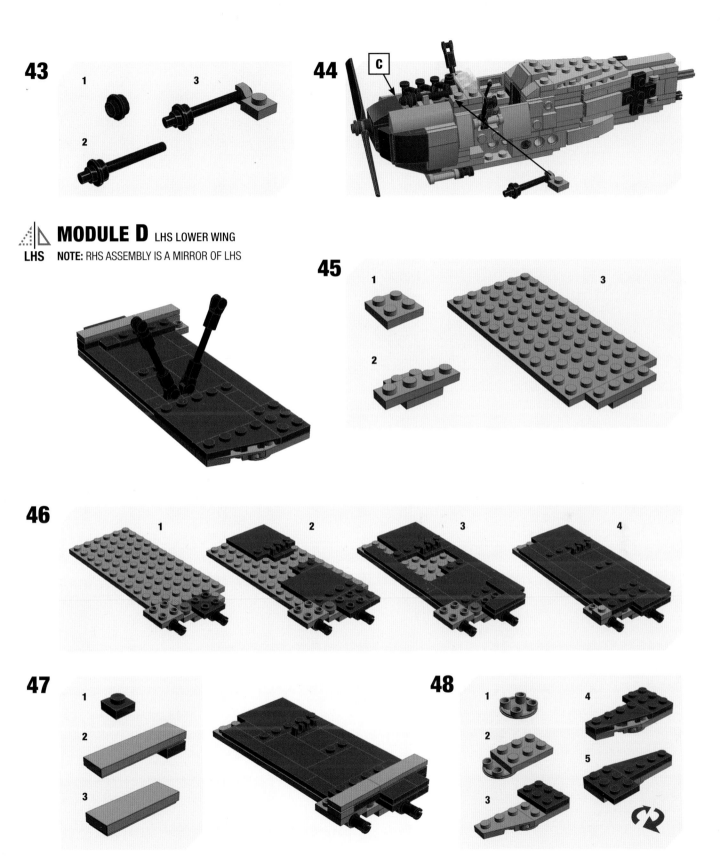

**MODULE D** LHS LOWER WING

**LHS** · **NOTE:** RHS ASSEMBLY IS A MIRROR OF LHS

**45**

**46**

**47**

**48**

**49**

**50**

**51**

2x

## MODULE E LHS UPPER WING

**LHS** NOTE: RHS ASSEMBLY IS A MIRROR OF LHS

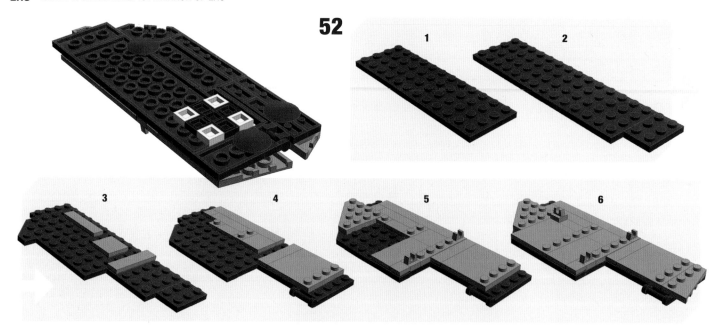

**52**

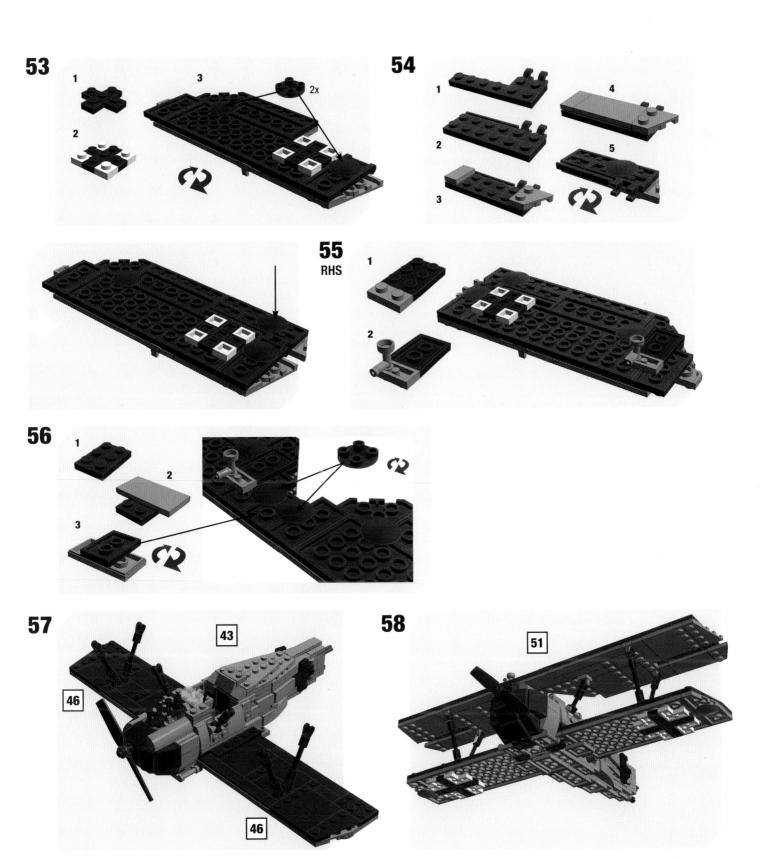

# MODULE F TAIL ASSEMBLY

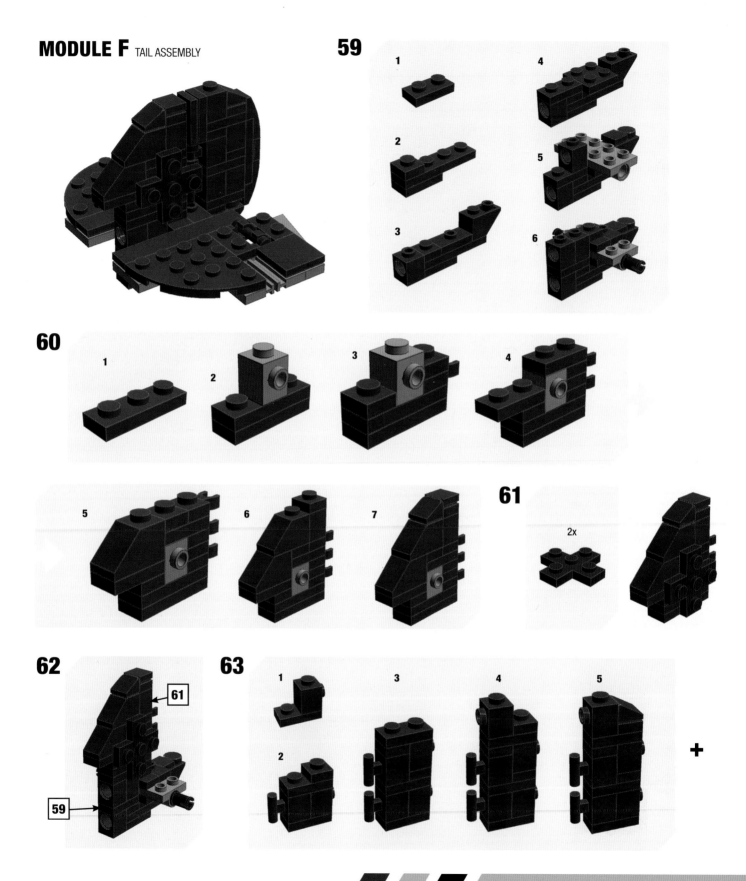

**59**

**60**

**61**

2x

**62**

61
59

**63**

+

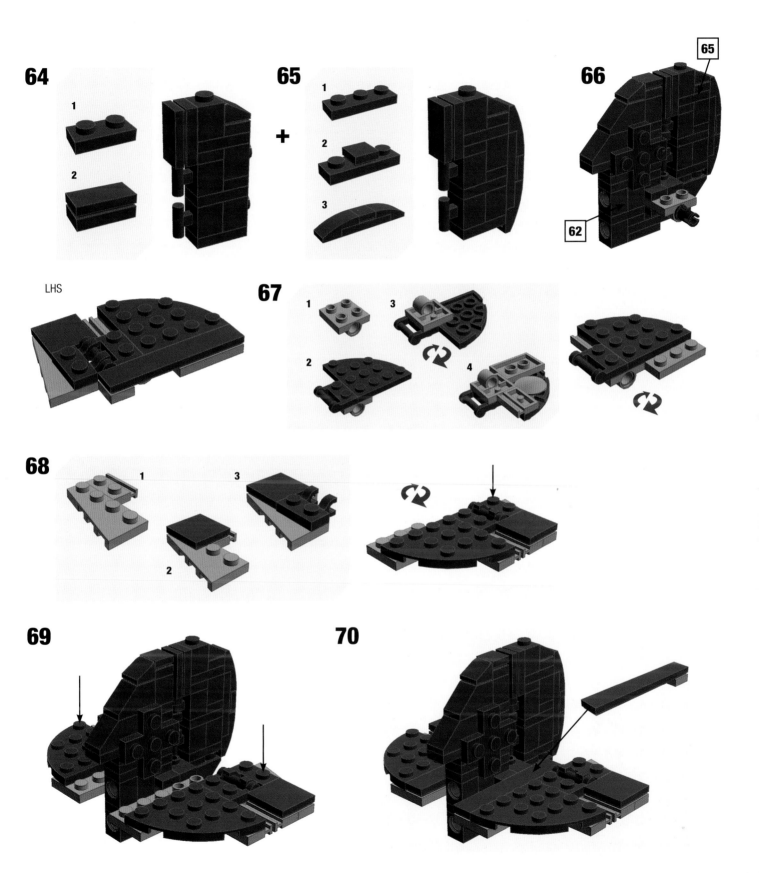

# MODULE G LANDING GEAR

**71**

LHS

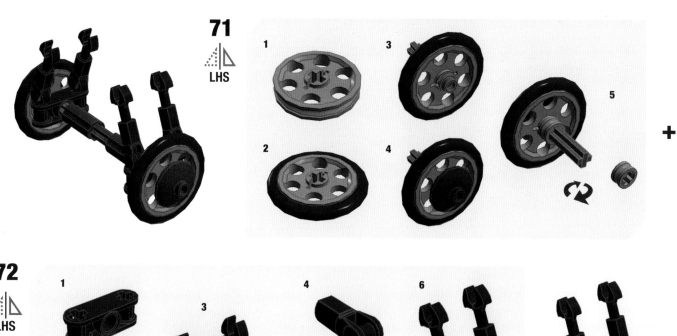

**72**

LHS

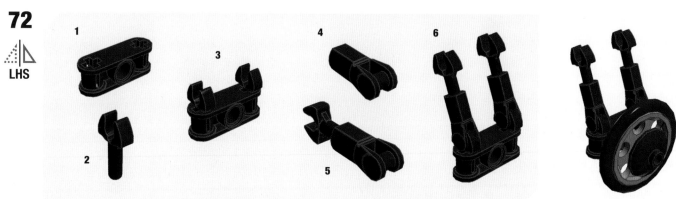

**73**

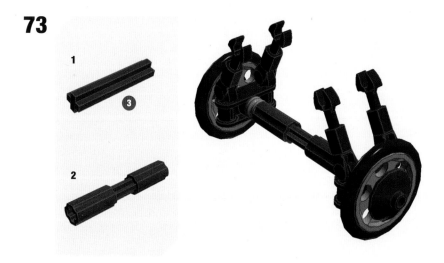

**74**

**75**

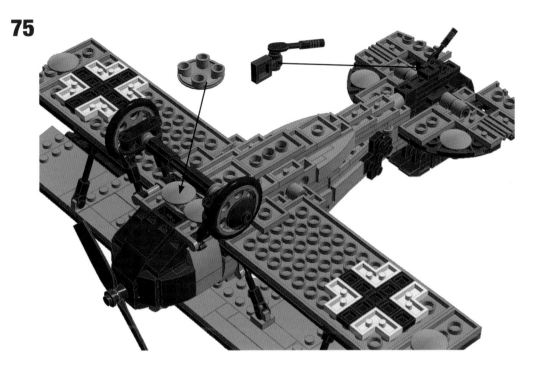

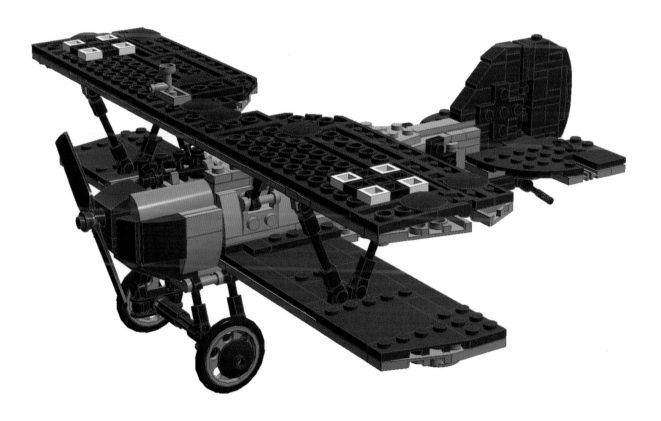

# SUPERMARINE
# SPITFIRE Mk VB

scale: 1:32

The Spitfire is possibly the most famous of all World War II–era fighter planes, designed as a short-range, high-speed, single-seat interceptor. It was built in large numbers (20,351) over many design iterations for a lengthy production period (1938–1948).

The Spitfire is notable for its wing design, which allowed the aircraft to achieve extremely high speeds during dive maneuvers. In 1952, a Spitfire Mk 19 was flown to an altitude of 51,550 feet (15,710 m), and once pilot Edward Powles regained control of the aircraft, he landed it intact. Instruments indicated that the Spitfire had achieved a speed of 690 miles per hour (1,110km/h), Mach 0.96! Other test flights included dive maneuvers that also approached Mach 0.9, although this sometimes resulted in damage to the aircraft's wings, including sweeping them backward somewhat on the frame.

Mention of the Spitfire must also include its Rolls-Royce Merlin V-12 engine. The instructions and technical features for the Merlin engine are found on page 56.

Spitfires were flown in most war theaters, predominantly in Europe, but also in North Africa and in the Pacific (operated by the Royal Air Force and Royal Australian Air Force) against the Japanese A6M "Zero." The Spitfire's weakness was greatest there, as its short range did not suit the long-distance engagement of the Pacific theater.

The model shown here has typical painted summer camouflage, though alternatives for winter and desert theaters can be achieved with color substitutions.

**COUNTRY OF ORIGIN:** United Kingdom

**PRODUCTION:** 1938–1948

**RETIRED:** 1961

**NUMBER MADE:** 20,351

**LENGTH/WINGSPAN:** 29' 11" (9.12 m) / 36' 10" (11.23 m)

**LOADED MASS:** 6,622 lb. (3000 kg)

**POWERPLANT:** 1 × Rolls-Royce Merlin 45 supercharged V-12 aero engine

**THRUST:** 1,470 hp (1,096 kW)

**MAXIMUM SPEED:** 370 mph (595 km/h)

**COMBAT RADIUS:** 470 miles (595km)

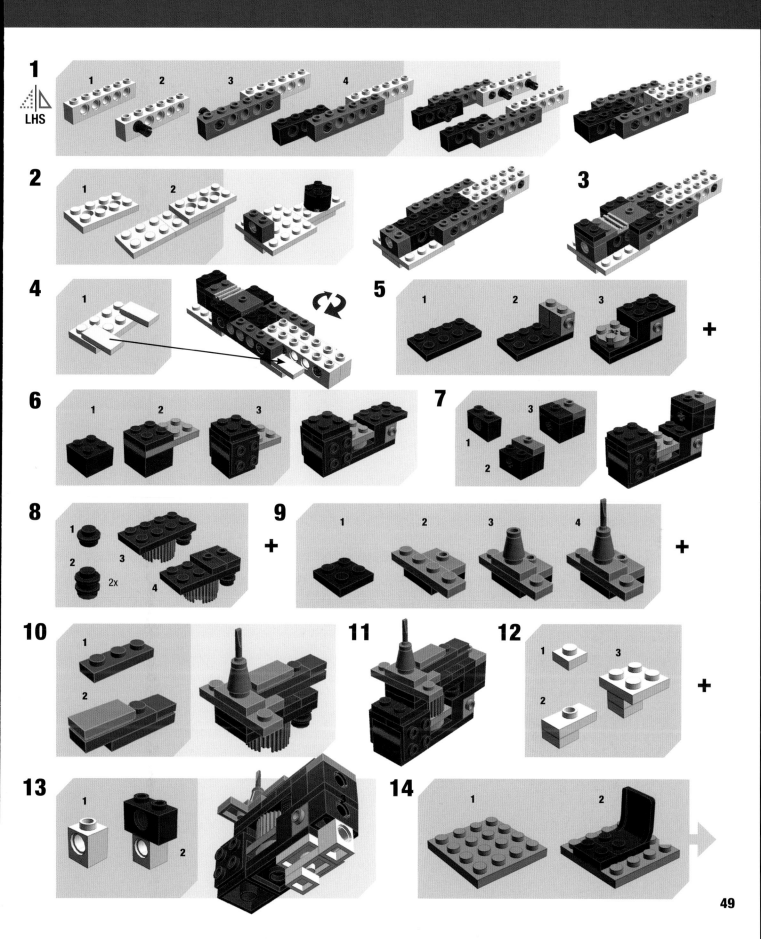

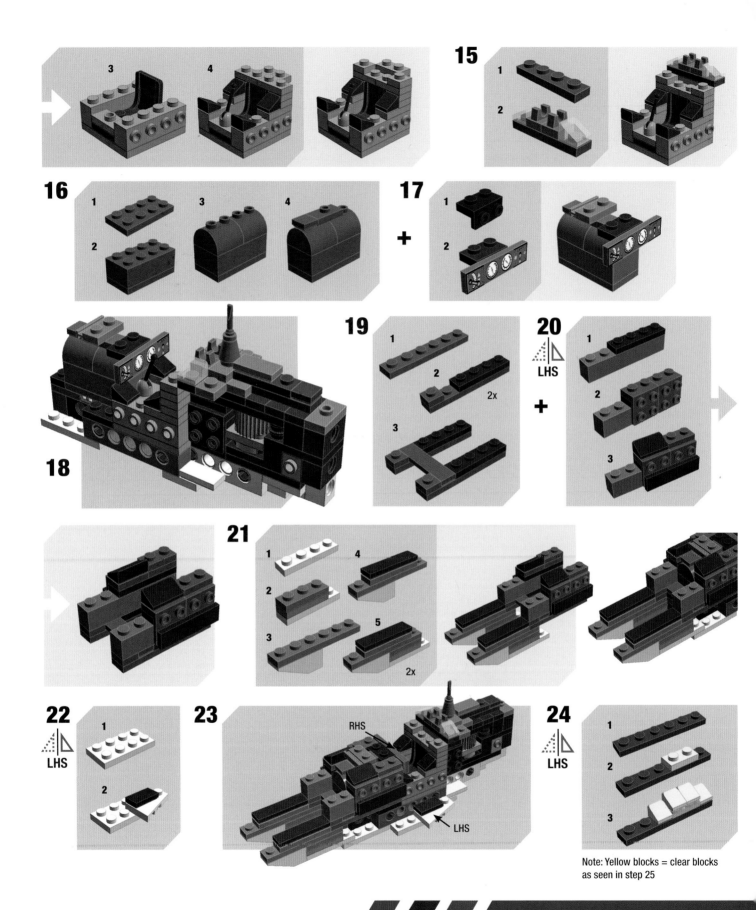

Note: Yellow blocks = clear blocks as seen in step 25

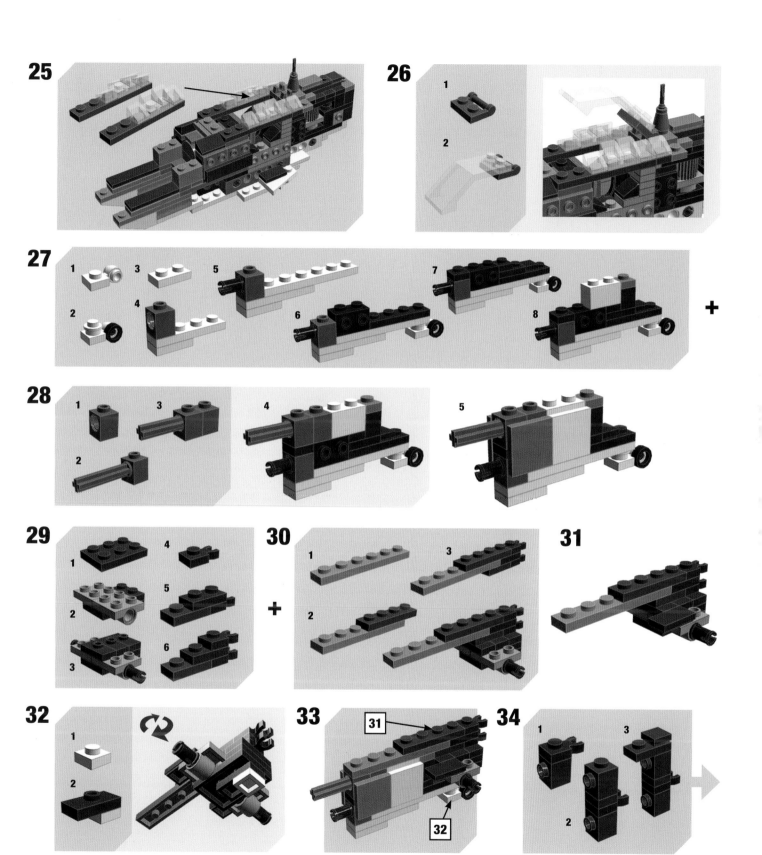

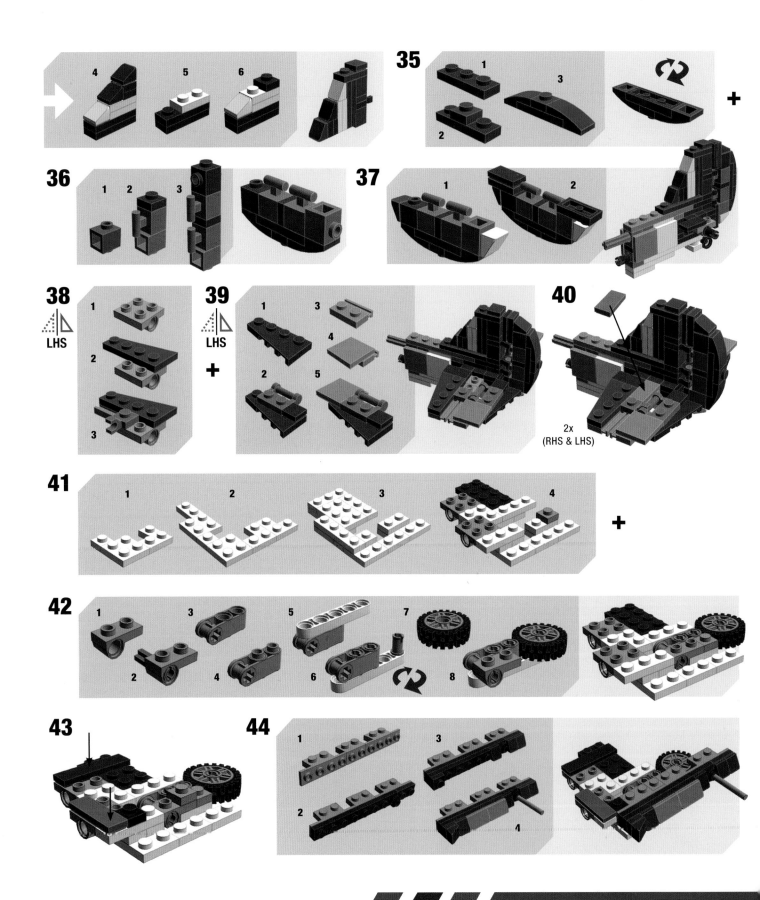

**35**

**36**

**37**

**38** LHS

**39** LHS

**40** 2x (RHS & LHS)

**41**

**42**

**43**

**44**

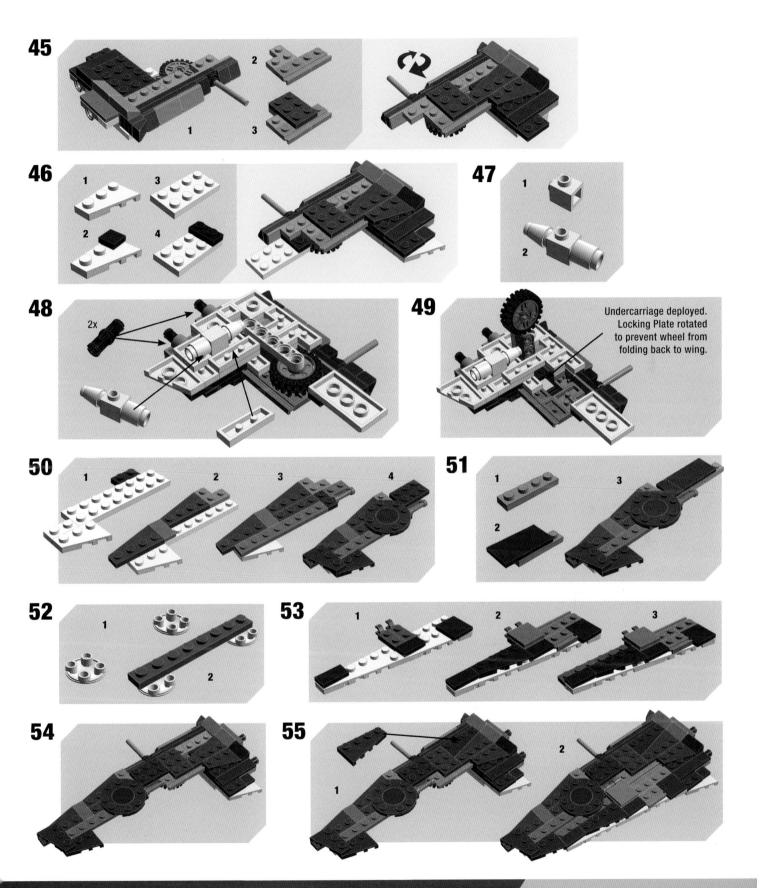

**45**

**46** **47**

**48**

2x

**49** Undercarriage deployed.
Locking Plate rotated
to prevent wheel from
folding back to wing.

**50**

**51**

**52**

**53**

**54**

**55**

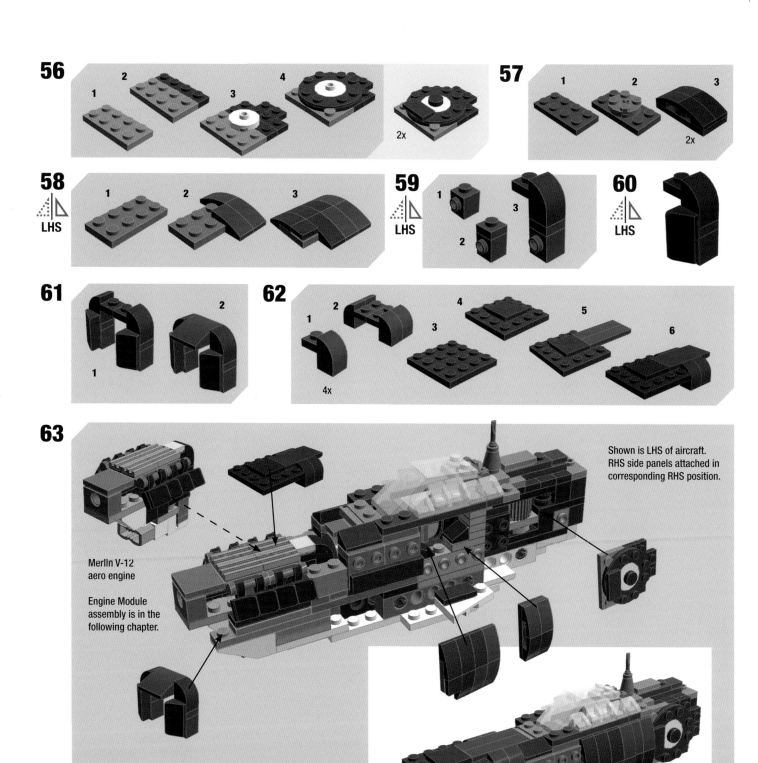

**56**
1  2  3  4
2x

**57**
1  2  3
2x

**58**
LHS
1  2  3

**59**
LHS
1  2  3

**60**
LHS

**61**
1  2
1

**62**
1  2  3  4  5  6
4x

**63**

Merlln V-12
aero engine

Engine Module
assembly is in the
following chapter.

Shown is LHS of aircraft.
RHS side panels attached in
corresponding RHS position.

**64**

**65**

**66**

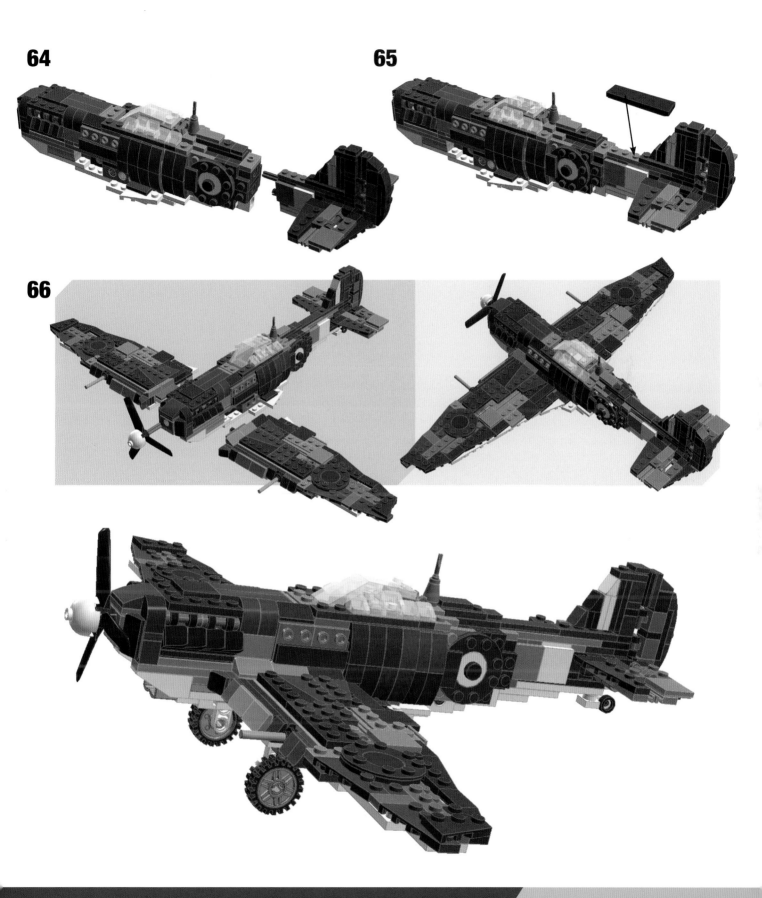

## ROLLS-ROYCE LIMITED
# MERLIN 61 V-12 ENGINE

**scale: 1:32**

The Rolls-Royce Merlin V-12 was designed in early 1933 and was soon adapted for military applications, including the Supermarine Spitfire and Hawker Hurricane.

Early versions produced 1,000 horsepower (746 kW) on 87 octane fuel, while later versions fitted to early Spitfires achieved 1,470 horsepower (1,096 kW) on 100 octane fuel due to the 1,649-cid (27 L) swept capacity. Deploying intercoolers for the superchargers saw this climb to 1,800 hp and topped out at over 2,000 horsepower in the de Havilland Hornet (this figure required special fuel).

Versions of the engine were even created for land-based tanks, while a licensed version was built in the United States by Packard for the North American P-51 Mustang; nearly 55,000 were built.

The Merlin is most closely associated with the Spitfire, however, and powered most of the 20,000 aircraft built.

An early shortcoming in the Merlin was that it was unable to follow the Luftwaffe Bf-109E (which used a fuel-injected engine) into an inverted dive due to its design. With a reduction in apparent gravity, the Merlin's carburetors were starved of fuel. Royal Australian Air Force (RAAF) pilots first countered this by half-rolling their aircraft into the dive, but later a solution was developed by aeronautical engineer Beatrice Shilling: a metal disk with a hole fitted to the fuel line. Eventually, a Bendix-manufactured pressure carburetor allowed better performance when inverted and improved high-altitude fueling.

The Merlin went on to power nearly fifty aircraft types in a production run that ended in 1950 and saw nearly 150,000 engines manufactured in total.

| | |
|---|---|
| **COUNTRY OF ORIGIN:** | United Kingdom |
| **MANUFACTURER:** | Rolls-Royce Limited |
| **PRODUCTION:** | 1936–1950 |
| **NUMBER MADE:** | 149,659 |
| **TYPE:** | 12-cylinder, supercharged, liquid-cooled 60° 'Vee' piston aircraft engine |
| **DISPLACEMENT:** | 1,649 cid (27 L) |
| **DRY WEIGHT:** | 1,640 lb (744 kg) |
| **POWER OUTPUT:** | 1,565 hp (1,167 kW) @ 3,000 rpm |
| **VARIANTS:** | Packard V-1650 Merlin |
| **MAJOR APPLICATIONS:** | Avro Lancaster |
| | de Havilland Mosquito |
| | Handley Page Halifax |
| | Hawker Hurricane |
| | Supermarine Spitfire |

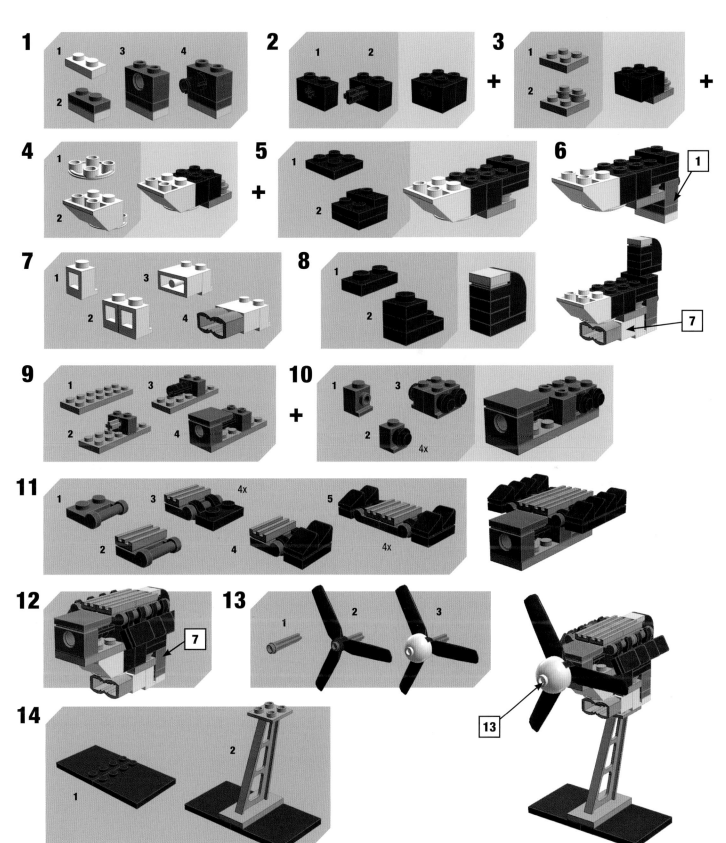

# A6M ZERO

scale: 1:32

"Tora! Tora! Tora!" was the attack signal over Japanese radio that began the strike against the United States in Pearl Harbor. This engagement brought the United States, which until this time been resisting entry into World War II, directly into conflict in the Pacific and, shortly afterward, in Europe.

The first two waves of the Pearl Harbor attack had been led by the Nakajima B5N and Aichi D3A bombers, which struck warships and air bases. The Mitsubishi A6M Zeros then joined the attack, focusing on air superiority.

The A6M was already well established prior to the attack, having entered service in 1940 as possibly the best long-range fighter in the world, and experienced and battle-tested due to engagements against Chinese- and Soviet-built aircraft in operation in China.

The A6M was fast, powerful, maneuverable, and had a formidable range (1,600 miles/2,600 km), whether launched from land or sea. The range also allowed them to stay engaged for longer periods of time and to be launched from aircraft carriers well beyond the range of Allied fighters or bombers.

The primary weakness of the Zero was its relative fragility; its lightness was helpful in most instances but left it vulnerable to fire from antiaircraft guns or US fighters. Its lightness also affected the Zero's armament, which was sometimes insufficient to down heavier Grumman Hellcats and the heavy Lockheed P-38 Lightning.

By the end of the war, the Zeros had finally become outclassed. They had one trick left, however: kamikaze operations.

**COUNTRY OF ORIGIN:** Japan

**PRODUCTION:** 1940–1945

**RETIRED:** 1945

**NUMBER MADE:** 10,939

**LENGTH/WINGSPAN:** 29' 8" (9.06 m) / 39' 4" (12.0 m)

**LOADED MASS:** 6,164 lb. (2,796 kg)

**POWERPLANT:** 1 × Nakajima Sakae-12 14-cylinder radial engine

**THRUST:** 940 hp (700 kW)

**MAXIMUM SPEED:** 332 mph (534 km/h)

**COMBAT RADIUS:** 964 miles (1,552 km)

**NOTE:** This build is done in a series of 3 modules.

# MODULE A COCKPIT ASSEMBLY

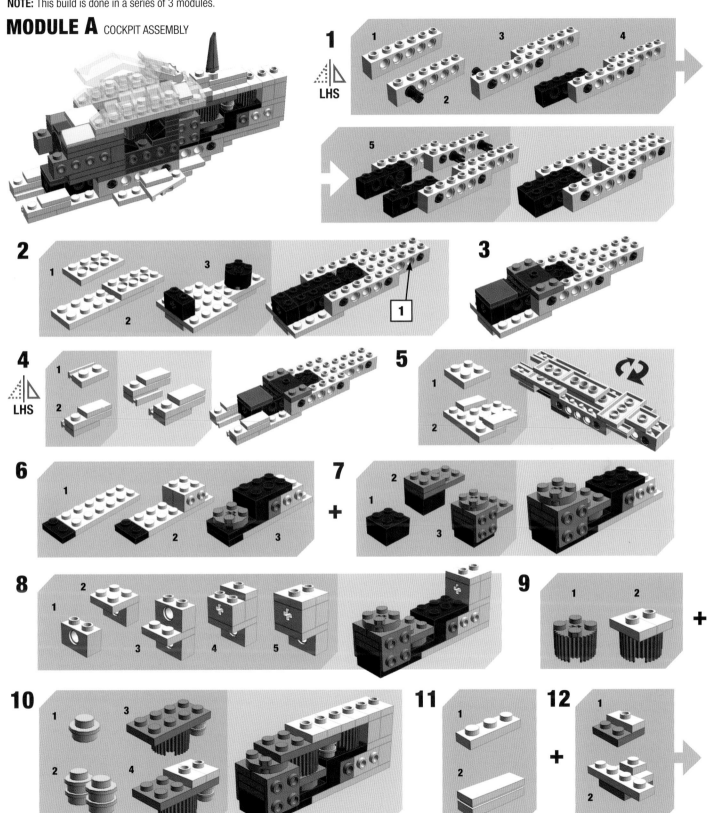

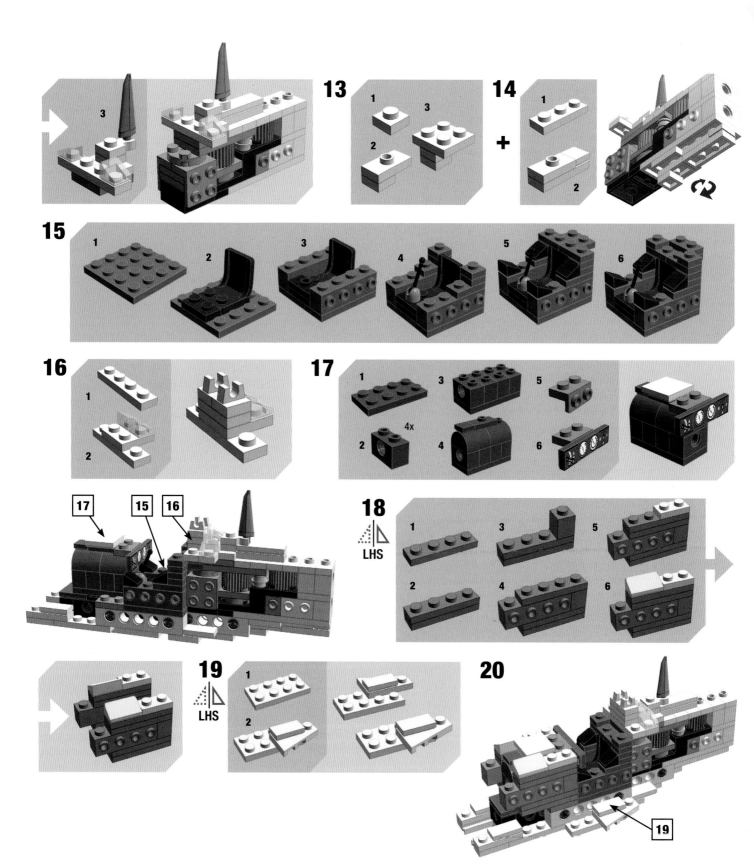

13

14

15

16

17

18
LHS

19
LHS

20

**21**

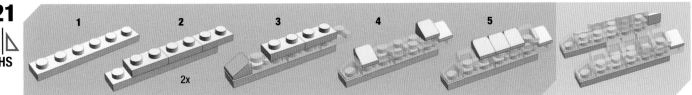

Note: Yellow blocks = clear blocks as seen in step 24

**22**

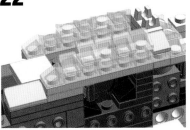

**23**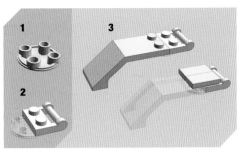

**24**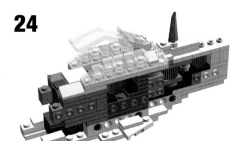

# MODULE B TAIL ASSEMBLY

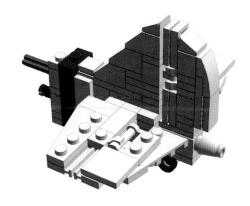

**25**

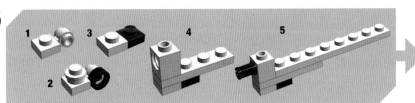

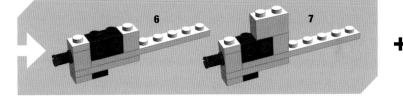

**+**

**26**

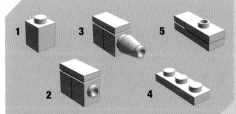

**27**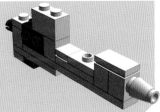

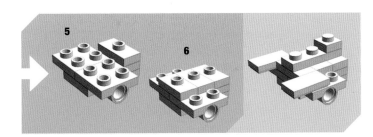

**28**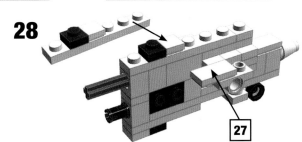

27

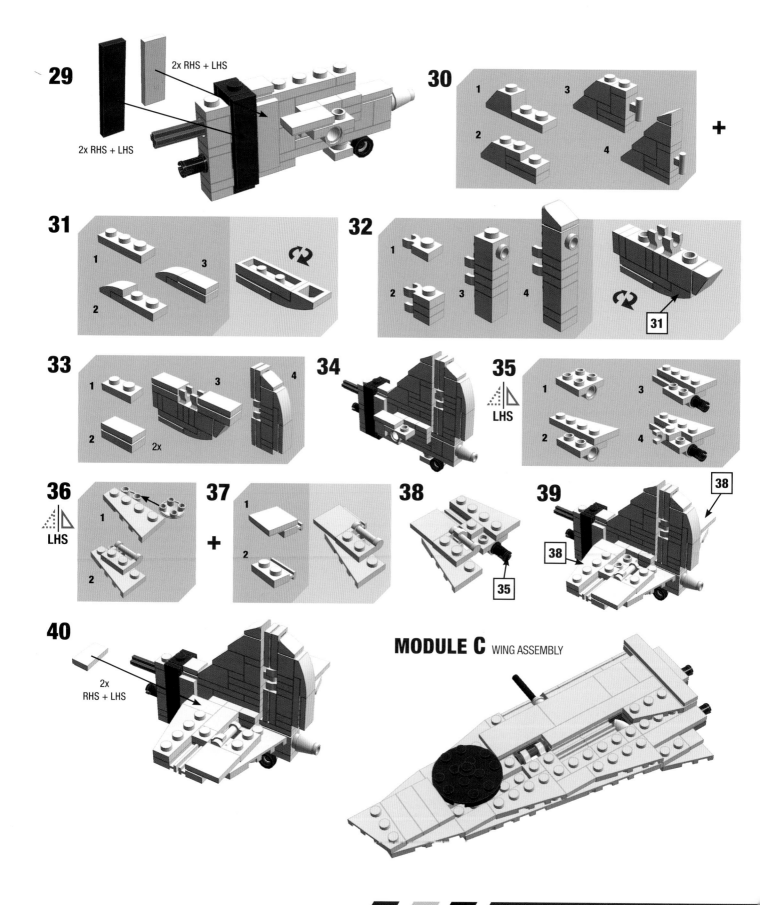

**29**

2x RHS + LHS

2x RHS + LHS

**30**

1   3

2   4

+

**31**

1   3

2

**32**

1   3   4

2

31

**33**

1   3   4

2   2x

**34**

**35**

LHS

1   3

2   4

**36**

LHS

1

2

**37**

1

2

+

**38**

35

**39**

38

38

**40**

2x
RHS + LHS

**MODULE C** WING ASSEMBLY

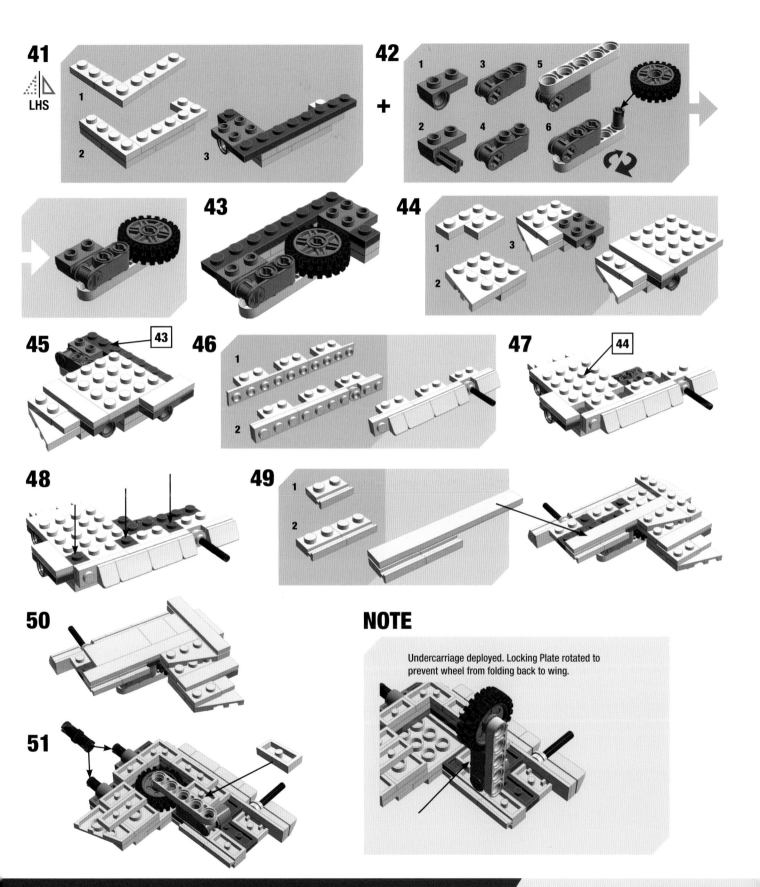

**41**

LHS

1

2

3

**42**

1    3    5

2    4    6

+

**43**

**44**

1    3

2

**45**    43

**46**

1

2

**47**    44

**48**

**49**

1

2

**50**

**51**

**NOTE**

Undercarriage deployed. Locking Plate rotated to prevent wheel from folding back to wing.

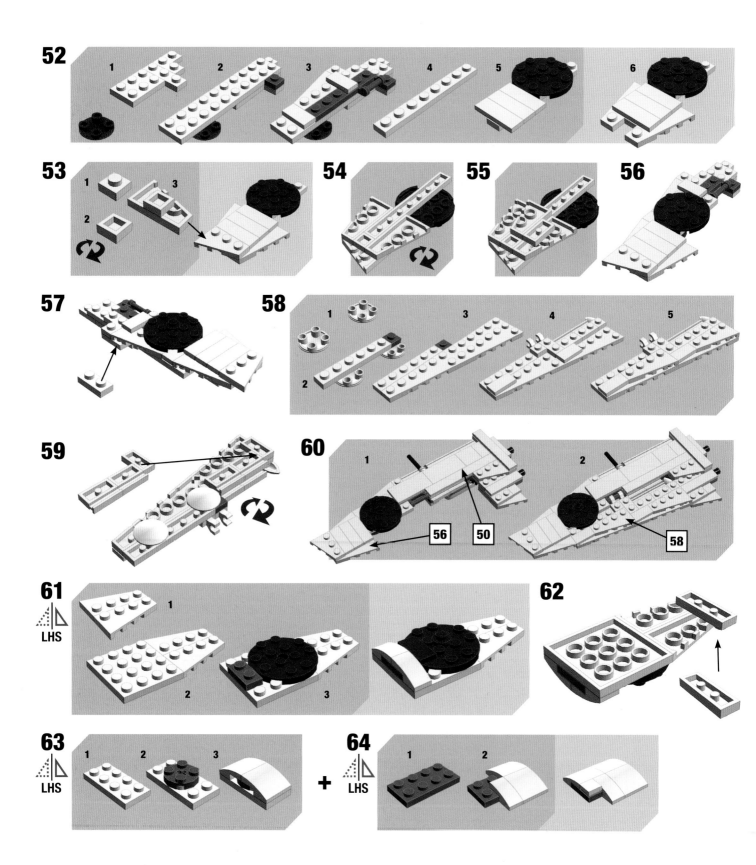

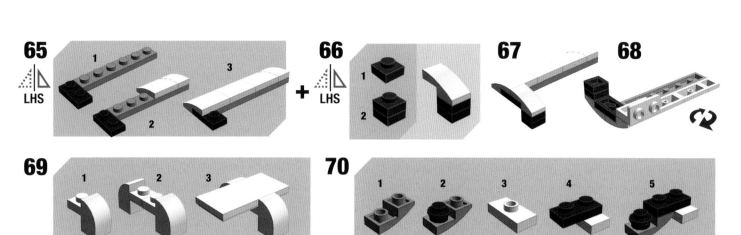

**65**
LHS

1 2 3

**+**

**66**
LHS

1 2

**67**

**68**

**69**

1 2 3

**70**

1 2 3 4 5

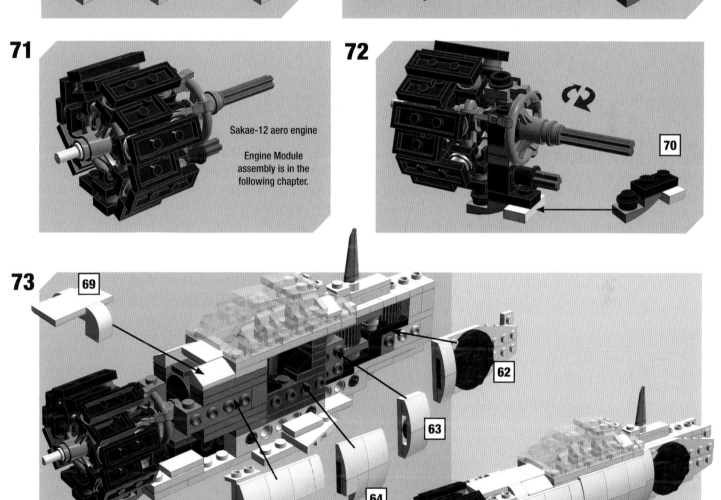

**71**

Sakae-12 aero engine

Engine Module assembly is in the following chapter.

**72**

70

**73**

69

62

63

64

68

Shown is LHS of aircraft. RHS panels are attached in corresonding RHS position.

**74**

**75**

1

2

3

**76**

RHS ONLY

**77**

C

C

**78**

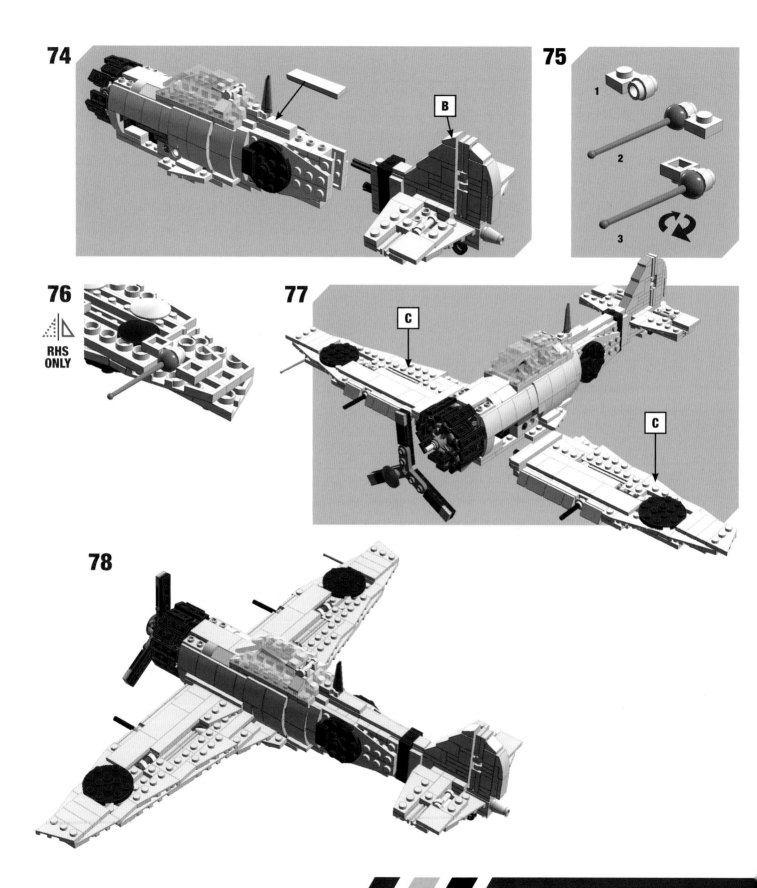

**79**

1  2  3  4  5  6  7  8

9  10  11

**80**

79

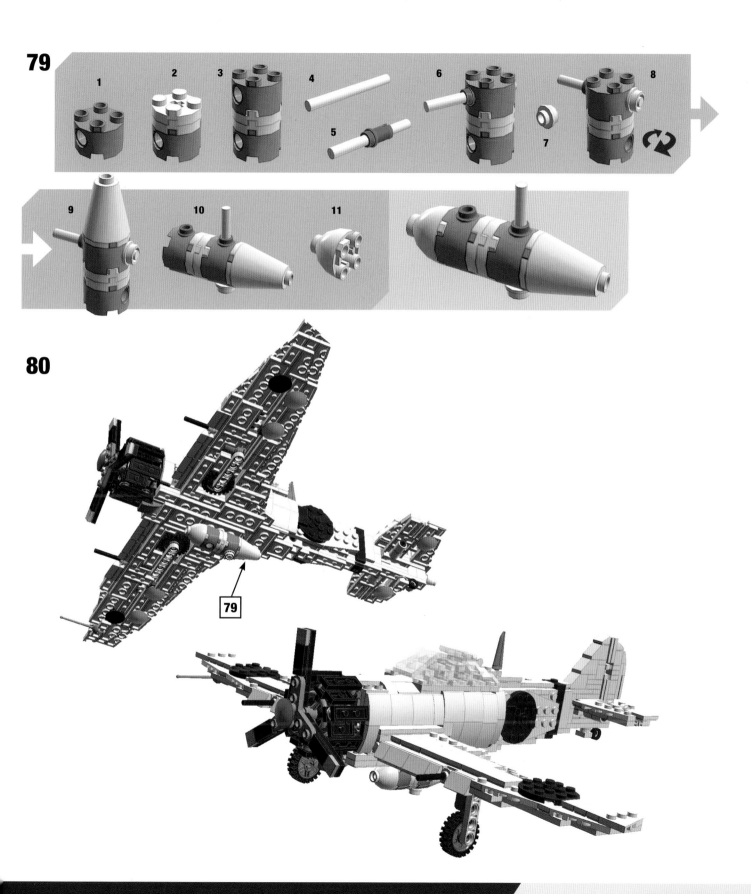

# NAKAJIMA AIRCRAFT COMPANY
# NK1C SAKAE-12

scale: 1:32

The Nakajima Sakae-12 radial aero engine began production in 1939, and about 30,000 Sakae-12 and derivatives were built and used in Europe, the United States, and Japan prior to and after World War II. This engine was used in many World War II Japanese fighter and bomber aircraft.

A key design feature of the engine are the radial engine rows. In the Sakae-12, there are two rows of 7-cylinder radial pistons. Four-stroke radial engines always have odd numbers of cylinders in each row, usually 5, 7, or 9. To create a larger engine, additional rows are added. The radial engine used a complex crank and conrod assembly.

The Sakae-12 engine fitted to the Mitsubishi A6M fighter (and other applications) used two rows of 7 cylinders for a total of 14 cylinders. The engine displaced 1,700-ci (27.9L) and produced 940 horsepower (700 kW). Later developments saw power rise to 1,210 horsepower (902 kW) using water-methanol injection.

One key advantage of a single- or double-row radial is the engine compactness. The Sakae-12 was a full 24 inches (600 mm) shorter than the Merlin V-12 engine fitted to the Spitfire.

**COUNTRY OF ORIGIN:** Japan

**MANUFACTURER:** Nakajima Aircraft Company

**PRODUCTION:** 1939–1945

**NUMBER MADE:** 30,233

**TYPE:** 14-cylinder air-cooled two-row radial aircraft engine

**DISPLACEMENT:** 1,700 cid (27.9 L)

**DRY WEIGHT:** 1,300 lb. (590 kg)

**POWER OUTPUT:** 940 hp (701 kW) @ 3,000 rpm

**MAJOR APPLICATIONS:** Mitsubishi A6M Zero, C5M2
Kawasaki Ki-45, Ki-48, Ki-56
Makagima B5N2, Ki-43, Ki-115
Tachikawa Ki-74

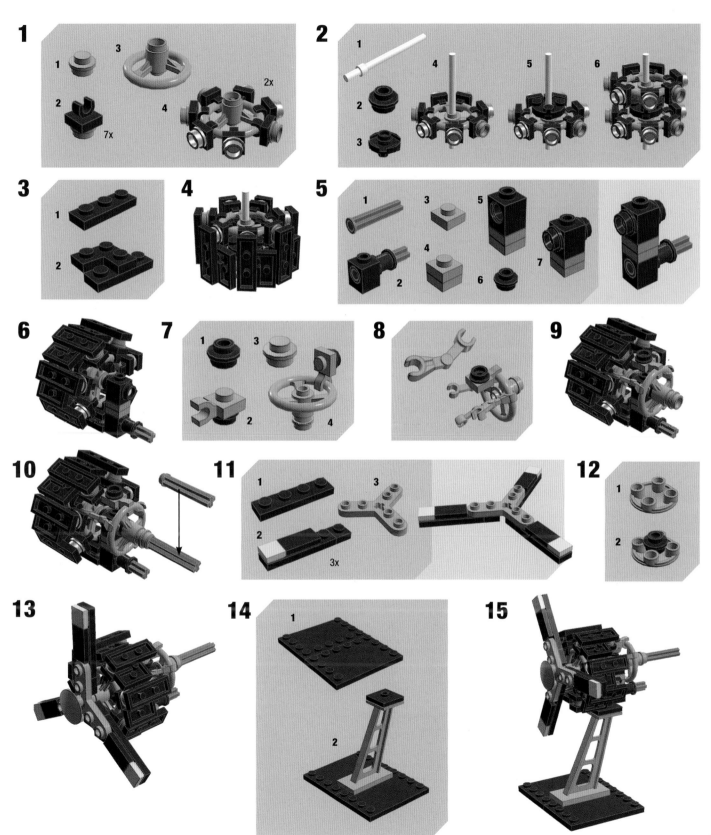

**1**
1
2 7x
3
4 2x

**2**
1
2
3
4
5
6

**3**
1
2

**4**

**5**
1
2
3
4
5
6
7

**6**

**7**
1
2
3
4

**8**

**9**

**10**

**11**
1
2
3
3x

**12**
1
2

**13**

**14**
1
2

**15**

# DASSAULT
# MIRAGE IIIO

**scale: 1:48**

After World War II, the Allied powers were the best prepared to continue aeronautical engineering advancements. Great Britain, the United States, and France all developed aircraft using the latest turbojet engine technology to create ever faster aircraft. The increase in speed during this period was phenomenal.

The most prominent fighter aircraft from France was the Mirage III. The Mirage first flew in 1956 and was already capable of Mach 1.85 by 1957. By the following year, the maximum speed at level flight had reached Mach 2.2, making it the first European aircraft to pass Mach 2. This was the version that went into production, deploying in 1961.

The form of the Mirage was also new compared to World War II–era aircraft. Common to some other fighter aircraft of the period, the wings formed a large delta, almost to the rear of the fuselage. The tall tail lacked horizontal stabilizers. The shape required a fast takeoff and long runways but permitted high maximum speeds and cruising speeds.

The Mirage III and its derivatives was the primary fighter deployed in France in the Armée de l'Air (AdA), though it was also successfully exported. The largest foreign operator was the RAAF in Australia; the plane was produced under license by the Commonwealth Aircraft Corporation (CAC) as the Mirage IIIO (the aircraft modeled here) for a total of 114 aircraft. Upon retirement, about half this fleet was sold to Pakistan in 1990, supplementing their earlier procurements from France. Israel was another large operator of the Mirage III and had 76 in total.

**COUNTRY OF ORIGIN:** France

**PRODUCTION:** 1961

**RETIRED:** In Service

**NUMBER MADE:** 1,422

**LENGTH/WINGSPAN:** 49' 4" (15.03 m) / 27' 0" (8.22 m)

**LOADED MASS:** 21,164 lb. (9,600 kg)

**POWERPLANT:** 1 × SNECMA Ata 09C after-burning turbojet engine
1 × SEPR 841 liquid-fuelled rocket engine

**THRUST:** 9,440 lb.f (42 kN)—jet engine
3,300 lb.f (14.7 kN)—rocket engine

**MAXIMUM SPEED:** Mach 2.2 (1,460 mph, 2,350 km/h)

**COMBAT RADIUS:** 746 miles (1,200 km)

**NOTE:** This build is done in a series of 5 modules.

# MODULE A FUSELAGE ASSEMBLY

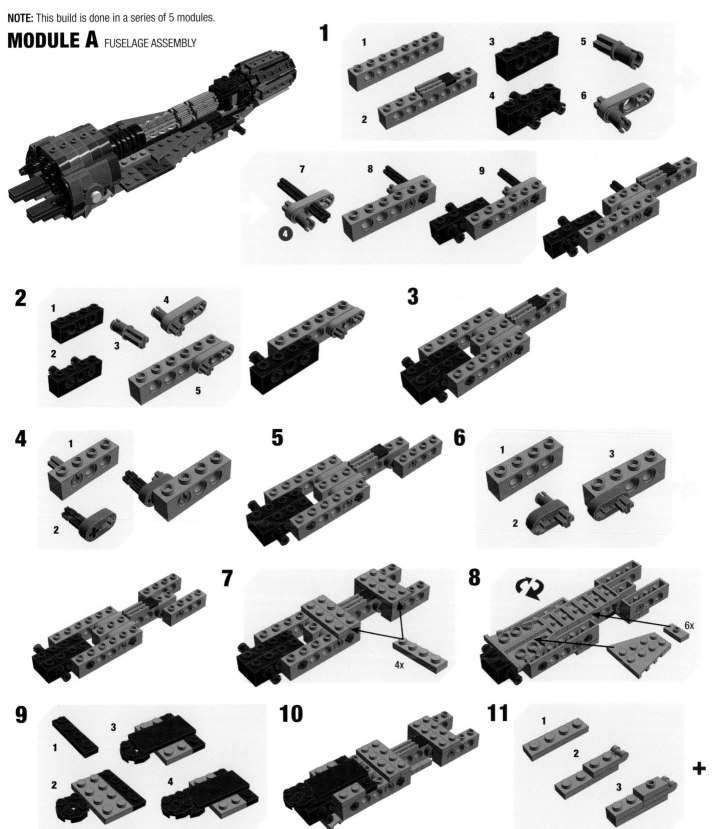

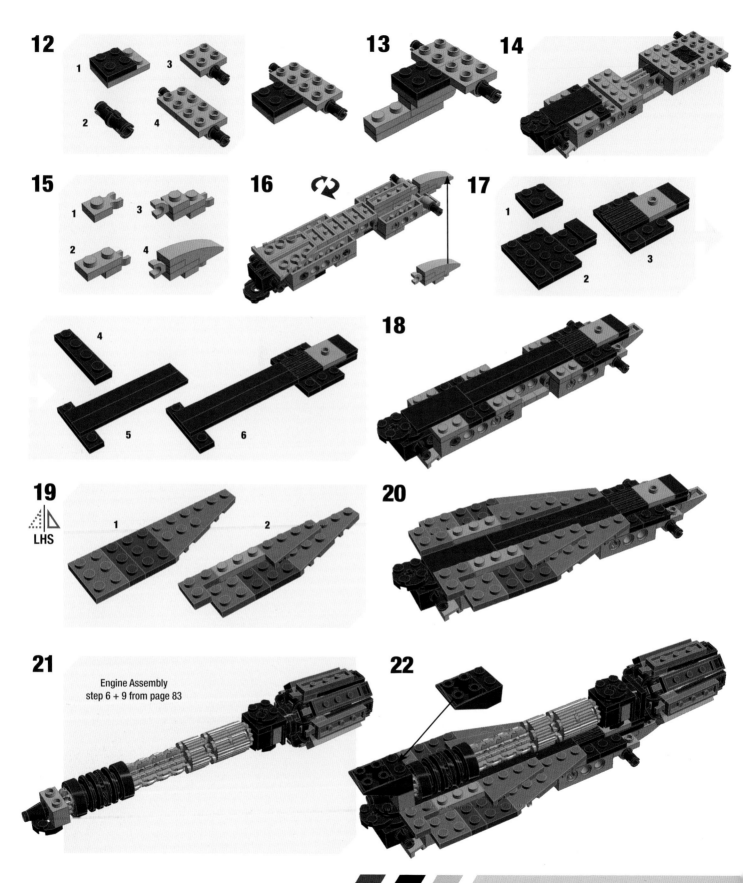

**12**

**13**

**14**

**15**

**16**

**17**

**18**

**19**

LHS

**20**

**21**

Engine Assembly
step 6 + 9 from page 83

**22**

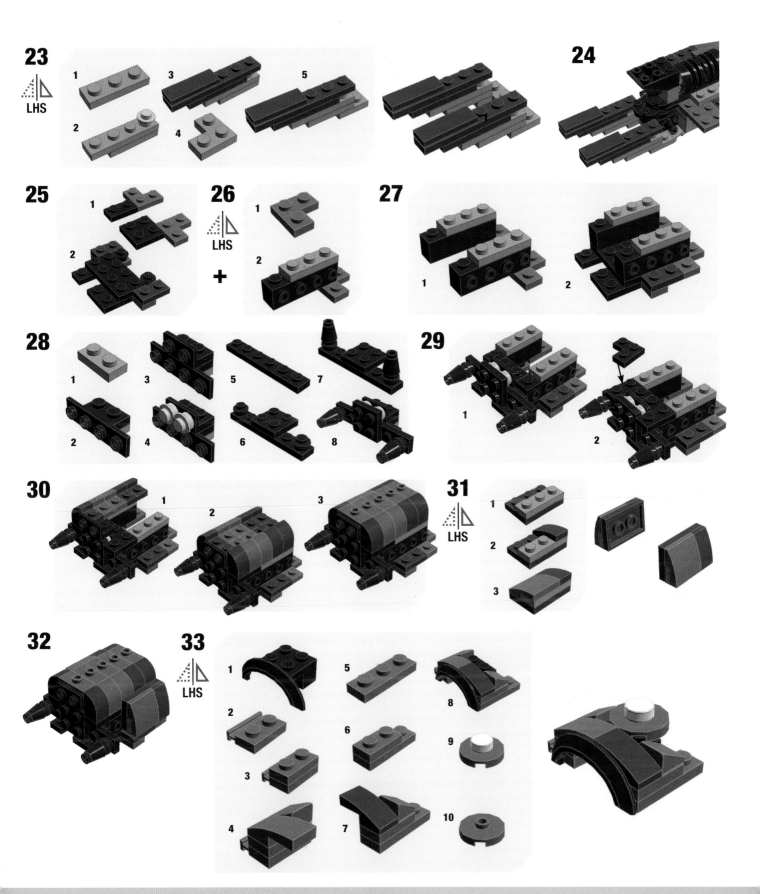

**23**

LHS

1  2  3  4  5

**24**

**25**

1  2

**26**

LHS

+

1  2

**27**

1  2

**28**

1  2  3  4  5  6  7  8

**29**

1  2

**30**

1  2  3

**31**

LHS

1  2  3

**32**

**33**

LHS

1  2  3  4  5  6  7  8  9  10

**34**

**35**

**MODULE B**

**36**

1

3

5

2

4

4x

**37**

LHS

1

2

3

4

**38**

**39**

1

2

3

4

5

**40**

LHS

1

2

3

4

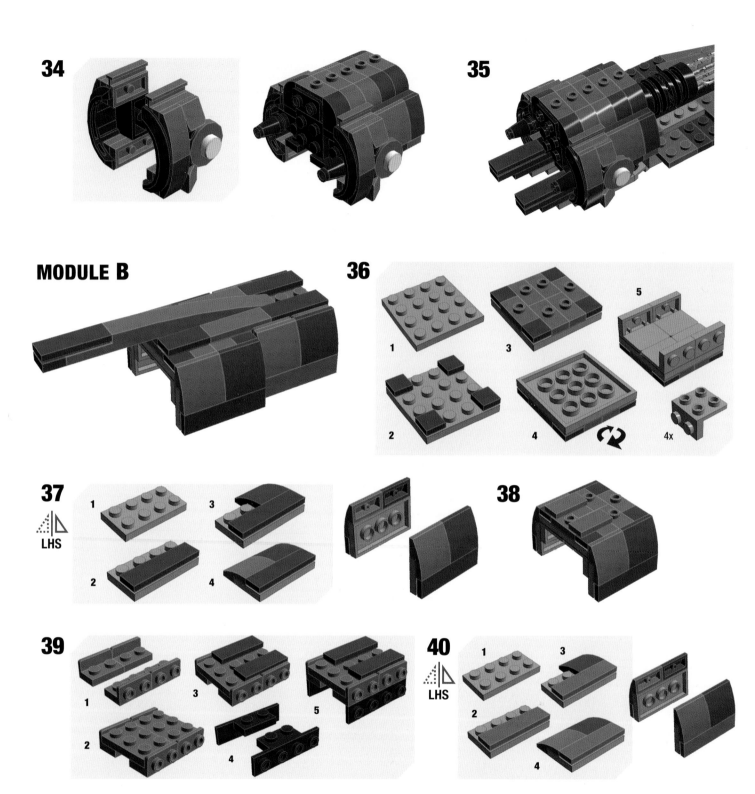

**41**

**42**

1

2

3

**43**

2x

**44**

**45**

## MODULE C

**46**

LHS

1

2

3

**47**

**48**

1

2

**49**

LHS

1

2

**50**

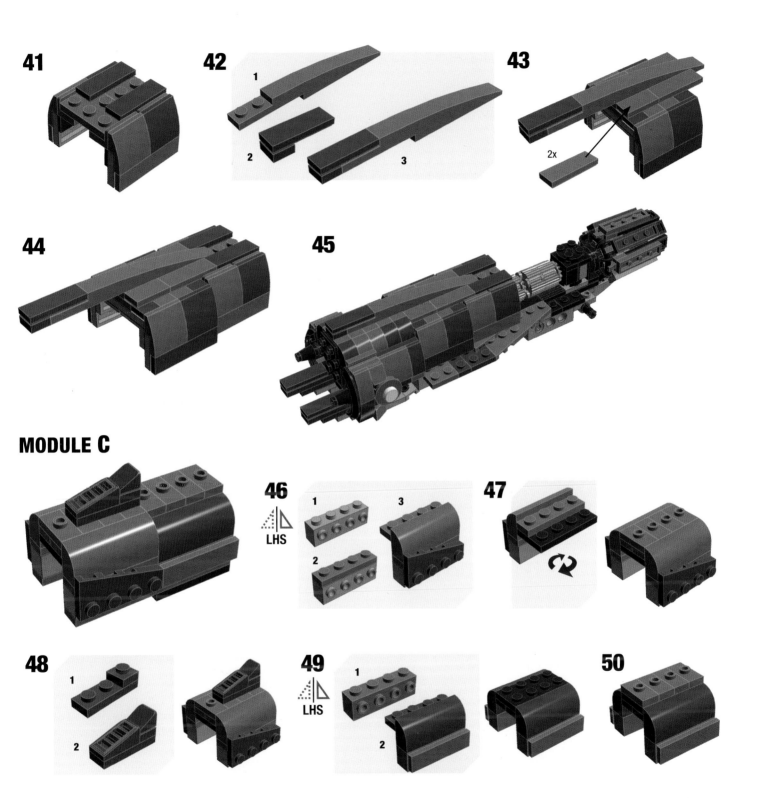

**51**

1

2

2x

**52**

48

51

**53**

# MODULE D

Main Wing LHS

RHS Assemblies are a mirror of LHS

**LHS**

**54**

1

2

3

4

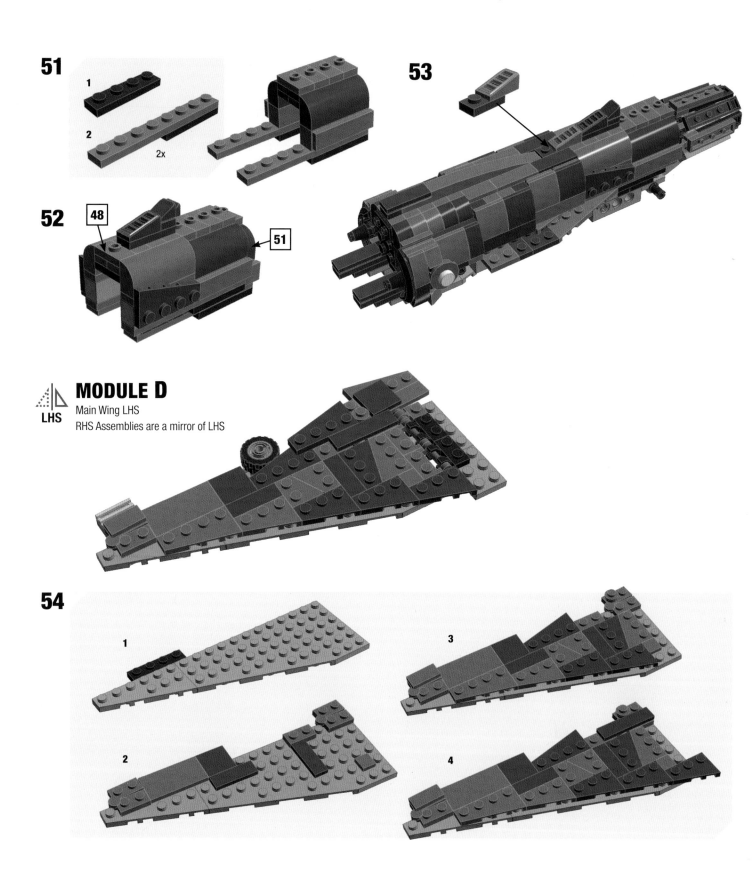

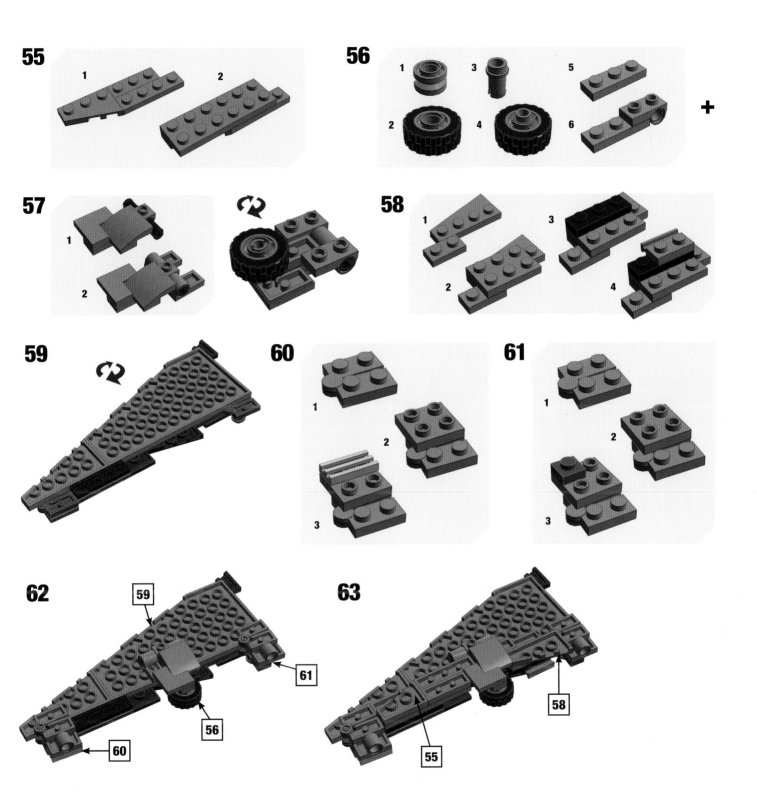

**64**

**65**

**66**

**67**

**68**

**69**

**70**

**71**

RHS

LHS

Assemble Wings RHS and LHS [70] to Fuselage [53]

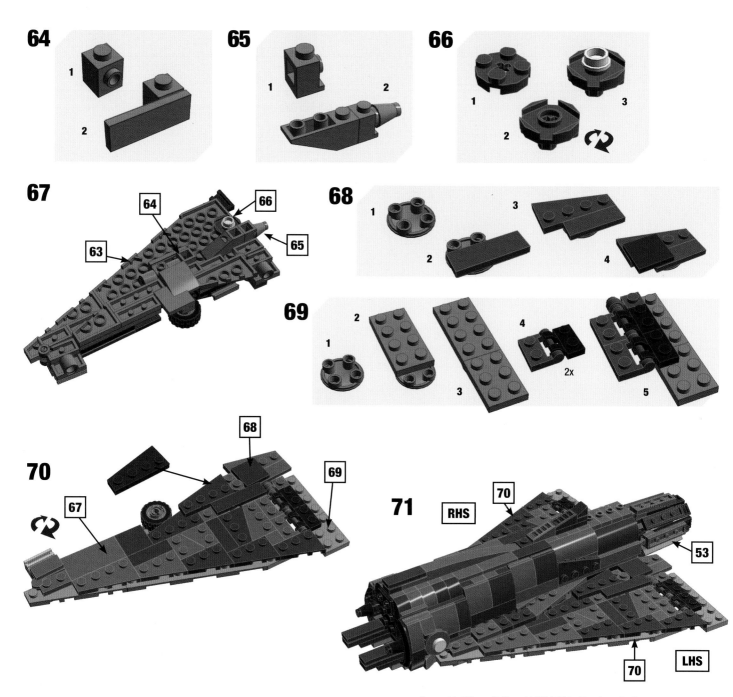

# MODULE E
TAIL ASSEMBLY

**72**
1
2
3
4
5
6

+

**73**
1
2
3
4
5
6

**74**

**75**
1
2
3

**76**

**77**
1
2
3
4

**78**

**79**

**80**

# MODULE F
COCKPIT ASSEMBLY

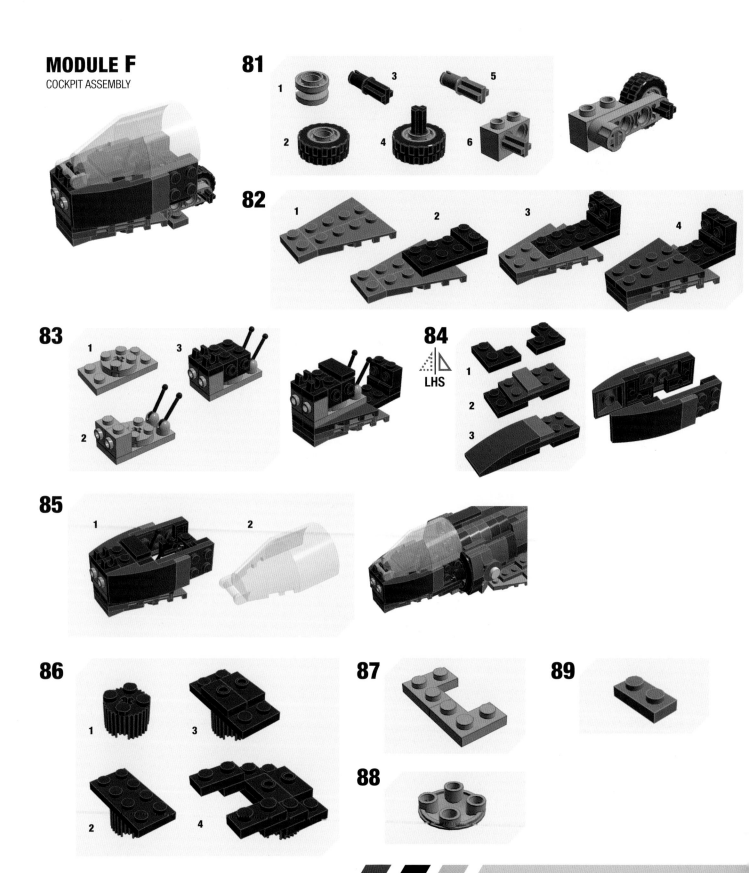

**81**

1
2
3
4
5
6

**82**

1
2
3
4

**83**

1
2
3

**84**

LHS

1
2
3

**85**

1
2

**86**

1
2
3
4

**87**

**88**

**89**

**90**

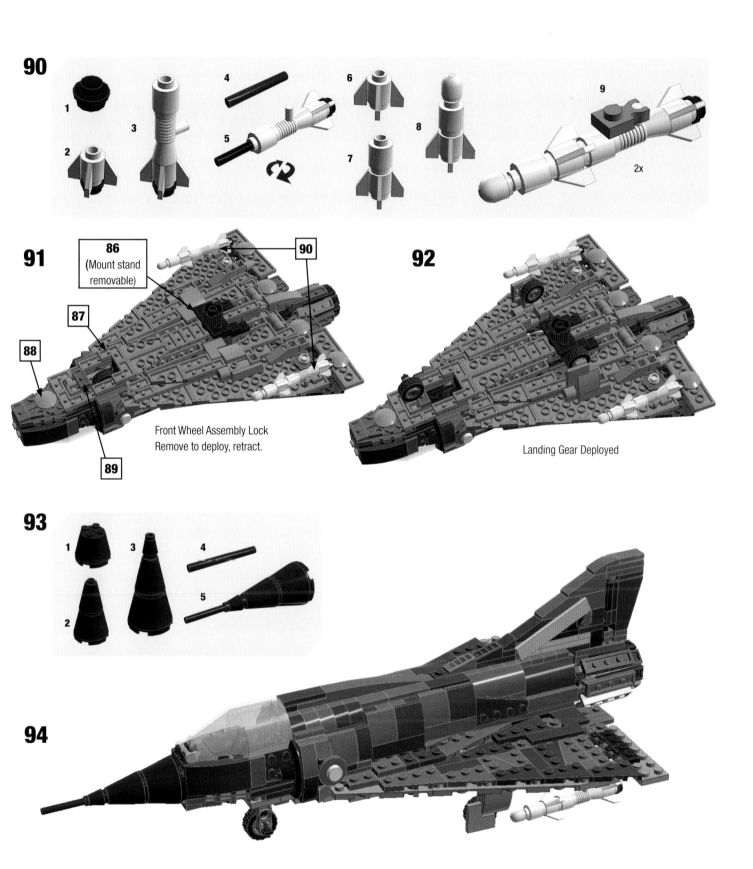

**91**

**86**
(Mount stand removable)

**90**

**87**

**88**

**89**

Front Wheel Assembly Lock
Remove to deploy, retract.

**92**

Landing Gear Deployed

**93**

**94**

## SNECMA
# ATAR 09C JET ENGINE

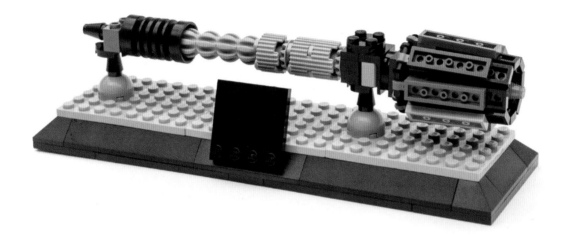

**scale: 1:48**

Turbojet engines had been in development prior to World War II but did not find their superiority to piston engines until the very end of the war. By that time, it was too late for any significant buildup of jet-powered air fleets.

Postwar, however, was a different matter, and the major Allied countries continued making the engines ever more powerful and the aircraft they powered ever faster.

France was lagging, primarily due to the Occupation, but began development of a turbojet based on the technologies obtained from the defeated Germans, notably the BMW 018 axial-flow turbojet. France also inherited the German engineers, who continued to develop the engine for French authorities. By 1948, the Atar 101 engine prototypes were capable of 4,900 pounds (21.6 kN) of force thrust, thanks to improved high-temperature metal alloys.

Further evolution to the Atar 08 and 09 in 1954 and 1957, respectively, saw increases to 13,200 pounds (58,800 N) of force, and the engine was ready for deployment to aircraft. The Dassault Mirage IIIA test aircraft had been in concurrent development, and when paired with the Atar 09B engine, the aircraft reached Mach 2.2, making it the first European aircraft to attain this speed.

Further development to the Atar 09D replaced the afterburner section with one of titanium, allowing for continuous operation above Mach 2.0 (a major improvement over the 09C's Mach 1.4).

The Atar 09C also powered the Mirage V evolution of the Mirage III and other French-designed fighter and fighter-bomber aircraft.

**COUNTRY OF ORIGIN:** France

**MANUFACTURER:** SNECMA

**PRODUCTION:** 1957–1972

**NUMBER MADE:** 1,500

**TYPE:** 19-Stage axial compressor, annular combuster, two-stage turbine jet after-burning aircraft engine

**DRY WEIGHT:** 3,210 lb. (1,456 kg)

**POWERPLANT:** 9,440 lb.f (42.0 kN)
13,240 lb.f (58.9 kN) with afterburner

**VARIANTS:** ATAR 101, 08, 08B, 08K-50, 09, 09K, Plus

**MAJOR APPLICATIONS:** Dassault Etendard, Mirage (and variants)
Sud-EstBarouder
Nord Gerfaut

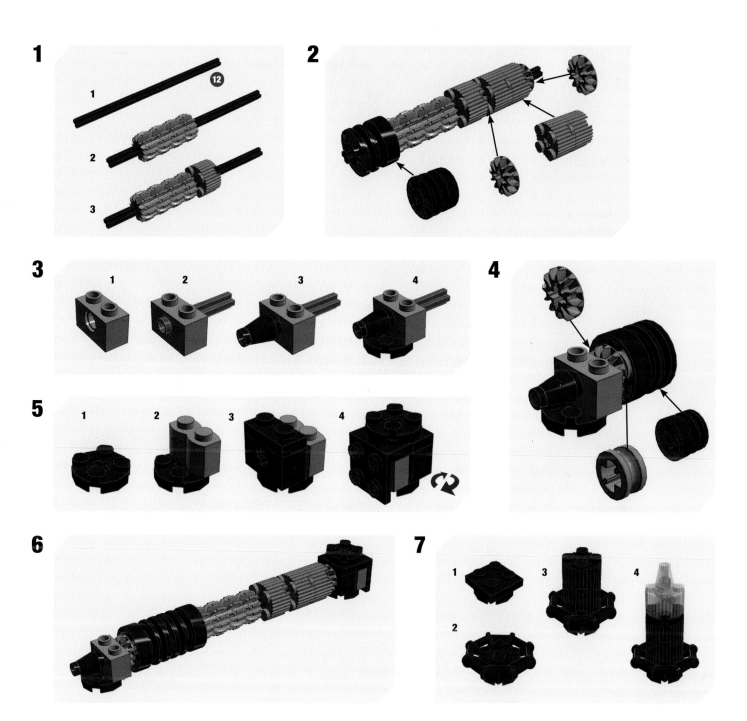

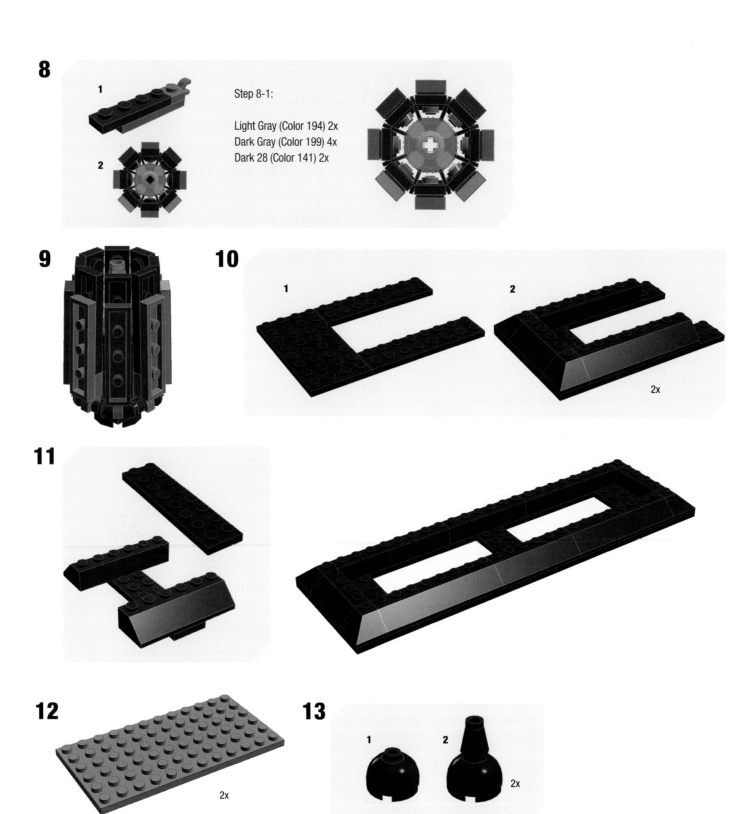

**8**

**1**

**2**

Step 8-1:

Light Gray (Color 194) 2x
Dark Gray (Color 199) 4x
Dark 28 (Color 141) 2x

**9**

**10**

**1**

**2**

2x

**11**

**12**

2x

**13**

**1**

**2**

2x

**14**

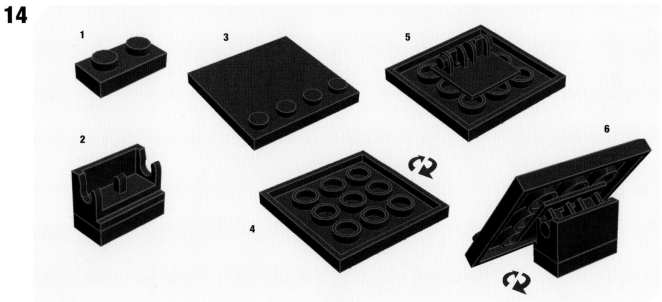

**15**

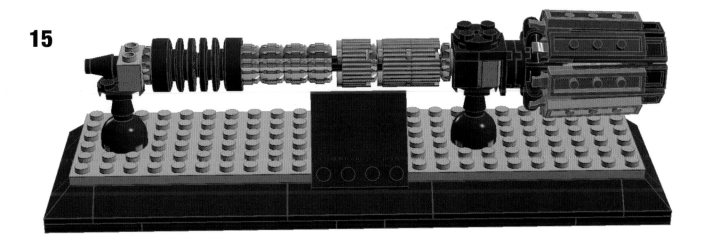

## LOCKHEED-MARTIN
# F-35B LIGHTNING II

**scale: 1:48**

The F-35 is the very latest US fifth-generation fighter. It looks similar to the earlier F-22 Raptor, though it is noticeably smaller in size. The fifth-generation fighter technology refers not only to its "stealth" shape and subtle aerodynamic features, but also to the advanced warfare electronic features that cannot be seen and the pathway for air to travel around and through the aircraft so that its heat signature cannot be detected.

This Lockheed Martin F-35 chapter brings you three planes in one, as it is produced in three principle versions: the A, B, and C. The F-35 is the result of the Joint Strike Fighter (JSF) project, a conglomeration of technical partnerships and strategic international partners (principally the United States, United Kingdom, Italy, Netherlands, Australia, Canada, Denmark, Norway, and Turkey) to produce an airframe with sufficiently technical breadth and modular flexibility to allow for the manufacture of the three distinct F-35 versions as replacements for a large number of legacy aircraft.

The JSF project has been the most expensive fighter aircraft project undertaken in the Western Hemisphere, with program delays and cost overruns dogging the project. But its intent was to provide cost savings throughout the airframe's thirty-plus-year life cycle.

The F-35 is a high-speed aircraft capable of over Mach 1.6, but it differs from the F-22 Raptor (an air-superiority fighter) in that its intended role is to attack ground-based targets and less capable aircraft after initial air defenses have been swept away by F-22s.

| | |
|---|---|
| **COUNTRY OF ORIGIN:** | United States |
| **PRODUCTION:** | 2015 |
| **RETIRED:** | In Service |
| **NUMBER MADE:** | 231 (March 2017) |
| **LENGTH/WINGSPAN:** | 50' 6" (15.67 m) / 35' 0" (10.7 m) |
| **LOADED MASS:** | 49,441lb. (22,426 kg) |
| **POWERPLANT:** | 1 × Pratt & Witney F135 after-burning turbofan |
| **THRUST:** | 28,000 lb.f (125 kN) |
| | 43,000 lb.f (191 kN) with afterburner |
| **MAXIMUM SPEED:** | Mach 1.6+ (1,200 mph, 1,930 km/h) |
| **COMBAT RADIUS:** | 669 miles (1,239 km) |

**NOTE:** This build is done in a series of 7 modules.

# MODULE A

Fuselage for:

F-35B Lightning STOVL

*For the following, complete instructions to 26 then continue at Module B:*

F-35A Lightning CTOL

F-35C Lightning Carrier Version

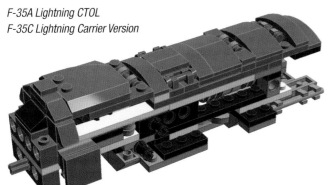

**1**

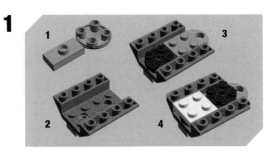

**2**

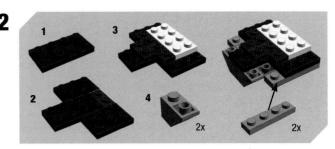

**3**

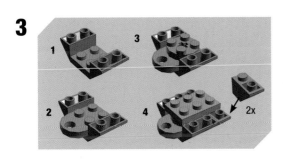

**4**

+

**5**

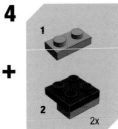

**6**

RHS

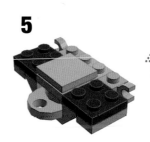

**7**

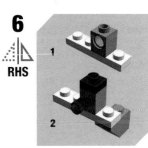

**8**

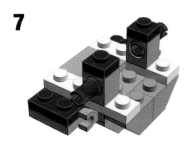

**9**

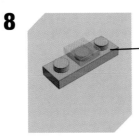

**10**

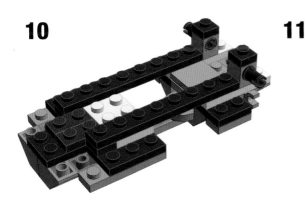

**11**

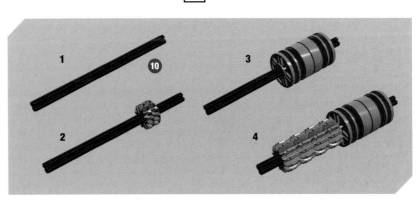

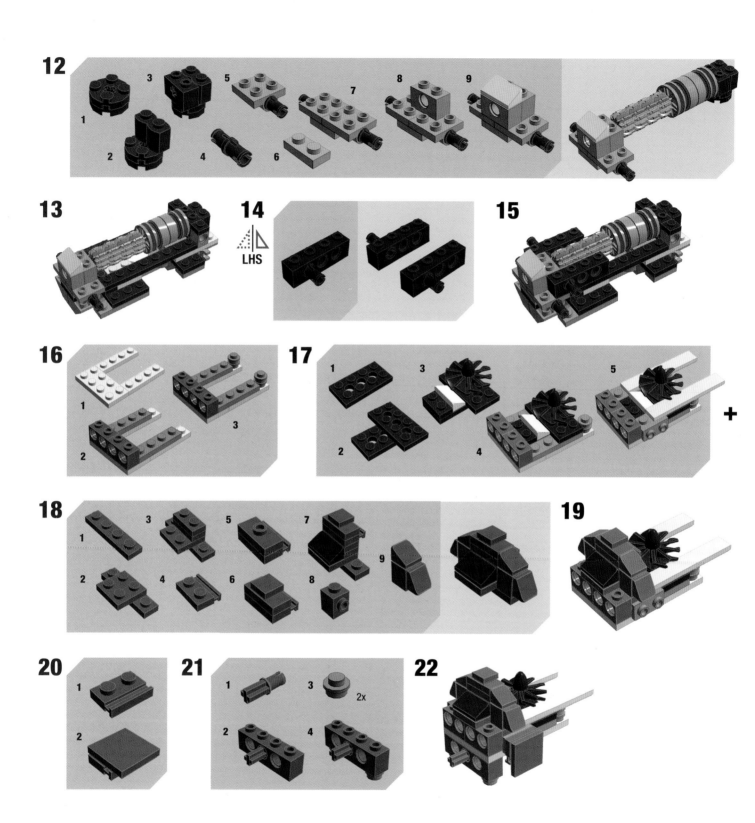

**12**

**13** **14** LHS **15**

**16** **17** +

**18** **19**

**20** **21** 2x **22**

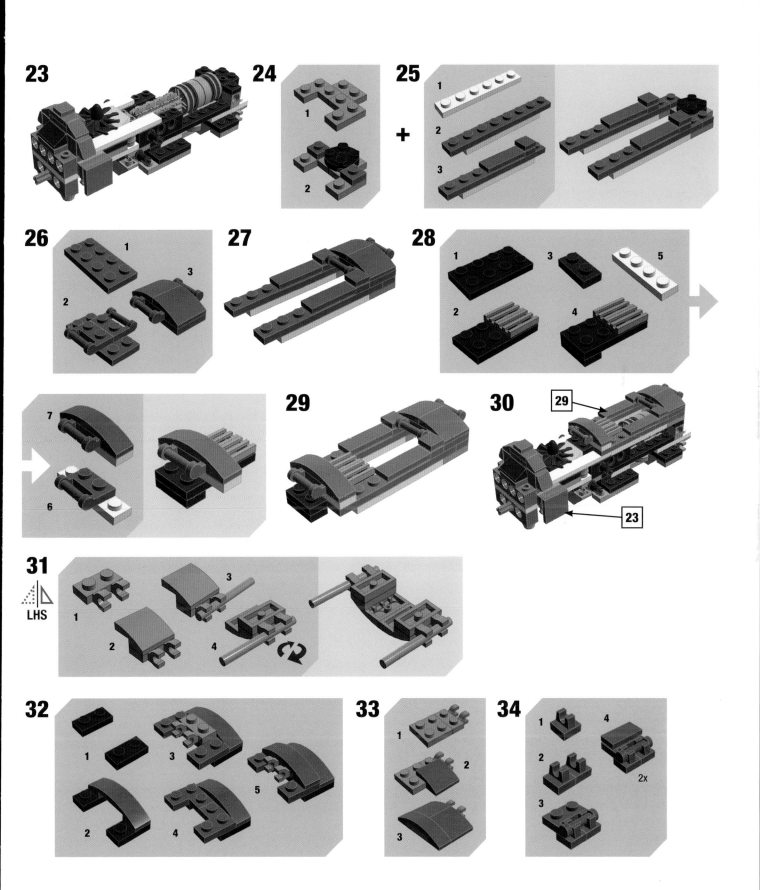

**35**

1

2

3

**36**

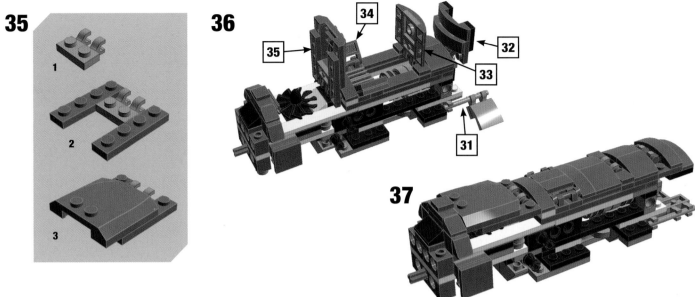

34

35

32

33

31

**37**

## MODULE B

Fuselage for:

F-35A Lightning CTOL
F-35C Lightning Carrier Version

**38**

Remove 3 parts

Remove Fan

23

**39**

1

2

**40**

1

2

3

2x

**41**

1

2

3

4

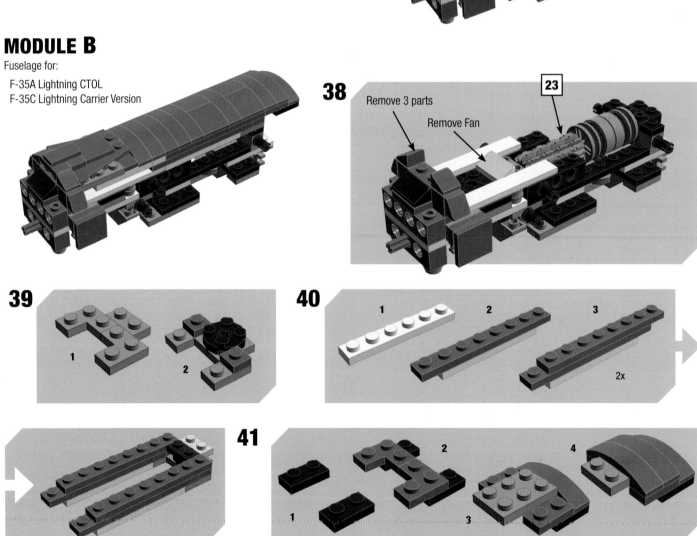

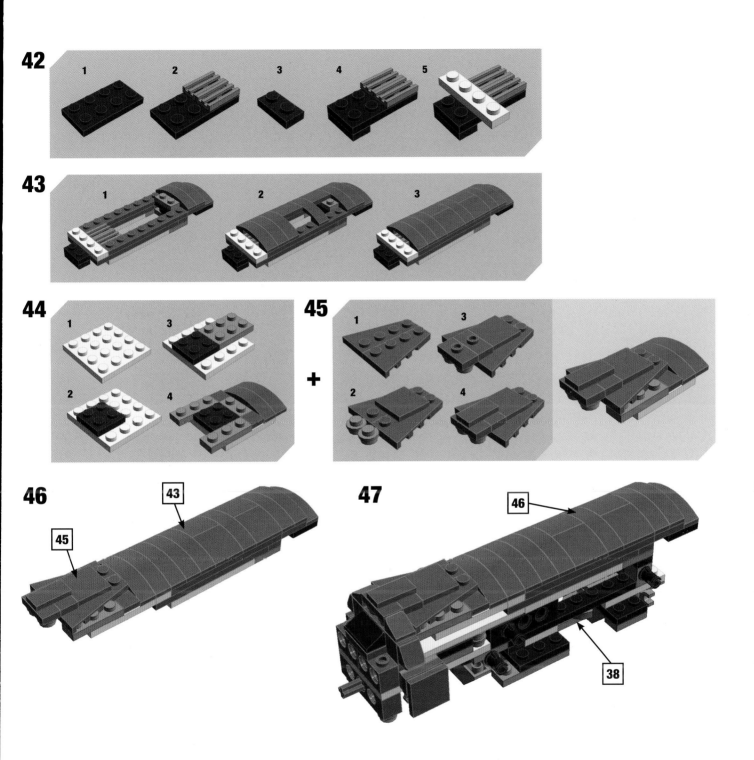

# MODULE C

Engine Exhaust Nozzle for:

F-35B Lightning STOVL

*For F-35A Lightning CTOL and F-35C Lightning Carrier Version complete instructions to 48-3 then continue at Module D.*

# MODULE D

Engine Exhaust Nozzle for:

F-35A Lightning CTOL
F-35C Lightning Carrier Version

# MODULE E

Fuselage Sides, Main Wing, Vertical Tail, and Tail Plane LHS for:

F-35A CTOL
F-35B Lightning STOVL

*RHS Assemblies are a mirror of LHS.*

**48**

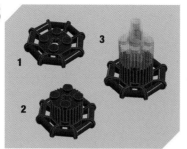

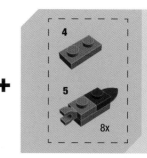

**49**

**50**

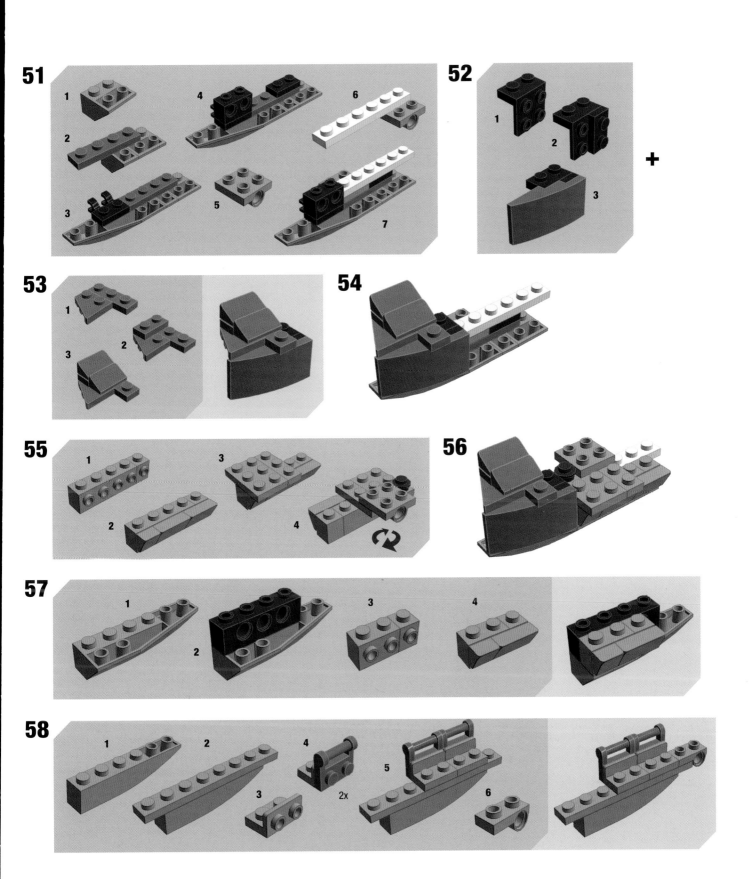

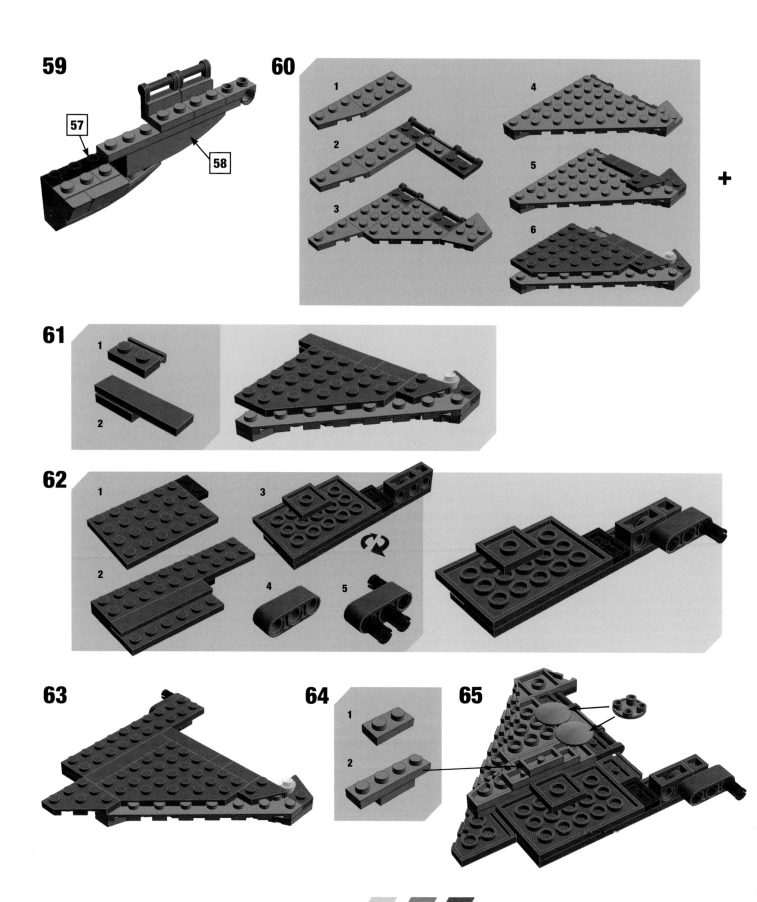

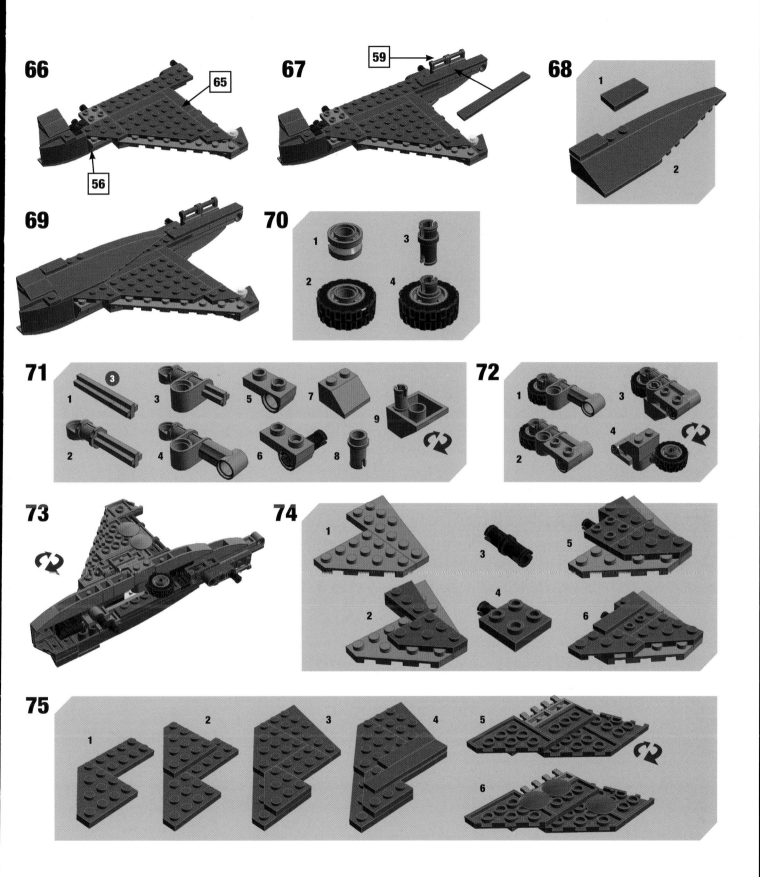

**66**

65

56

**67**

59

**68**

1

2

**69**

**70**

1

3

2

4

**71**

1

2

3

4

5

6

7

8

9

3

**72**

1

2

3

4

**73**

**74**

1

2

3

4

5

6

**75**

1

2

3

4

5

6

**76**

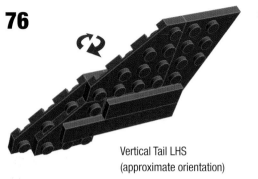

Vertical Tail LHS
(approximate orientation)

**77**

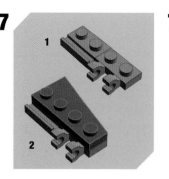

**78**

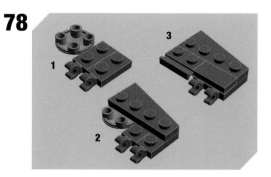

**79**

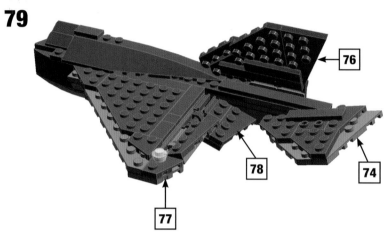

# MODULE F

Fuselage Sides, Main Wing, Vertical Tail, and Tail Plane LHS for:
 F-35A Carrier Version

*RHS Assemblies are a mirror of LHS.*

**80**

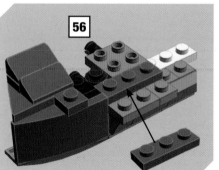

**81**

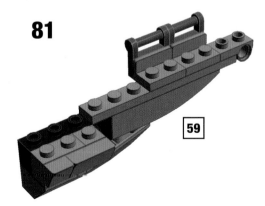

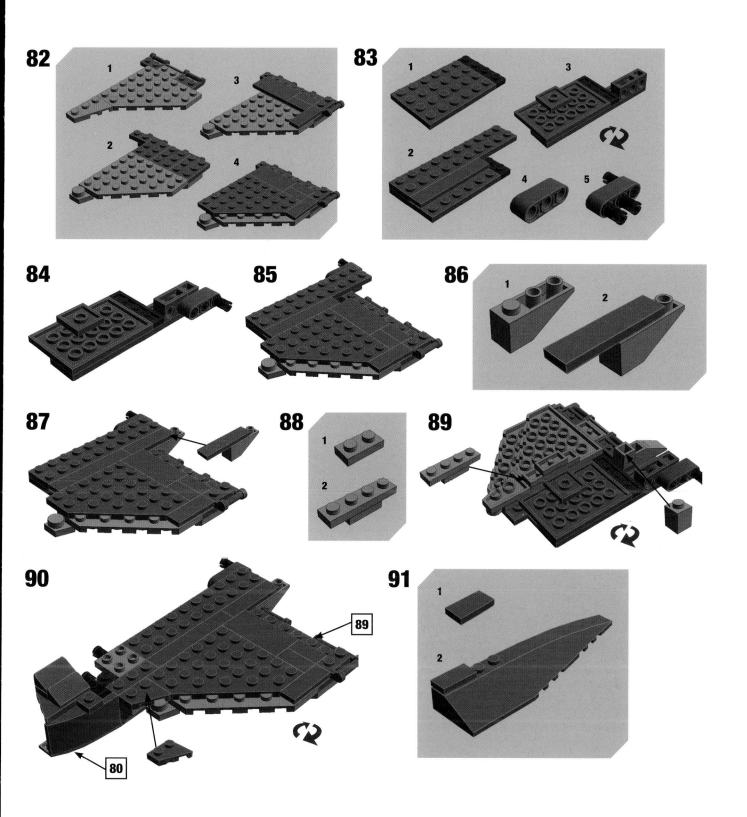

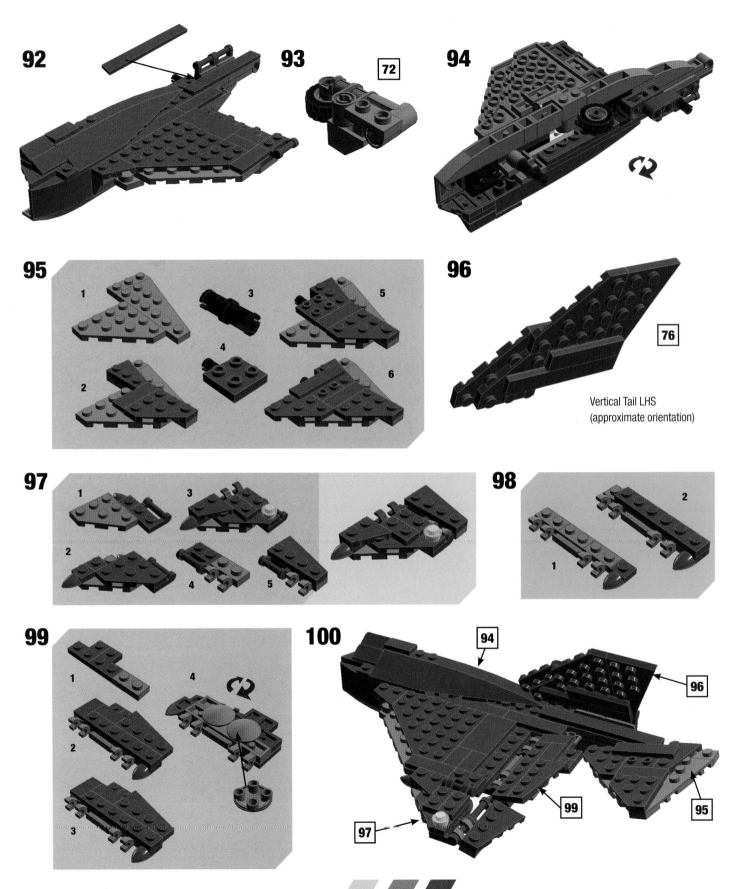

**92**

**93** 72

**94**

**95**

1
2
3
4
5
6

**96** 76

Vertical Tail LHS
(approximate orientation)

**97**

1
2
3
4
5

**98**

1
2

**99**

1
2
3
4

**100** 94
96
97
99
95

# MODULE G

Nosecone and Cabin:

F-35A CTOL

F-35B STOVL

F-35C Carrier Version

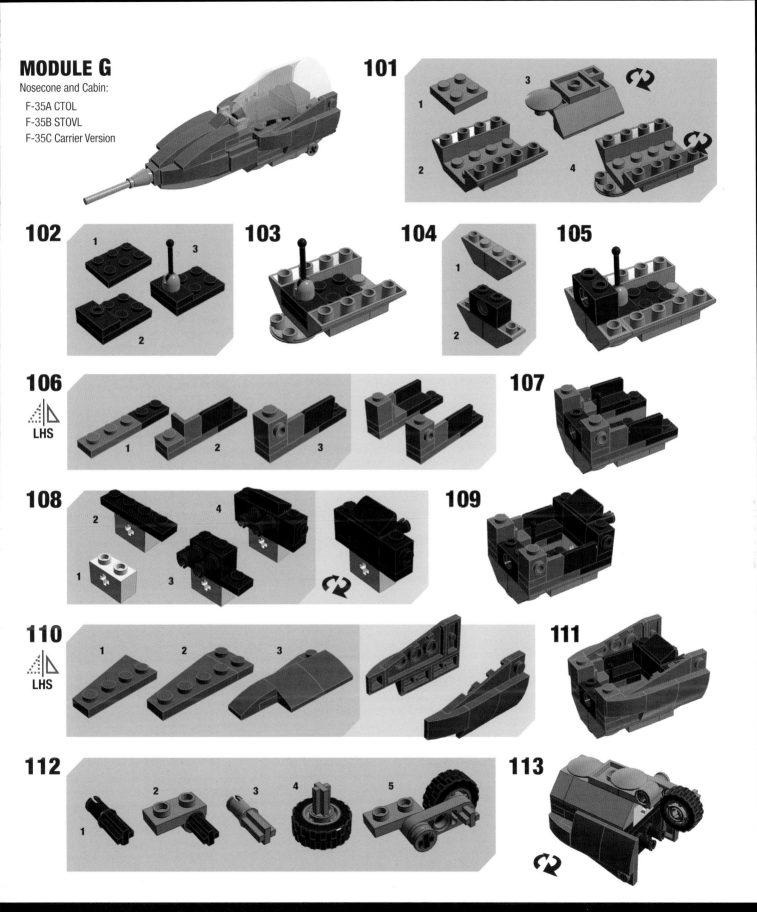

**101**

**102**

**103**

**104**

**105**

**106**
LHS

**107**

**108**

**109**

**110**
LHS

**111**

**112**

**113**

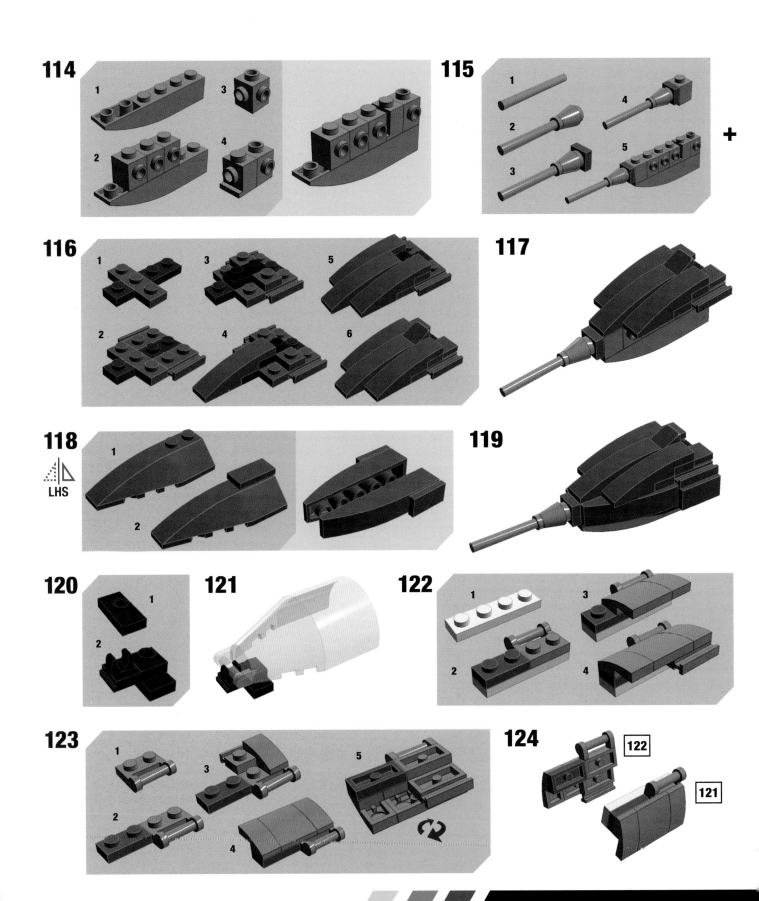

**114**

1

3

2

4

**115**

1

2

3

4

5

+

**116**

1

2

3

4

5

6

**117**

**118**

LHS

1

2

**119**

**120**

1

2

**121**

**122**

1

2

3

4

**123**

1

2

3

4

5

**124**

122

121

## 125

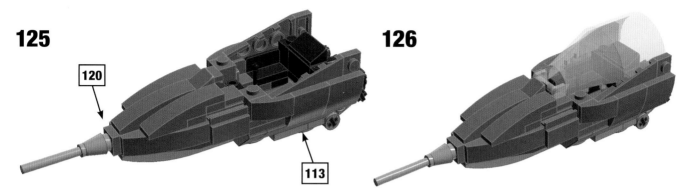

120

113

## 126

## 127

### MODULE A
F-35B STOVL

### MODULE B
F-35A CTOL
F-35C Carrier Version

### MODULE E
(RHS)
F-35A CTOL
F-35B STOVL

### MODULE F
(RHS)
F-35C Carrier Version

## 128

### MODULE C
F-35B STOVL

### MODULE D
F-35A CTOL
F-35C Carrier Version

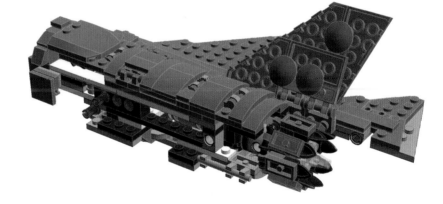

## 129

### MODULE E
(LHS)
F-35A CTOL
F-35B STOVL

### MODULE F
(LHS)
F-35C Carrier Version

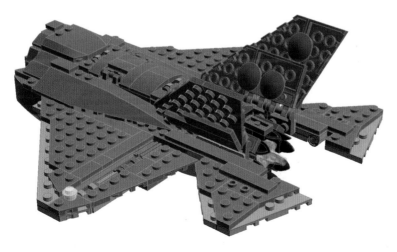

## 130
## MODULE G
F-35A CTOL
F-35B STOVL
F-35C Carrier Version

## 131

## 132
F-35B STOVL

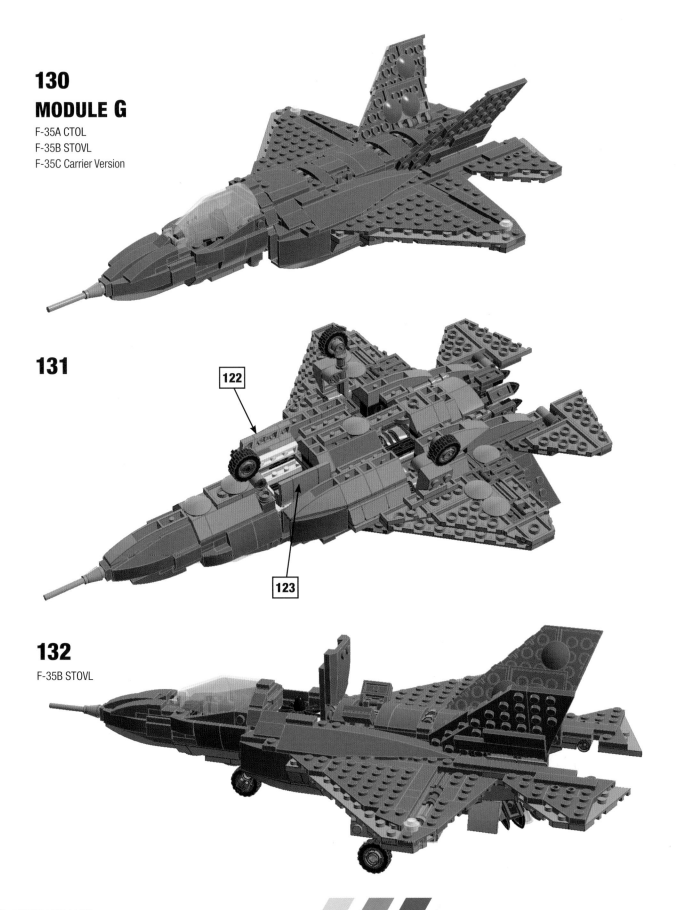

The JSF project uses a platform strategy to minimize the cost and development of various flight, avionics, and structural elements to produce the three principle F-35 versions summarized below.

The F-35A is a conventional takeoff and landing (CTOL) version of the F-35 intended for the US Air Force. This is the lightest version of the F-35 and can carry a combination of heavy fuel loads or military payload. The F-35A is intended to replace the F-15 and F-16 fighters.

F-35B, the short takeoff and vertical landing (STOVL) version of the F-35, is the heaviest, sacrificing a third of the fuel volume of the F-35A to accommodate a lift fan behind the cockpit. The jet engine exhaust is also able to be directed downward via a swivel nozzle at the rear of the aircraft. These two systems allow the F-35B to take off over very short distances, hover, and land vertically. The F-35B is principally used by the US Marine Corps to replace the F/A-18 Hornet and AV-8B Harrier II in fighter and ground-attack roles. The F-35B has similar shipborne roles to Harriers and is deployed on naval vessels with very short landing areas.

The F-35C (carrier version) is intended as the US Navy's replacement for F/A-18 Hornets. The base F-35C aircraft is modestly lighter than the F-35B version, with greater fuel capacity than the F-35A. This allows the F-35C the longest operational range of any of the three versions. This is also aided by an increased wing surface area of 20 percent. The F-35C uniquely has folding wingtips, allowing it to be packed more tightly aboard aircraft carriers.

Each of the three versions of the F-35 can be built from the instruction set presented here. The modular construction techniques have provided the conventional engine and fuselage as one version, with the vertical lift system fan and jet nozzle as an alternative. The folded wingtip, larger wings, and tail planes of the F-35C are also shown as an alternative to the standard wings found on the F-35A and B versions.

| F-35A – CTOL | | F-35B – STOVL | | F-35C – Carrier Version | |
|---|---|---|---|---|---|
| Span (ft) | 35 | Span (ft) | 35 | Span (ft) | 43 |
| Length (ft) | 51.4 | Length (ft) | 51.1 | Length (ft) | 51.4 |
| Wing Area (ft$^2$) | 460 | Wing Area (ft$^2$) | 460 | Wing Area (ft$^2$) | 668 |
| | | | | | |
| Weight Empty (lb) | 29,036 | Weight Empty (lb) | 32,161 | Weight Empty (lb) | 32,072 |
| Internal Fuel (lb) | 18,480 | Internal Fuel (lb) | 14,003 | Internal Fuel (lb) | 20,085 |

# ADVANCED

There are only two models in Section 3. I encourage you build these only after completing the Section 2 models. The P-38 in particular has many complex technical features and will keep the builder busy for at least a couple of days.

The two models here may not be well known to LEGO® hobbyist builders, but they should make a welcome addition to any aviation enthusiast's collection. These two aircraft represent the pinnacle of their times, the fifty-year-old Blackbird still being the fastest aircraft ever made. They are both large models: the SR-71 shares the same 1:48 scale as the two jets in Section 2, and the P-38 Lightning, modelled at Miniland scale (1:21), with over 2,000 parts, is possibly the most advanced LEGO brick aircraft available with instructions.

At this size, modelling in LEGO becomes a mechanical challenge. Many of the same issues confronting aeronautical engineers are also present in building these models—for example, how to keep the wings from snapping off! Aircraft engineering has to deal with four principle forces: thrust, lift, drag, and gravity. Dealing with gravity alone in these brick models shows how much harder adding the other three to the mix would be!

# LOCKHEED
# SR-71 BLACKBIRD

scale: 1:48

Fastest ever. Highest ever. The Lockheed SR-71, now fifty years old, still holds aeronautical records that may never be matched. The role of the SR-71 was to fly at extraordinary high speed and elevation to perform risky aerial reconnaissance missions.

How fast was the Blackbird? Try Mach 3.3+ (2,200+ mph/3,540+ km/h). No other aircraft could catch it, and no missile fired from another aircraft was fast enough to bring it down.

The Blackbird stretched all fields of aeronautical engineering. The body was made of titanium alloys. The SR-71 flew using special fuel—one that was non-flammable at ambient conditions on the ground—as the fuel tanks leaked profusely when the Blackbird parked because of its unique design; at high-speed flight, all the seams and joints sealed (the entire airframe heated significantly due to aerodynamic friction). The SR-71 had special Pratt & Whitney J58 engines with a semi-scramjet operating mode, with cones ("nacelles") at the inlet to control supersonic-to-subsonic intake air characteristics.

This extraordinary aircraft set unrivaled records, including a sustained altitude of 85,069 feet (25,929 m), at the edge of space. Along with absolute speed records, the SR-71 set records for "recognized courses," such as its trip from New York to London in 1 hour, 54 minutes at an average speed of 1,806.964 miles per hour (2,908.027 km/h). A number of SR-71 flights across the United States were timed at under 70 minutes.

The SR-71 was finally retired in 1996, its primary spy role taken over by low Earth–orbiting satellites.

| | |
|---|---|
| **COUNTRY OF ORIGIN:** | United States |
| **PRODUCTION:** | 1964 |
| **RETIRED:** | 1999 |
| **NUMBER MADE:** | 32 |
| **LENGTH/WINGSPAN:** | 107' 5" (32.74 m) / 55' 7" (16.94 m) |
| **LOADED MASS:** | 152,000 lb. (69,000 kg) |
| **POWERPLANT:** | 2 × Pratt & Whiney J58-1 after-burning turbojets |
| **THRUST:** | 34,000 lb.f (151 kN), each |
| **MAXIMUM SPEED:** | Mach 3.3 (2,200 mph, 3,540 km/h) |
| **COMBAT RADIUS:** | 1,840 miles (2,962 km) |

**NOTE:** This build is done in a series of 15 modules.

# MODULE A NOSE CONE ASSEMBLY

**1**

1
2
3
4
5

**2**

1
2
3

**3**

1
2
3

**4**

1
2
3

**5**

1
2

+   +

**6**

1
2

**7**

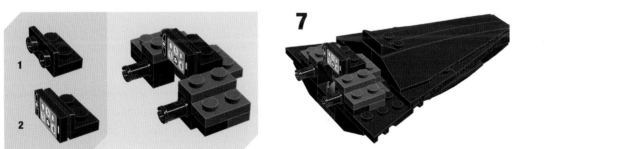

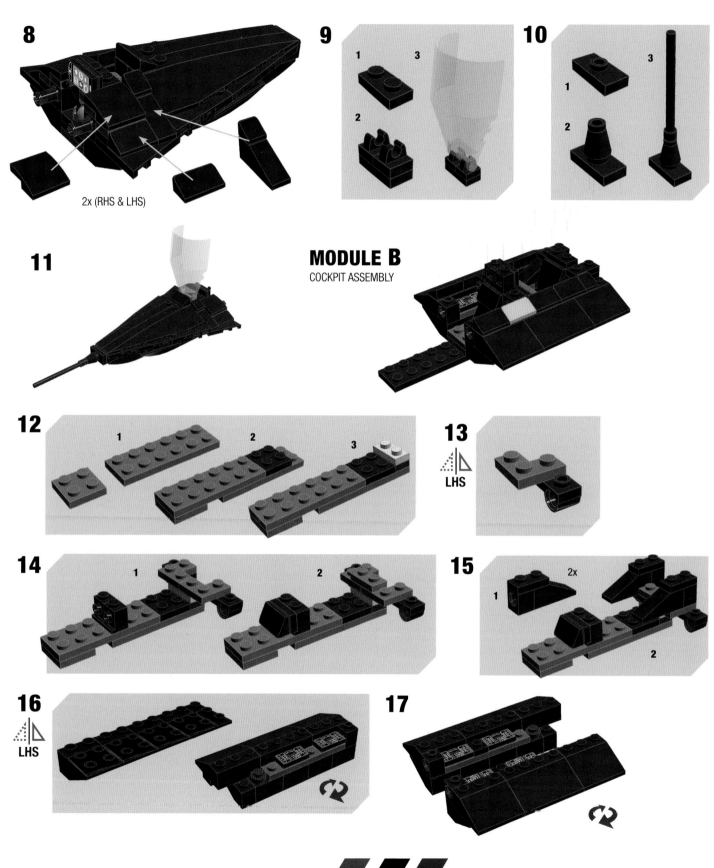

**8**

2x (RHS & LHS)

**9**

1  3

2

**10**

1  3

2

**11**

**MODULE B**
COCKPIT ASSEMBLY

**12**

1  2  3

**13**

LHS

**14**

1  2

**15**

2x

1

2

**16**

LHS

**17**

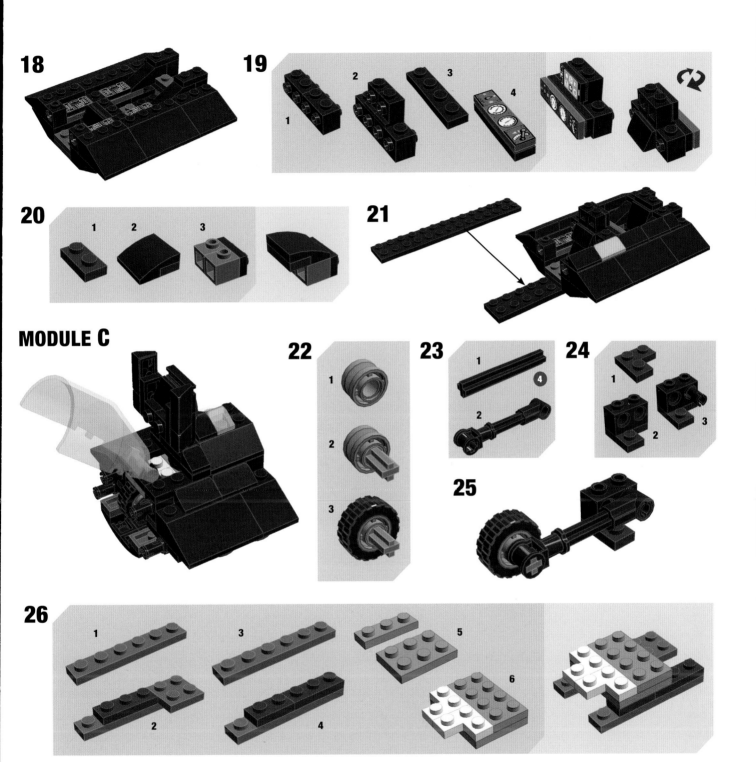

**18**

**19**

1  2  3  4

**20**

1  2  3

**21**

## MODULE C

**22**

1
2
3

**23**

1
4
2

**24**

1
2
3

**25**

**26**

1
2
3
4
5
6

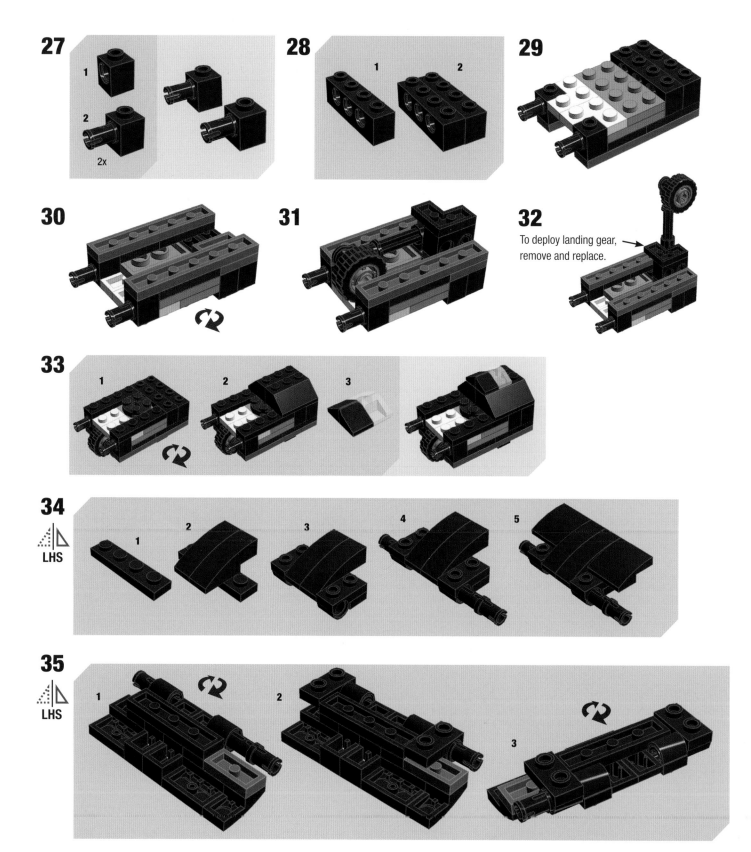

**27**

1

2

2x

**28**

1   2

**29**

**30**

**31**

**32**

To deploy landing gear, remove and replace.

**33**

1   2   3

**34**

LHS

1   2   3   4   5

**35**

LHS

1   2   3

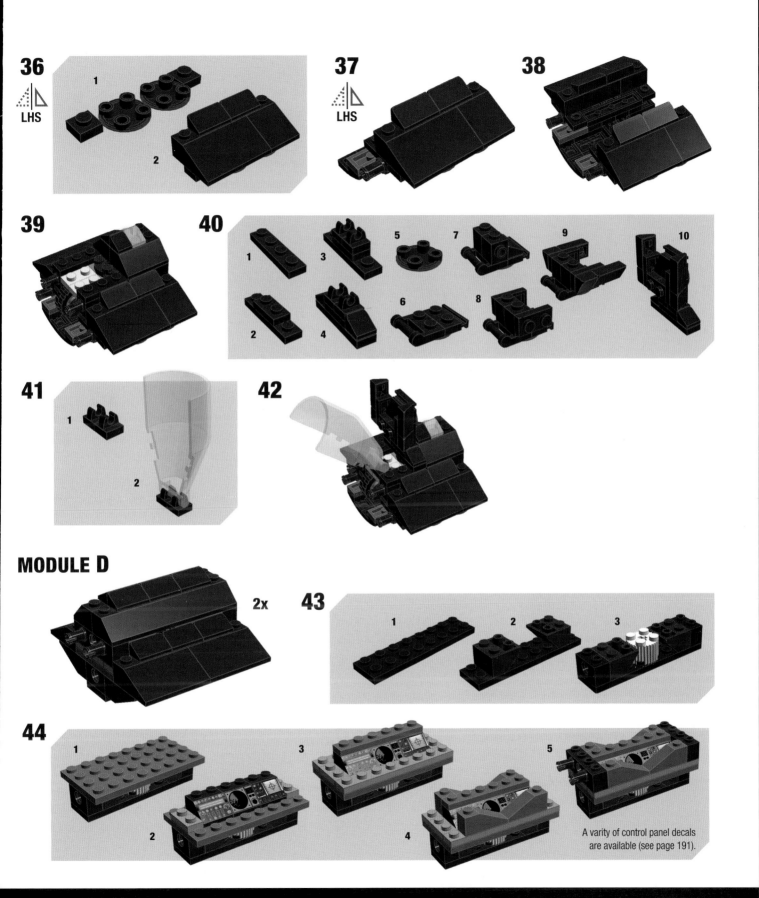

**36**

LHS

1

2

**37**

LHS

**38**

**39**

**40**

1
2
3
4
5
6
7
8
9
10

**41**

1
2

**42**

# MODULE D

2x

**43**

1
2
3

**44**

1
2
3
4
5

A varity of control panel decals are available (see page 191).

**45**

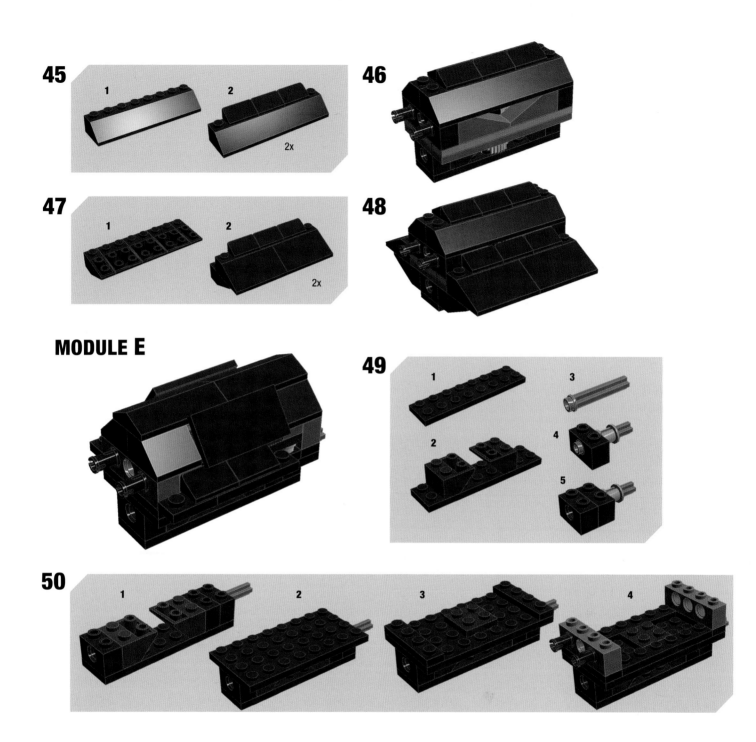

1
2
2x

**46**

**47**

1
2
2x

**48**

**MODULE E**

**49**

1
3
2
4
5

**50**

1
2
3
4

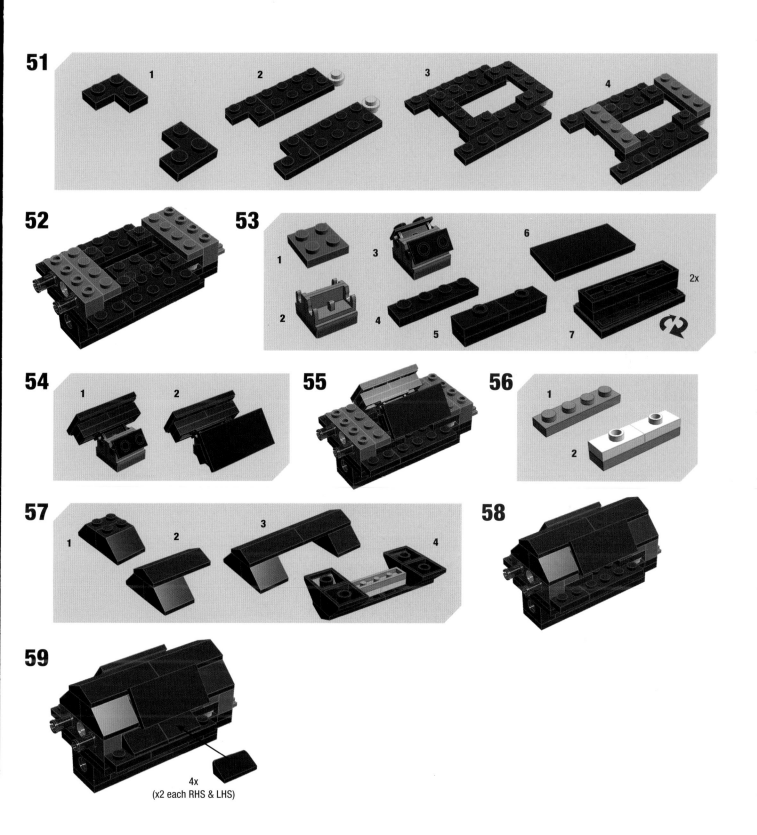

51

52

53

54

55

56

57

58

59

4x
(x2 each RHS & LHS)

# MODULE F

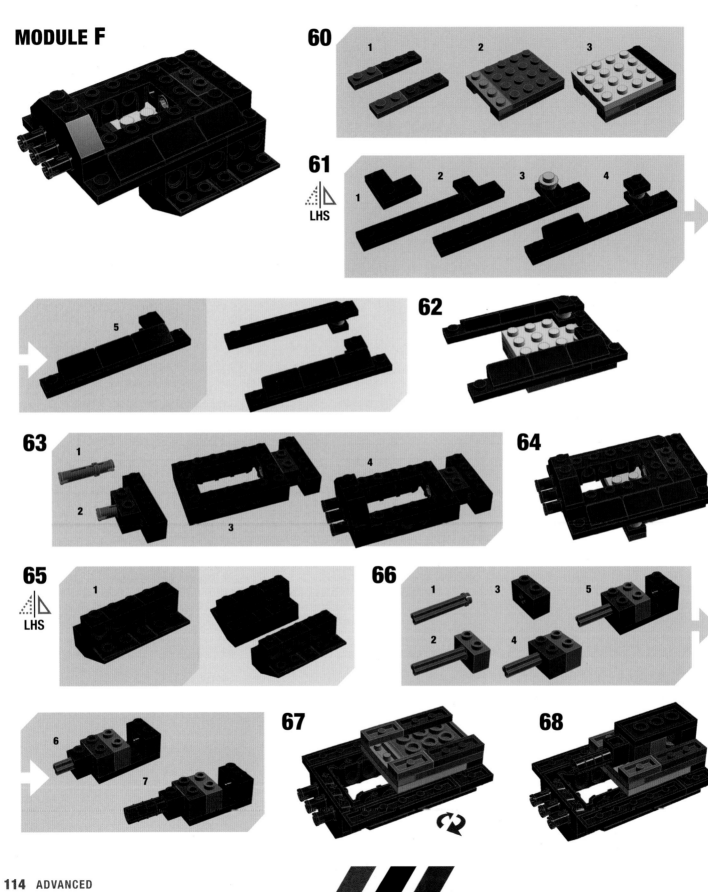

60

61
LHS

62

63

64

65
LHS

66

67

68

**69**

**70**

## MODULE G

**71**
1
2
3

**72**
1
2

**73**
1
2
3
4

**74**
1
2

**75**
1  4x
2
3
3x

**76**
LHS

**77**

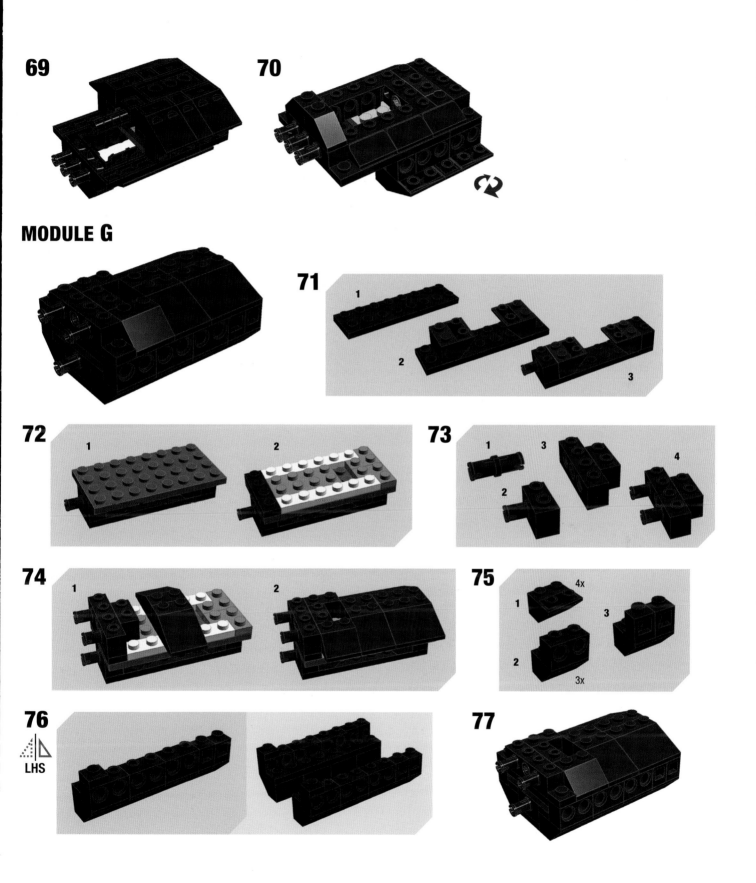

# MODULE H

**78**

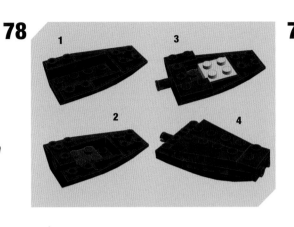

**79**

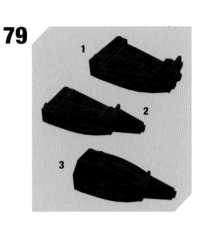

# MODULE I

Forewing LHS

*RHS Forewing is a mirror assembly.*

**80**

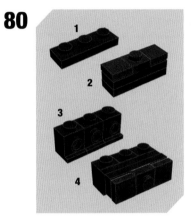

**81**

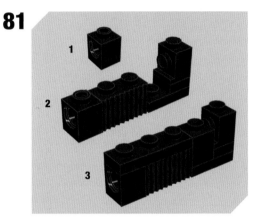

**82**

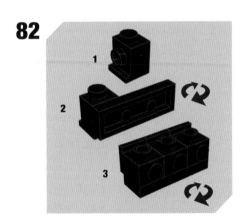

**83**

**84**

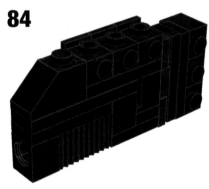

**85**

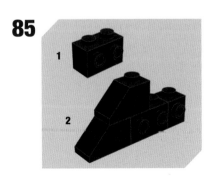

**86**

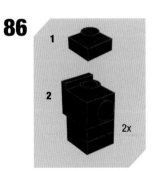

2x

**87**

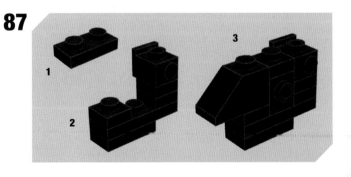

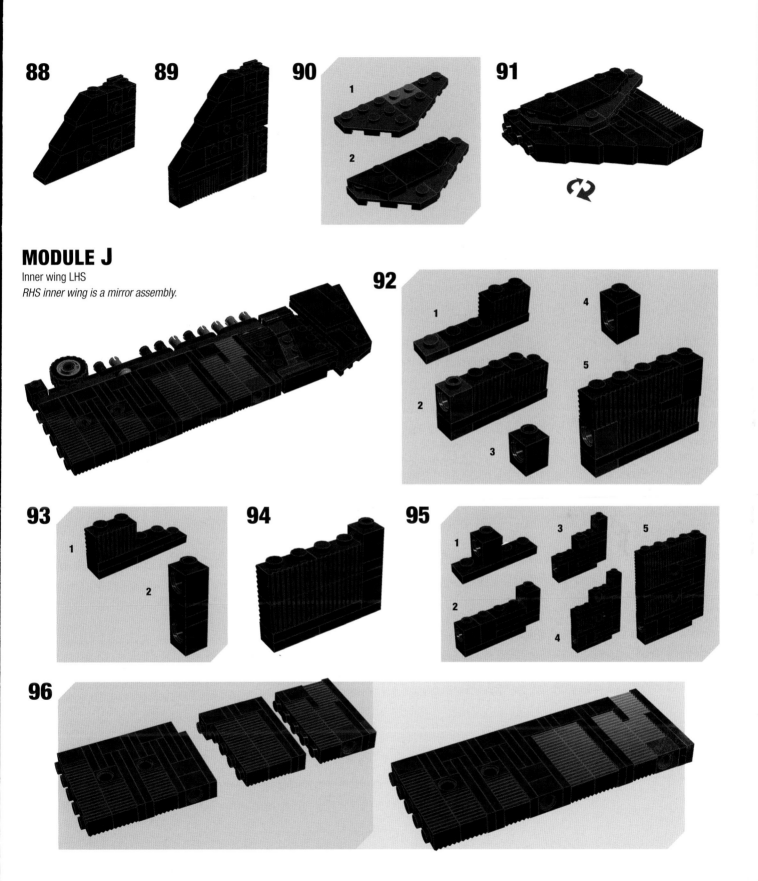

**88**

**89**

**90**
1
2

**91**

## MODULE J
Inner wing LHS
*RHS inner wing is a mirror assembly.*

**92**
1
2
3
4
5

**93**
1
2

**94**

**95**
1
2
3
4
5

**96**

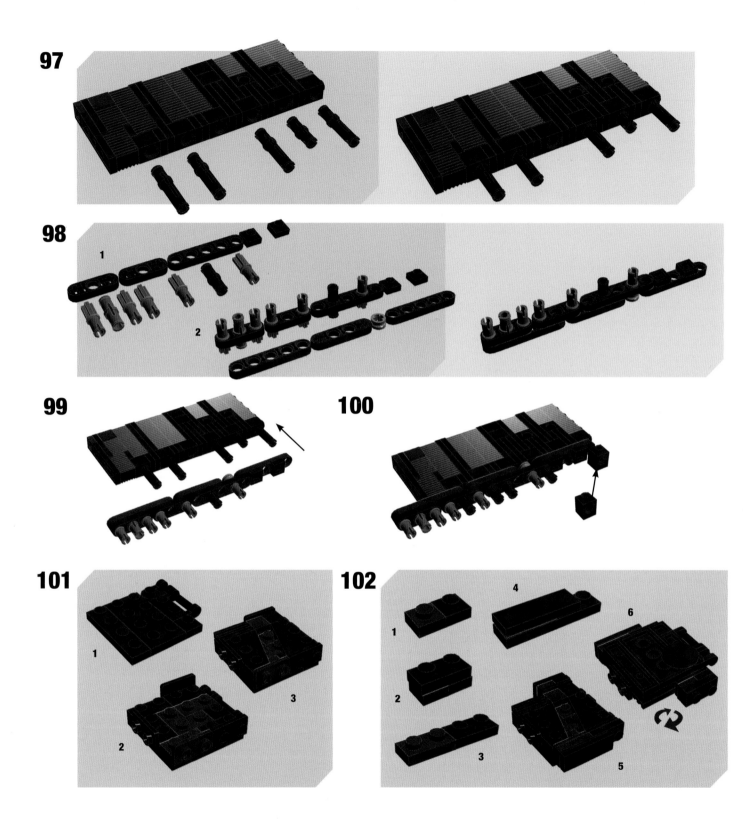

**97**

**98**

**99**

**100**

**101**

**102**

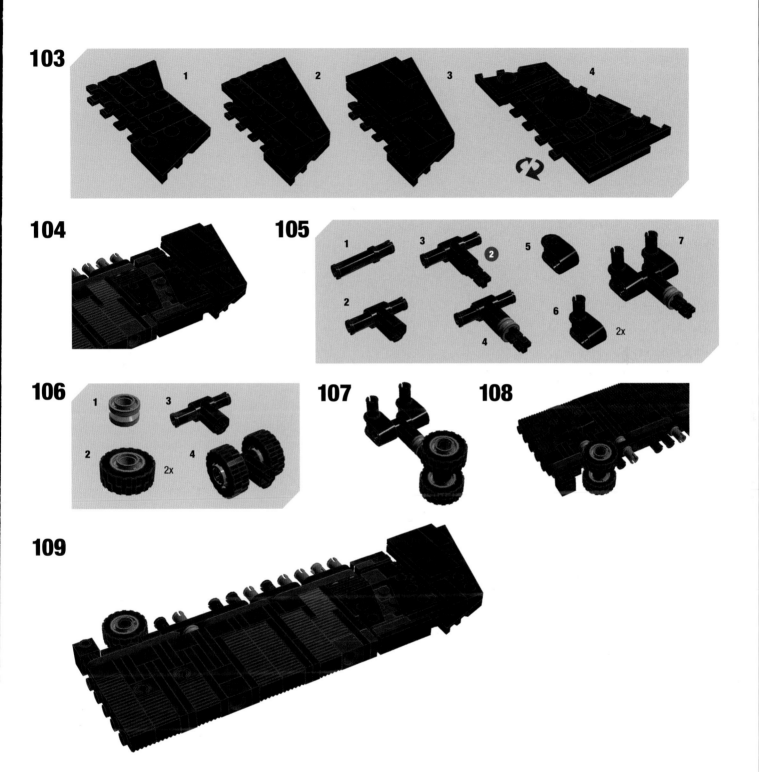

**103**

**104**

**105**

**106**

**107**

**108**

**109**

# MODULE K  A

Engine Module LHS
*RHS Engine Module is a mirror assembly
(connector peg is the only difference).*

**110**

**111**

**112**

**113**

**114**

**115  A**

**116  A**

**117  A**

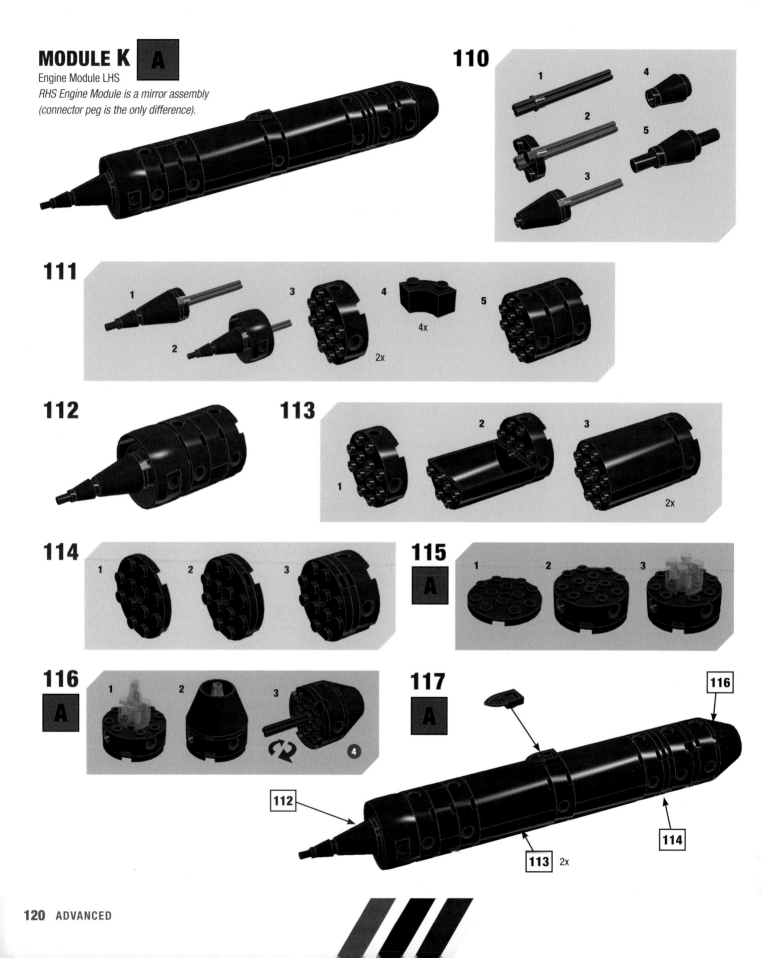

**118**
**B**

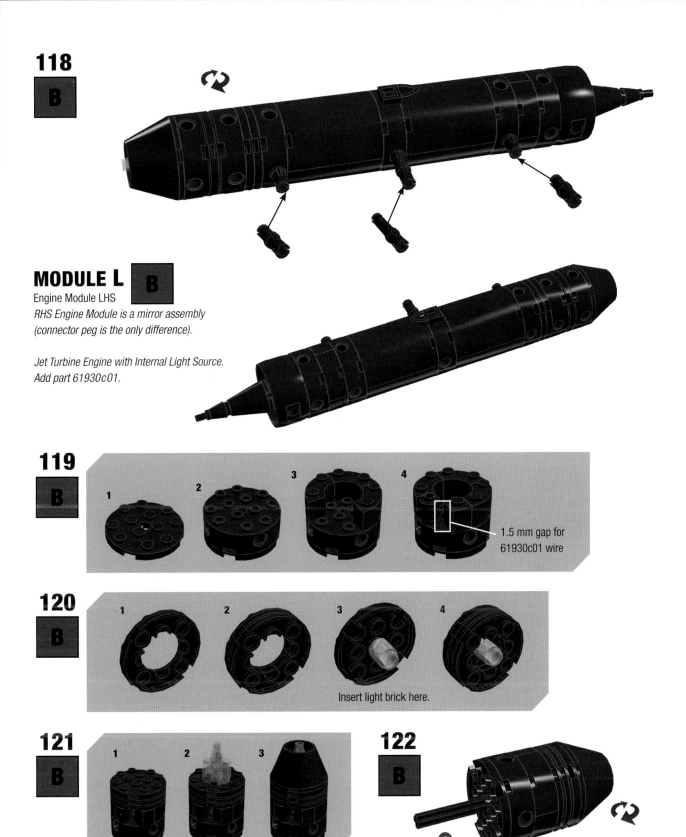

# MODULE L **B**
Engine Module LHS
*RHS Engine Module is a mirror assembly*
*(connector peg is the only difference).*

*Jet Turbine Engine with Internal Light Source.*
*Add part 61930c01.*

**119**
**B**

1 2 3 4

1.5 mm gap for
61930c01 wire

**120**
**B**

1 2 3 4

Insert light brick here.

**121**
**B**

1 2 3

**122**
**B**

4

## 123

**B**

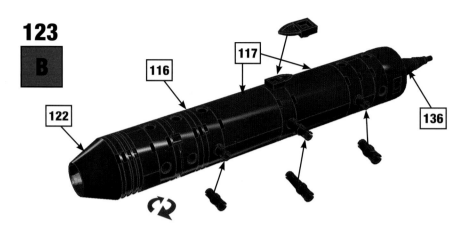

## MODULE M

Outer wing LHS

*RHS outer wing is a mirror assembly.*

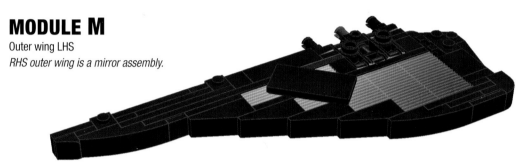

## 124

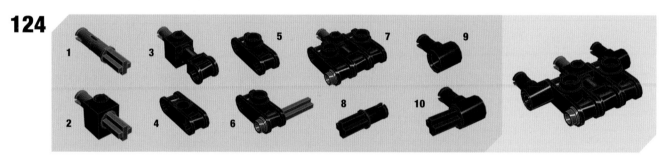

## 125

## 126

## 127

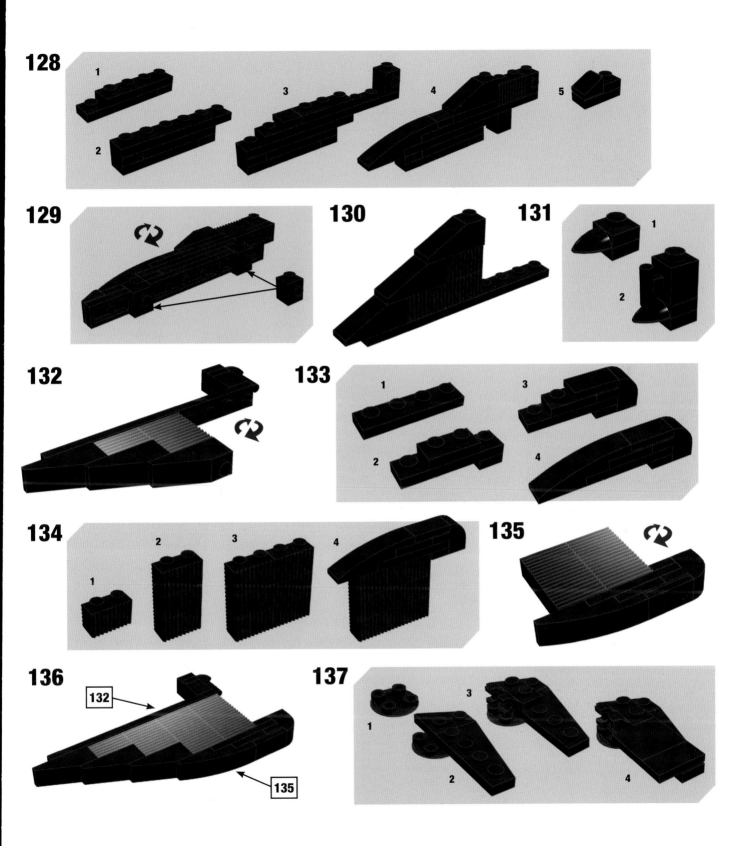

**138**

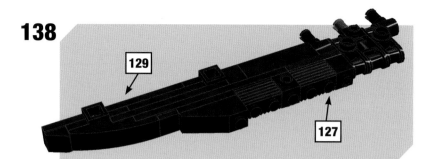

**139**

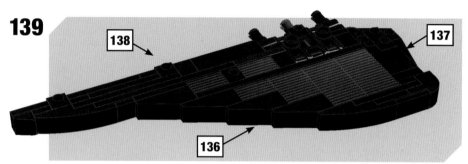

**140**

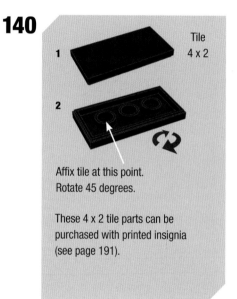

Tile
4 x 2

Affix tile at this point.
Rotate 45 degrees.

These 4 x 2 tile parts can be purchased with printed insignia (see page 191).

**141**

Attach 4 x 2 tile to lower face at same part.

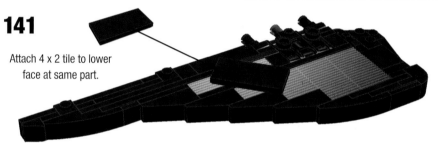

# MODULE N

Vertical Tail LHS

*RHS vertical tail is a mirror assembly.*

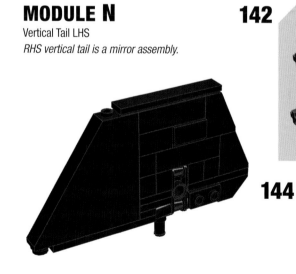

**142**

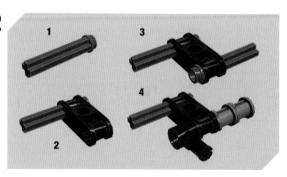

**143**

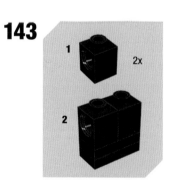

2x

**144**

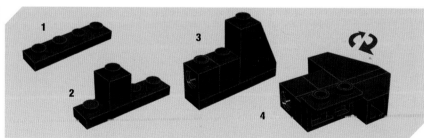

**145**

**146**

1
3
2

**147**

1
2

**148**

146
145

**149**

148
147

**MODULE O**

**150**

1
2

**151**

A
C
B

2x
(RHS & LHS)

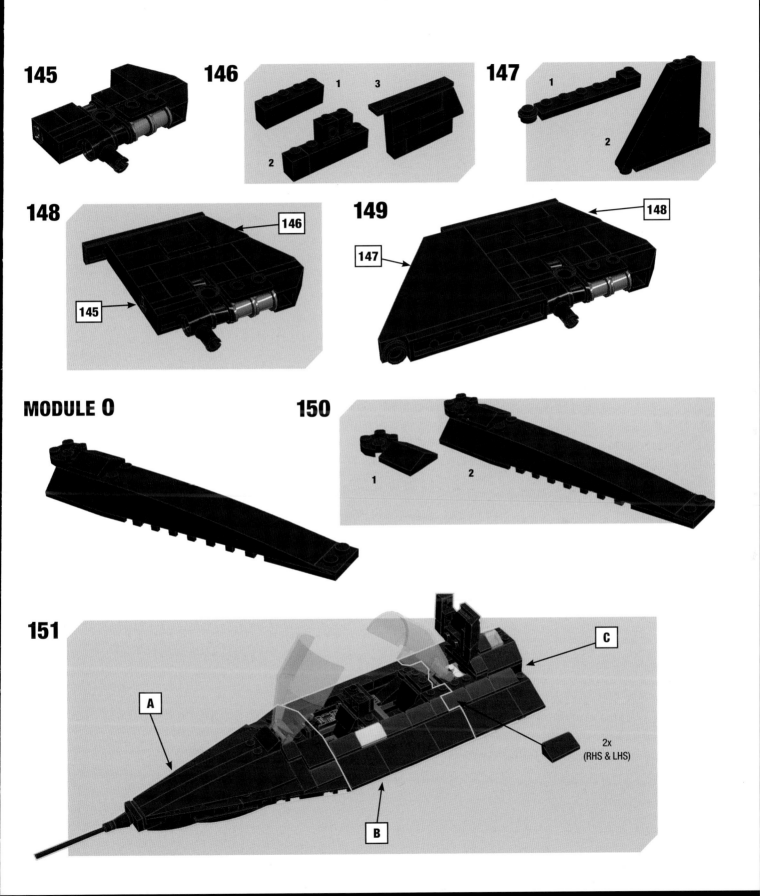

**152**

2x
(RHS & LHS)

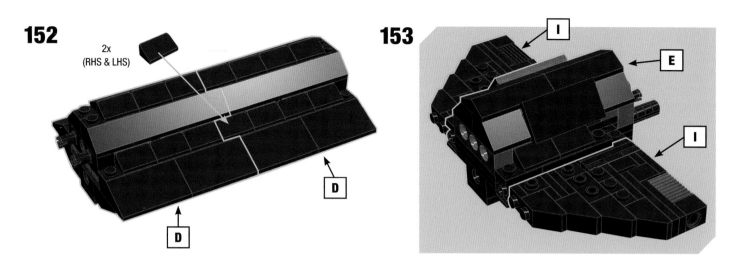

D

D

D

**153**

I

E

I

**154**

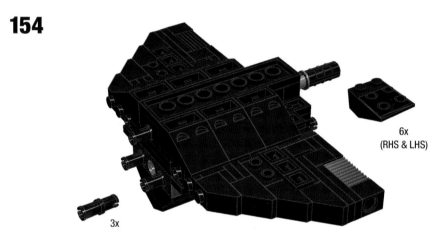

6x
(RHS & LHS)

3x

**155**

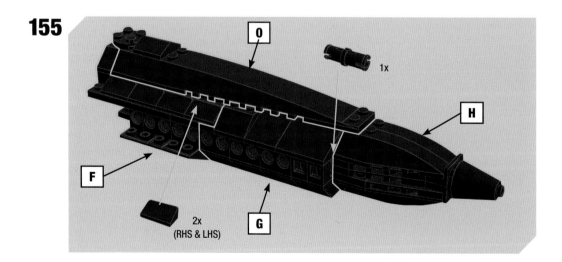

O

1x

H

F

G

2x
(RHS & LHS)

**156**

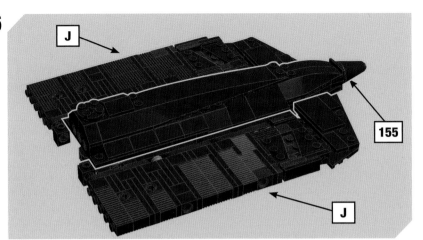

J

155

J

**157**

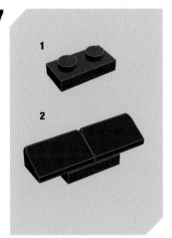

1

2

**158**

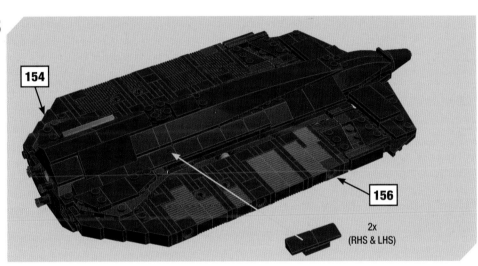

154

156

2x
(RHS & LHS)

**159**

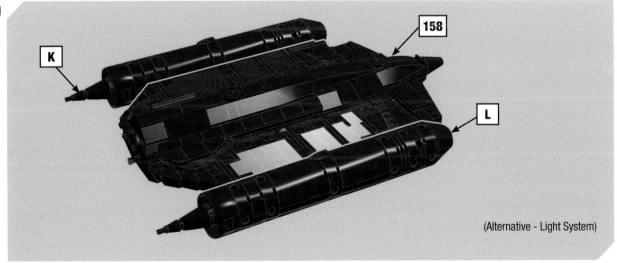

158

K

L

(Alternative - Light System)

**160**

M

M

2x
(LHS & RHS)

**161**

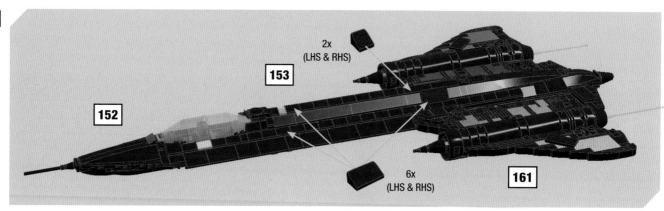

2x
(LHS & RHS)

153

152

6x
(LHS & RHS)

161

**162**

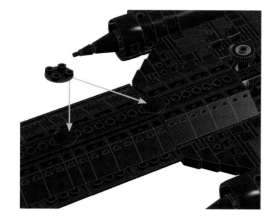

**163**

N

**164**

Incline approximately
20° inboard

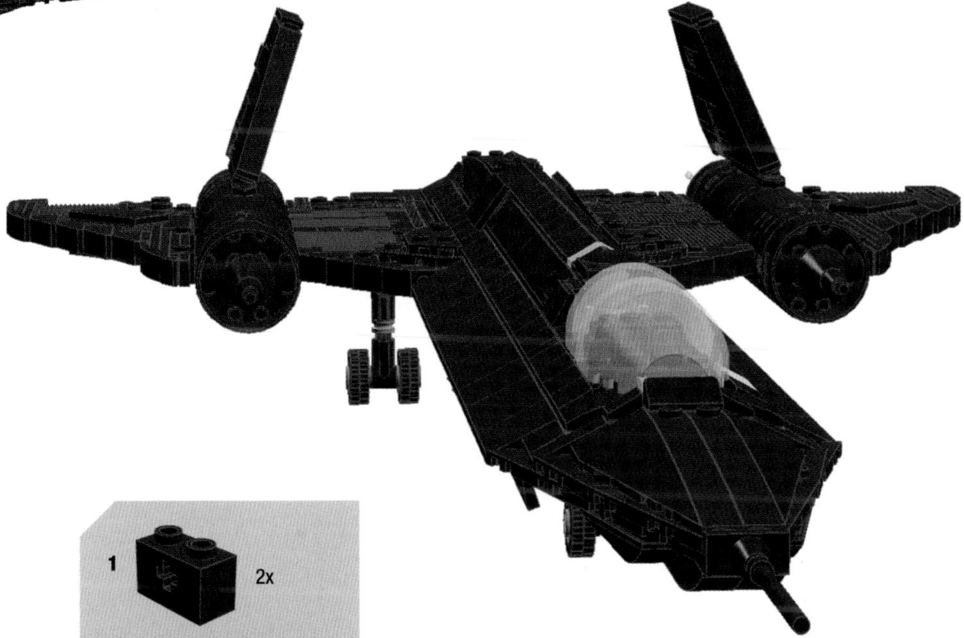

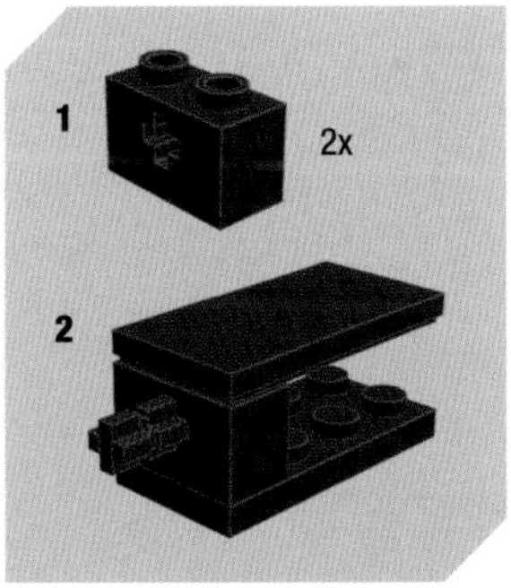

1    2x

2

The aircraft display stand used in the official LEGO® 10177 Boeing 787
Dreamliner can be used to display the Lockheed SR-71 Blackbird model
shown here using these modifications to the end form.

# P-38 LIGHTNING

scale: 1:21

The Lockheed P-38 Lightning was known by the Germans as *der Gabelschwanz-Tuefel* (the fork-tailed devil), a reference to the twin booms that housed the engines and the central nacelle containing the cockpit. The P-38 was designated as a heavy fighter, a bruiser.

And a bruiser it was. Although the P-38 was manufactured during the entire time the United States was engaged in World War II and flew in most theaters, it excelled in the Pacific, where its long range allowed it to inflict casualties over long distances. The power of the Lightning and its high climb rate allowed it to make diving and climbing attacks that did not expose it to enemy fighters, Mitsubishi A6M "Zeros" in particular. The P-38 was the first military aircraft to exceed 400 miles per hour (640 km/h) in level flight.

The Lightning was heavy, a consequence of two engines, metal-skinned construction, and a wide wingspan. This configuration also limited its effectiveness as a close-combat dogfighting aircraft; it lacked the nimbleness of smaller, lighter fighters. The P-38 suffered heavy losses in Europe against Luftwaffe Bf 109s, which it could not match for speed. The escort role was soon turned over to the P-51 Mustangs, and P-38s were assigned to reconnaissance missions (the black-and-white invasions stripes on this build indicate action in the Normandy campaign).

The United States had a large fleet of surviving P-38s after the war, though these rapidly became obsolete with the introduction of jets. Many P-38s were purchased to be converted into racers and stunt planes.

**COUNTRY OF ORIGIN:** United States

**PRODUCTION:** 1941

**RETIRED:** 1965

**NUMBER MADE:** 10,037

**LENGTH/WINGSPAN:** 37' 10" (11.53 m) / 52' 0" (15.85 m)

**LOADED MASS:** 17,500 lb. (7,940 kg)

**POWERPLANT:** 2 × Allison V-1710-111/113V12 supercharged piston aero engine

**THRUST:** 1,600 hp (1,193 kW) each

**MAXIMUM SPEED:** 414 mph (667 km/h)

**COMBAT RADIUS:** 885 miles (1,820 km)

# PART 1: OUTBOARD SYSTEMS

## MODULE A

LHS Engine

Use assemblies from V-1710 Engine
starting page 158:

Step 20 Engine Assembly
Step 21 Cowl
Step 22 Cowl
Step 25 Propeller
Step 27 Propeller Nose

**1**

LHS

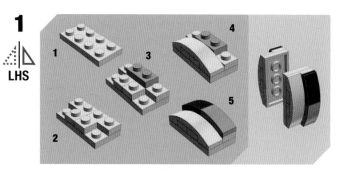

**2**

Remove red part for
assembly to engine.

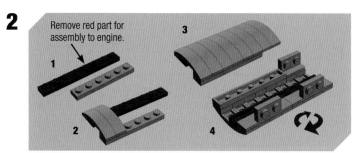

**3**

Remove red part for
assembly to engine.

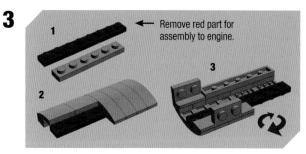

**4**

2x

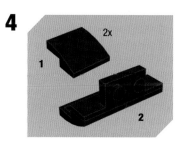

**5**

**6**

V-1710 Engine
Step 26

**7**

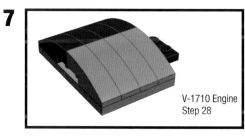

V-1710 Engine
Step 28

**8**

**9**

**10**

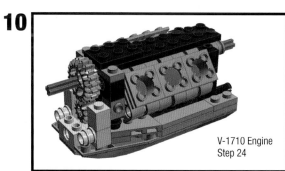

V-1710 Engine
Step 24

**11**

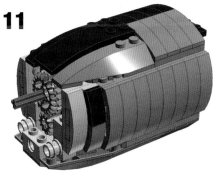

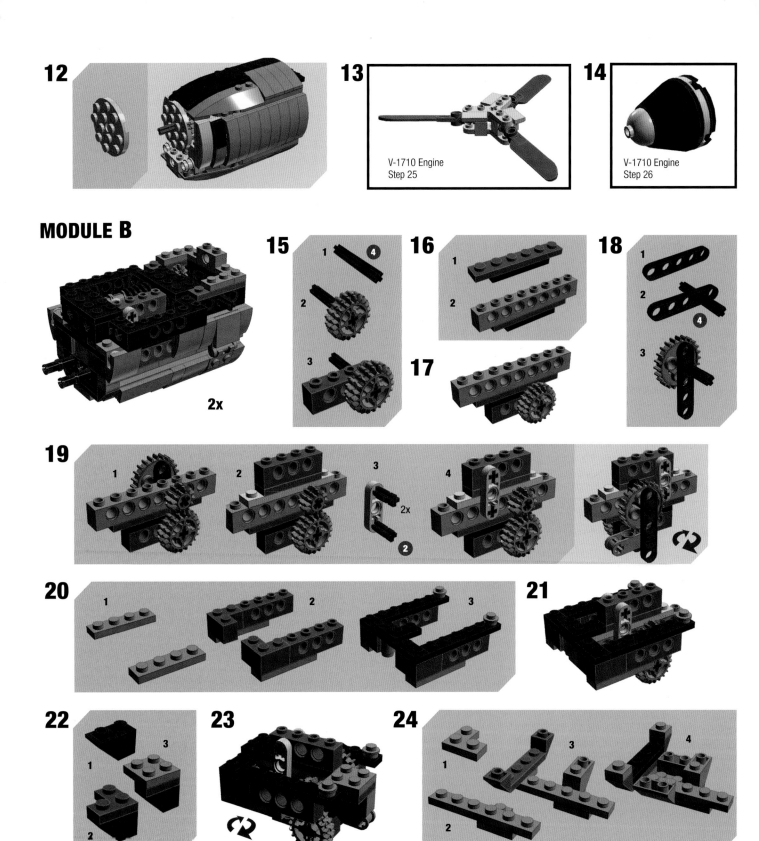

**12**

**13**

V-1710 Engine
Step 25

**14**

V-1710 Engine
Step 26

## MODULE B

2x

**15**

1    4

2

3

**16**

1

2

**17**

**18**

1

2    4

3

**19**

1    2    3    2x    4    2

**20**

1    2    3

**21**

**22**

1    3    2

**23**

**24**

1    3    4    2

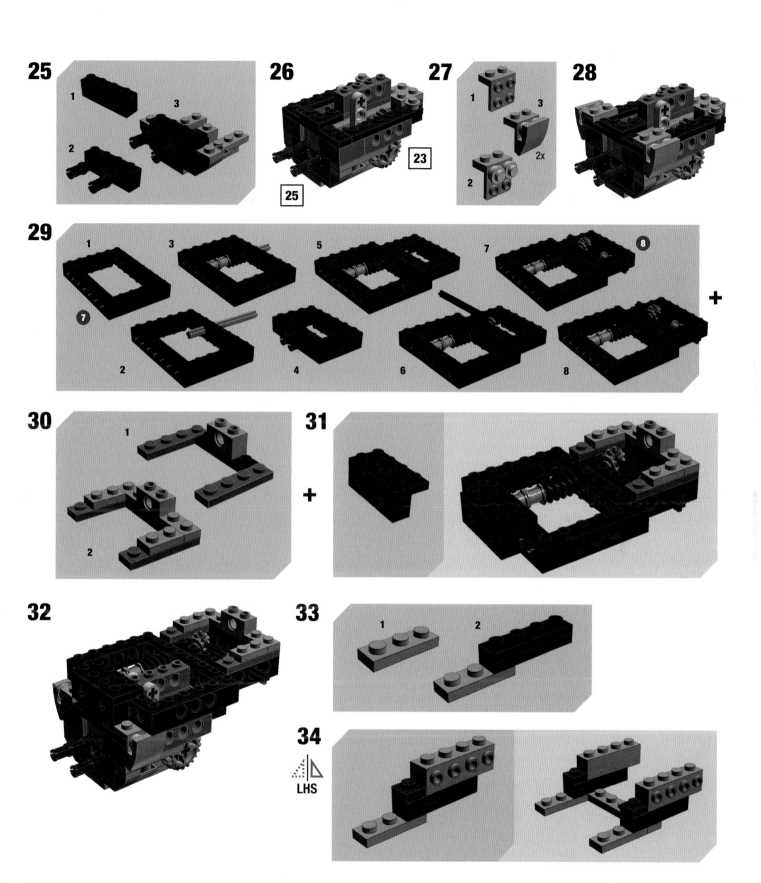

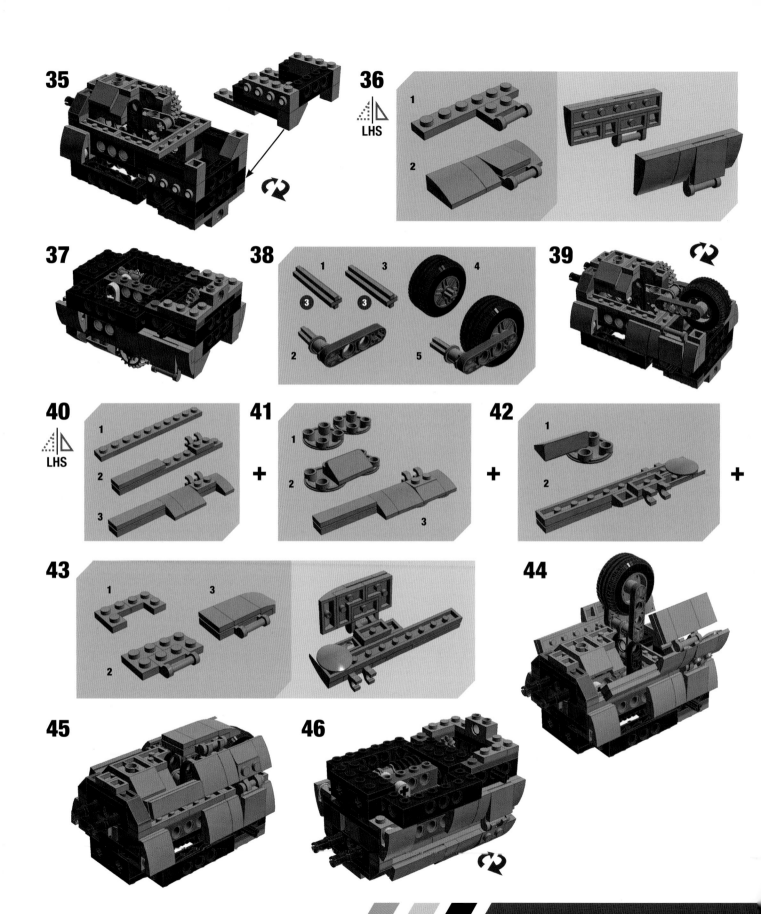

**35**

**36**
LHS
1
2

**37**

**38**
1 3 4
3 3
2 5

**39**

**40**
LHS
1
2
3

**+**

**41**
1
2
3

**+**

**42**
1
2

**+**

**43**
1 3
2

**44**

**45**

**46**

# MODULE C

**47**

**2x**

**+**

**48**

1    2    3    4

**2x**

**+**

**49**

1    2    3

**50**

**51**

**52**

# MODULE D

**53**

1    4    6    7

2    5

3    8    9

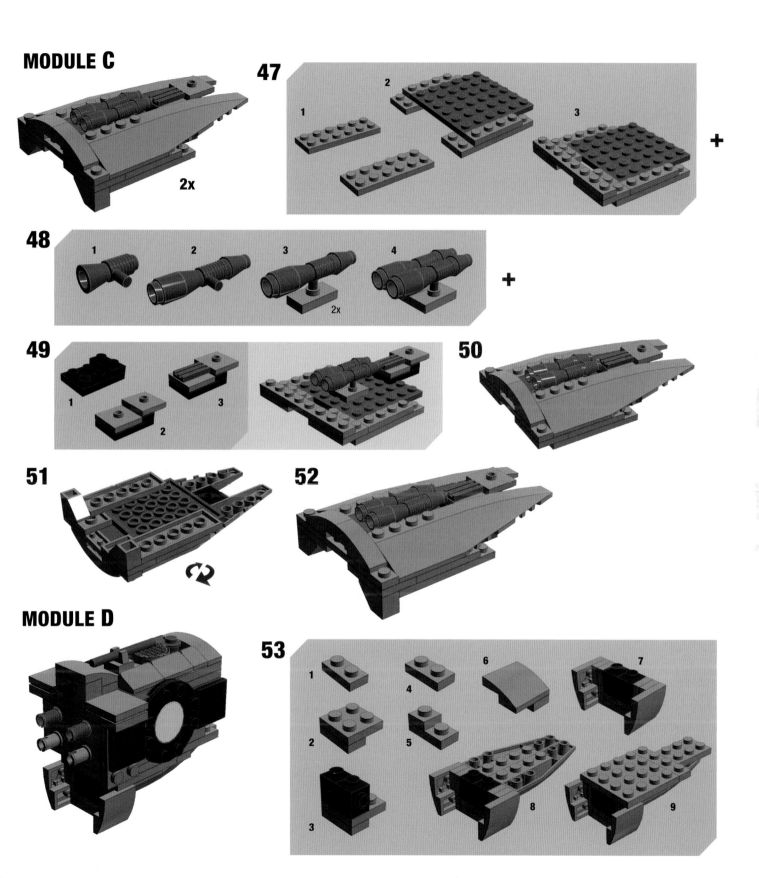

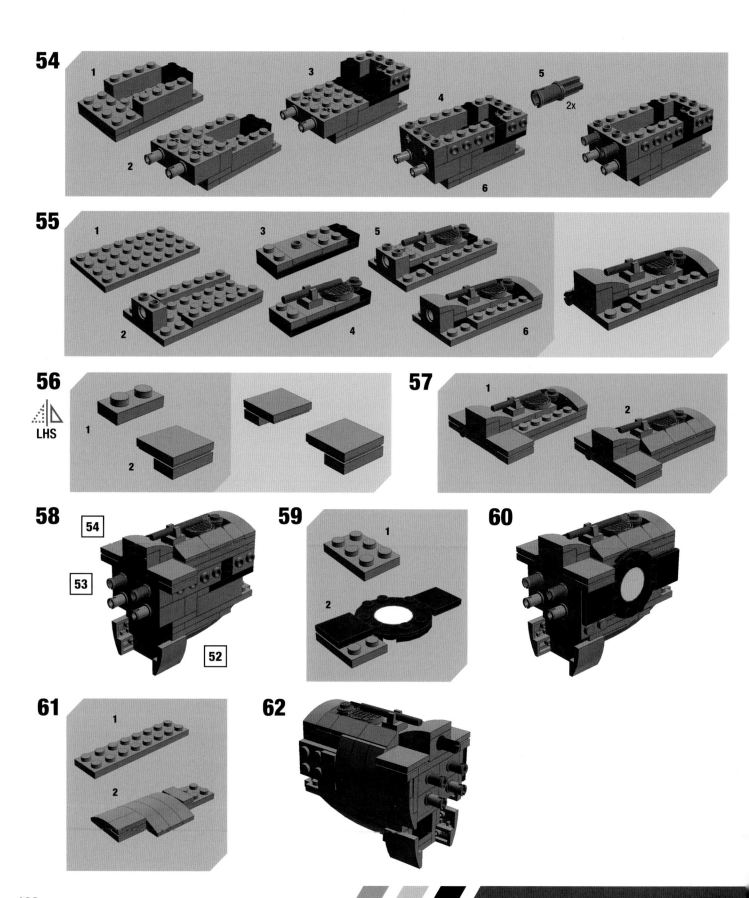

**54**

1

2

3

4

5    2x

6

**55**

1

2

3

4

5

6

**56**

LHS

1

2

**57**

1

2

**58**

54

53

52

**59**

1

2

**60**

**61**

1

2

**62**

# MODULE E

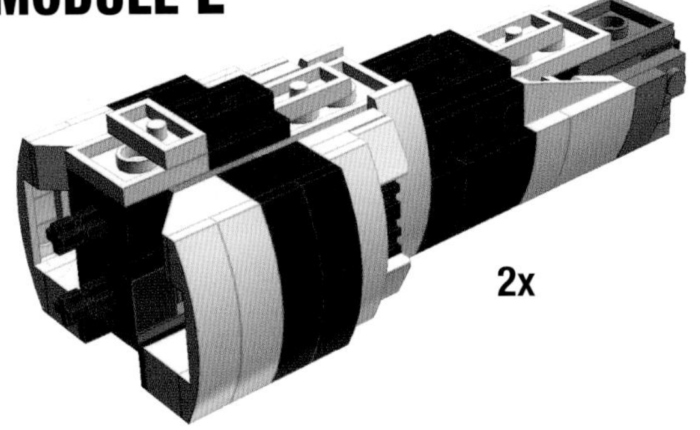

**63**

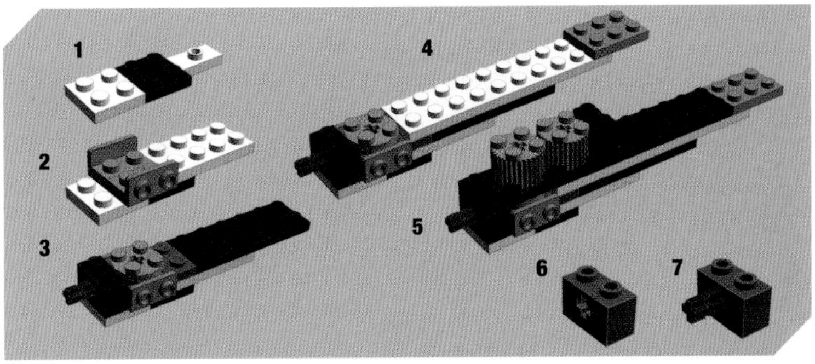

**64**

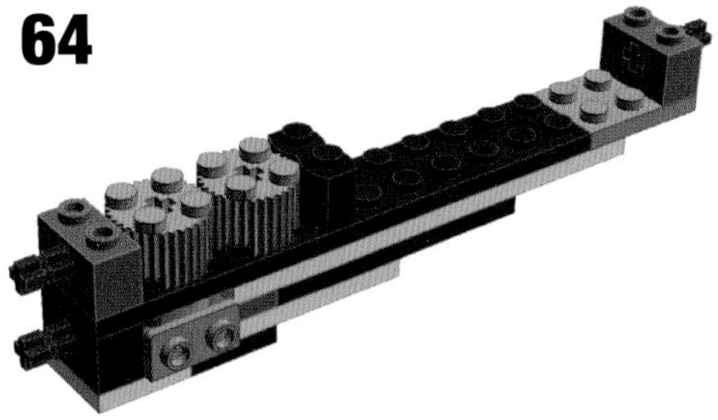

**65**

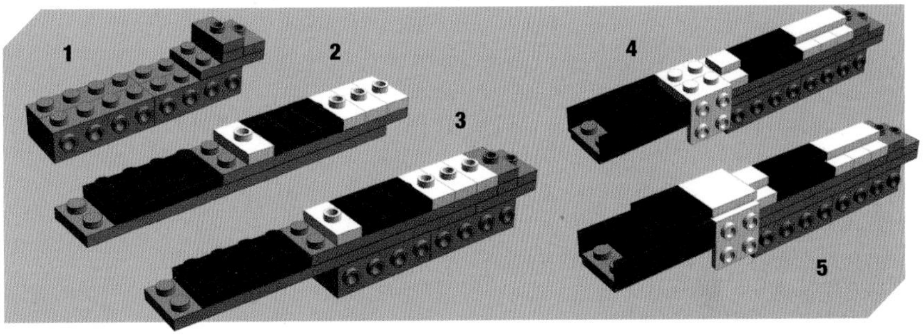

**66**

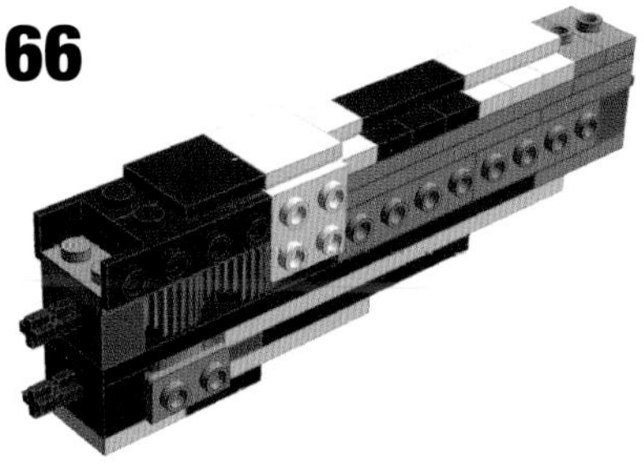

**67** LHS

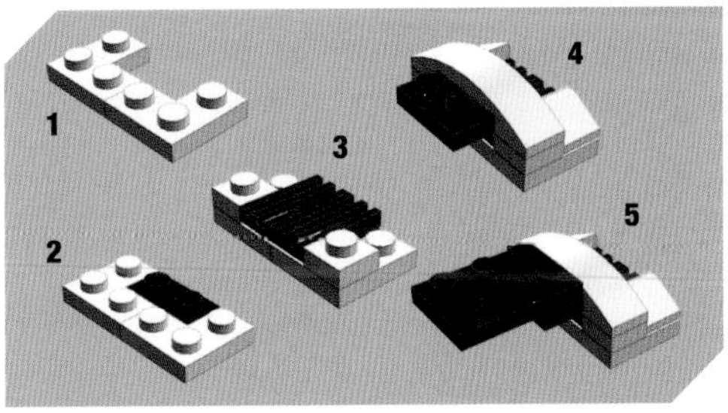

**68**

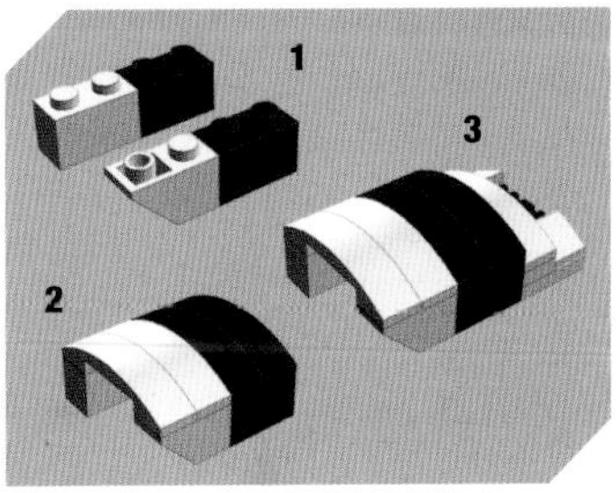

**69**

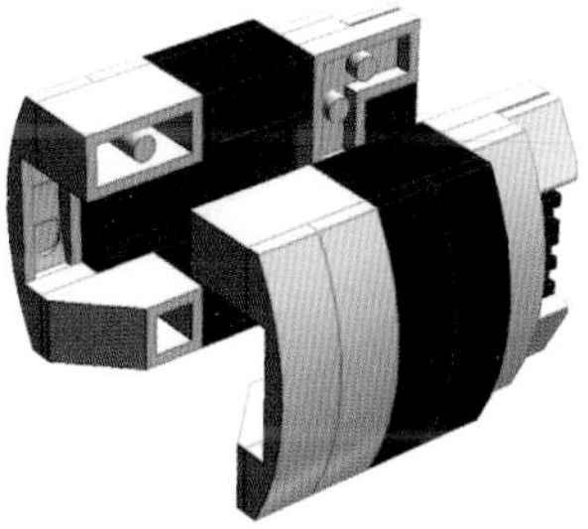

**70** LHS

**71** LHS

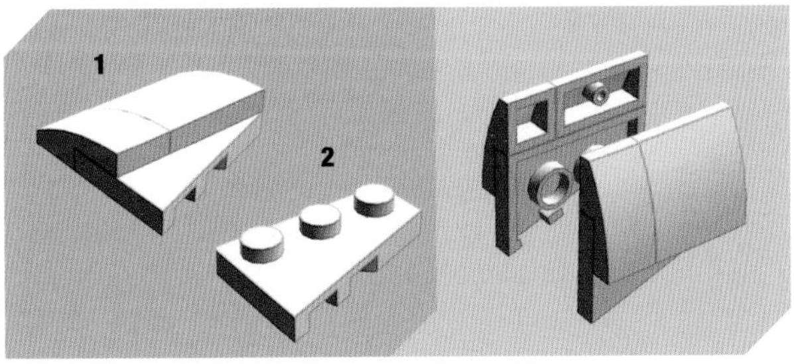

**72** LHS

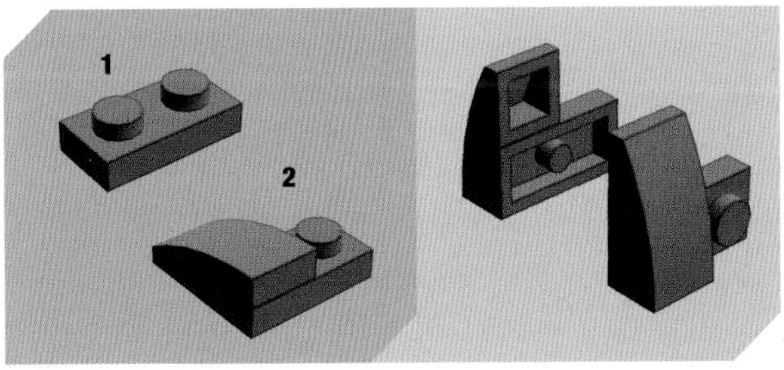

2x

**73**

72
71
70
69

**74**

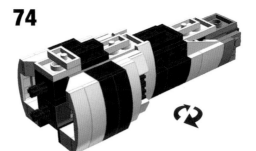

**75**

**MODULE F**

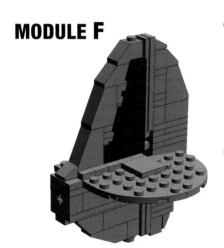

**76**

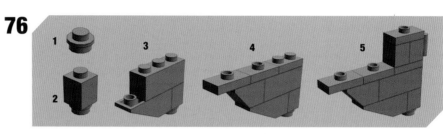

1
2
3
4
5

**77**

1
2
3
4

**78**

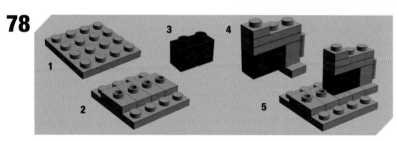

1
2
3
4
5

**79**

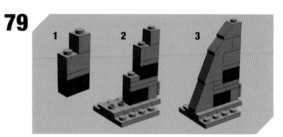

1
2
3

**80**

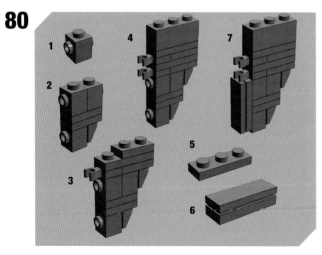

1
2
3
4
5
6
7

**81**

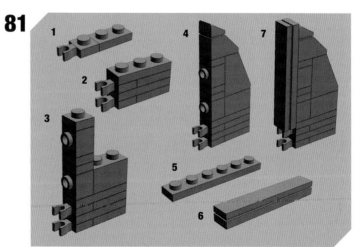

1
2
3
4
5
6
7

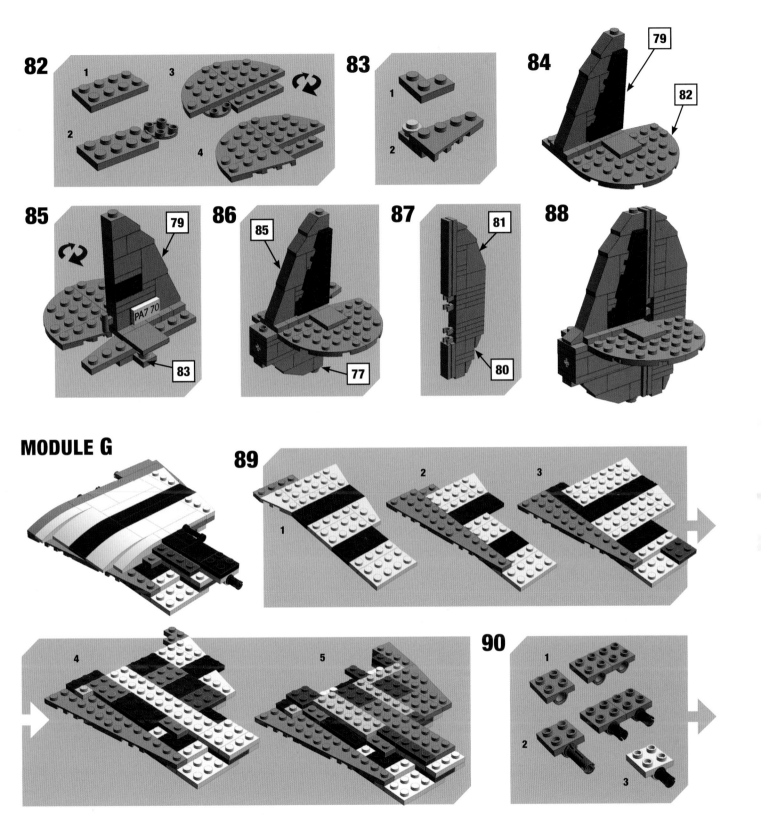

**82**

**83**

**84**

**85**

**86**

**87**

**88**

## MODULE G

**89**

**90**

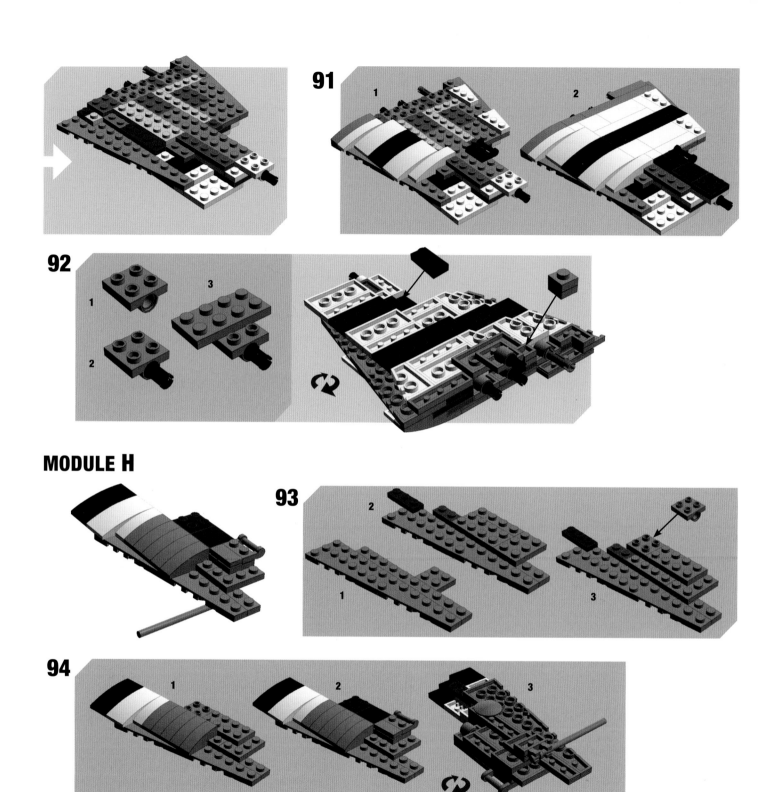

**91**

**92**

## MODULE **H**

**93**

**94**

# MODULE I

**95**

# MODULE J

**96**

**97**

**98**

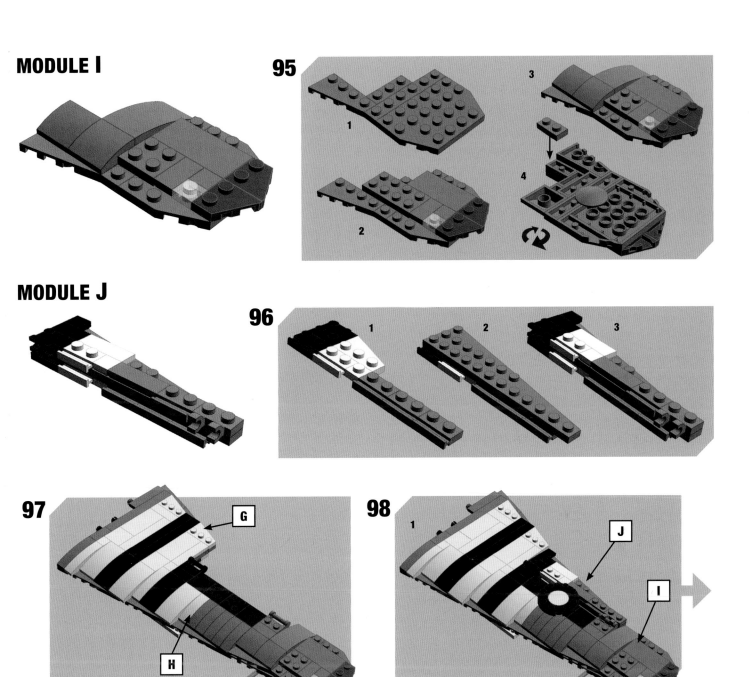

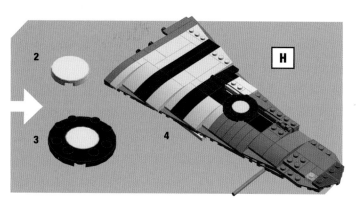

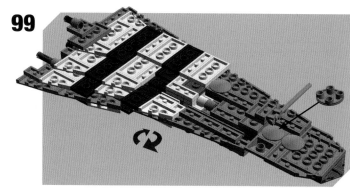

**99**

# PART 2: INBOARD SYSTEMS

## MODULE K

**1**

**2**

**3**

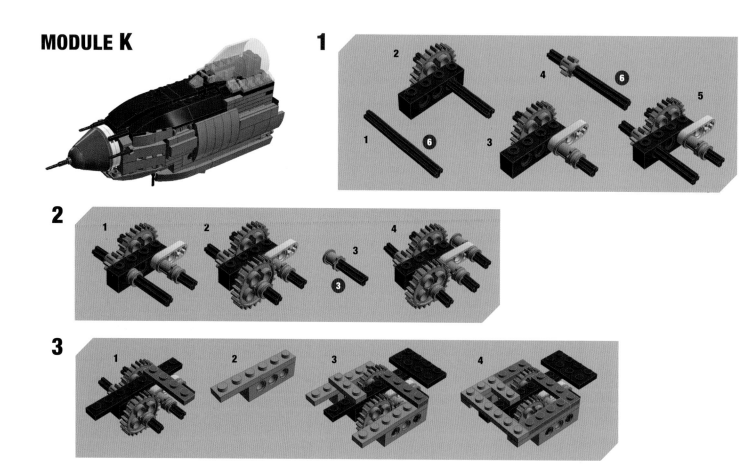

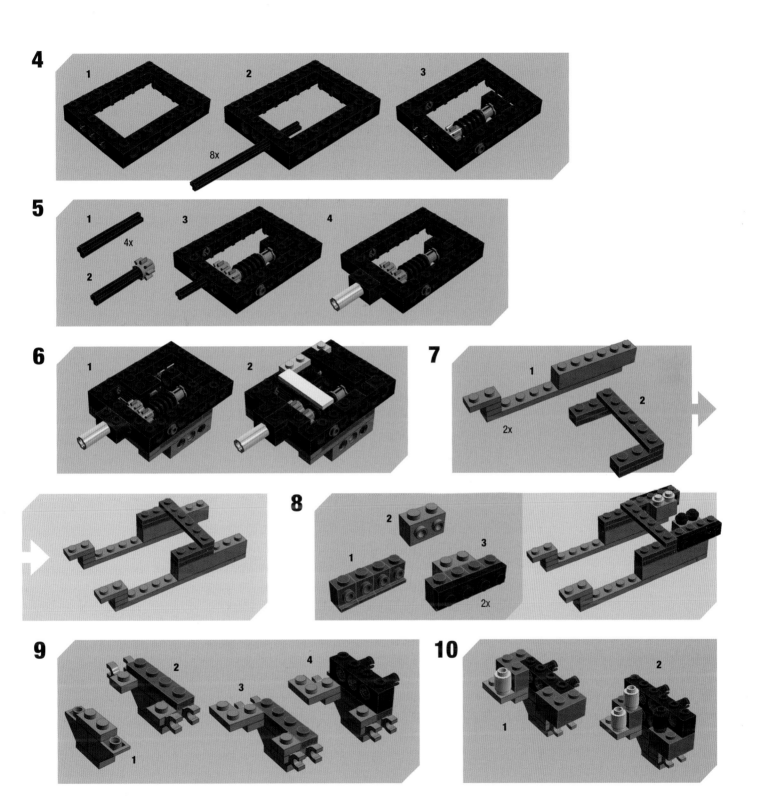

**11**

8

10

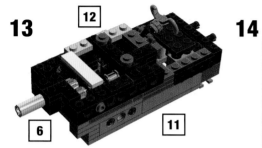

**12**

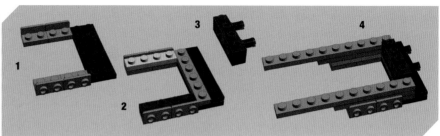

**13**

12

6

11

**14**

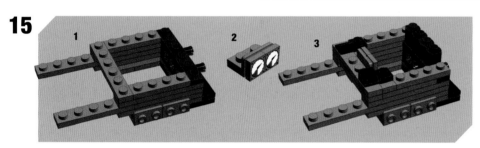

**15**

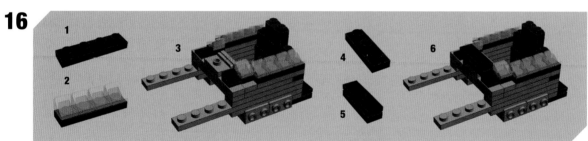

**16**

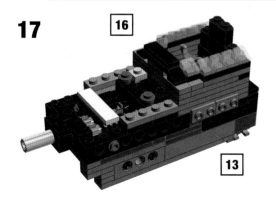

**17**

16

13

**18**

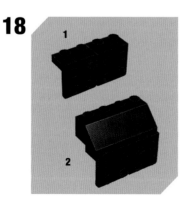

**19**

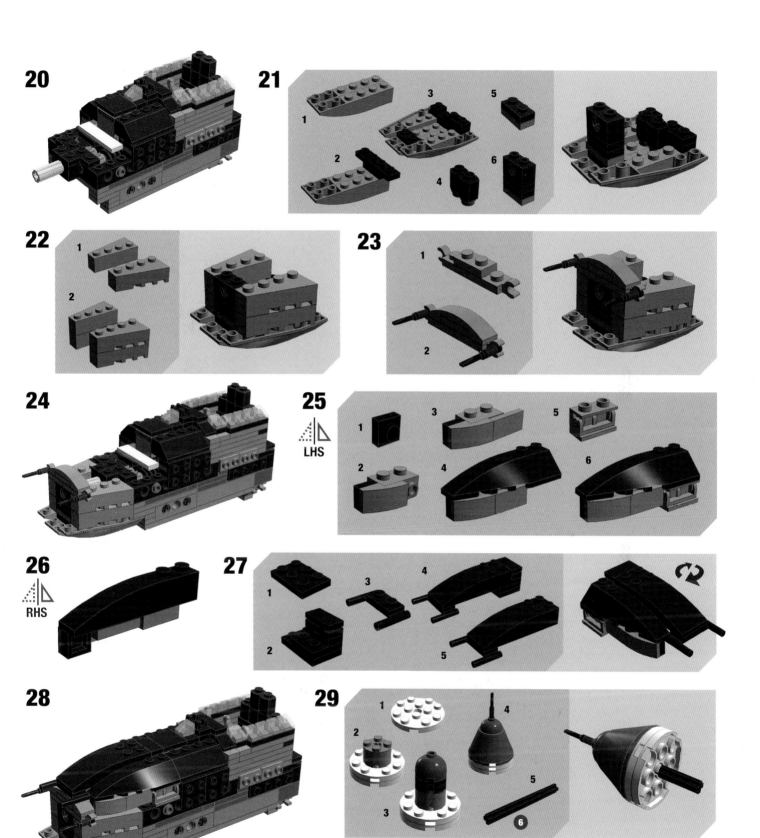

**20**

**21**
1 3 5 2 6 4

**22**
1 2

**23**
1 2

**24**

**25**
LHS
1 3 5 2 4 6

**26**
RHS

**27**
1 3 4 2 5

**28**

**29**
1 2 4 3 5 6

**30**

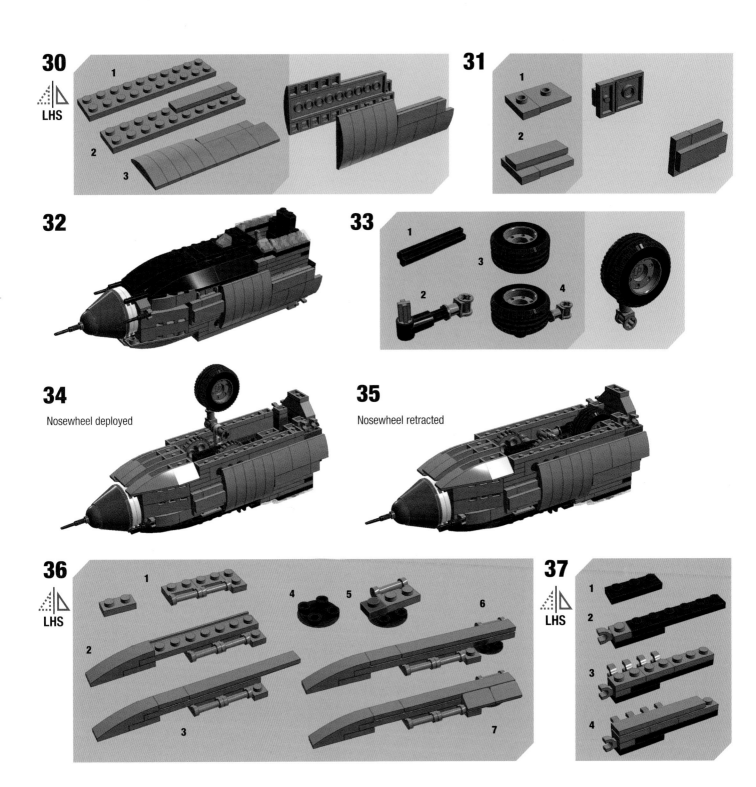

LHS

1
2
3

**31**

1
2

**32**

**33**

1
2
3
4

**34**

Nosewheel deployed

**35**

Nosewheel retracted

**36**

LHS

1
2
3
4
5
6
7

**37**

LHS

1
2
3
4

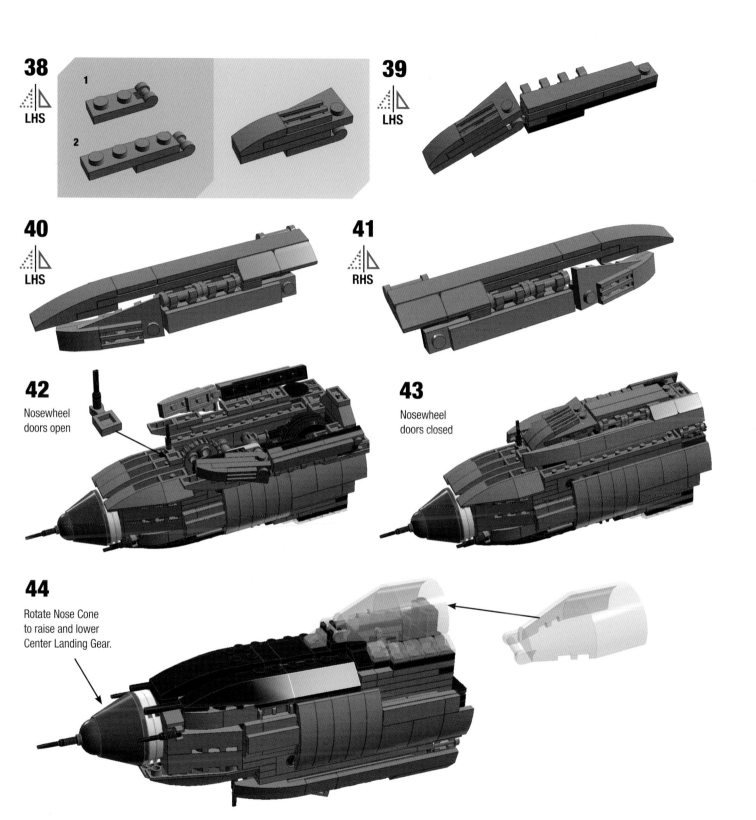

**38**

LHS

1

2

**39**

LHS

**40**

LHS

**41**

RHS

**42**

Nosewheel
doors open

**43**

Nosewheel
doors closed

**44**

Rotate Nose Cone
to raise and lower
Center Landing Gear.

# MODULE L

**45**

**46**

**47**

**48**

**49**

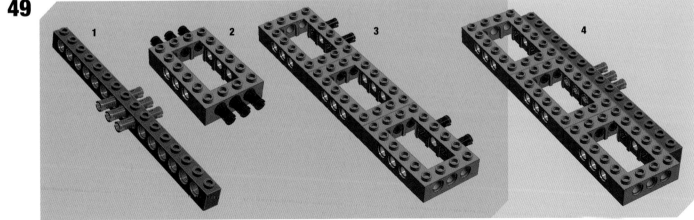

**50**

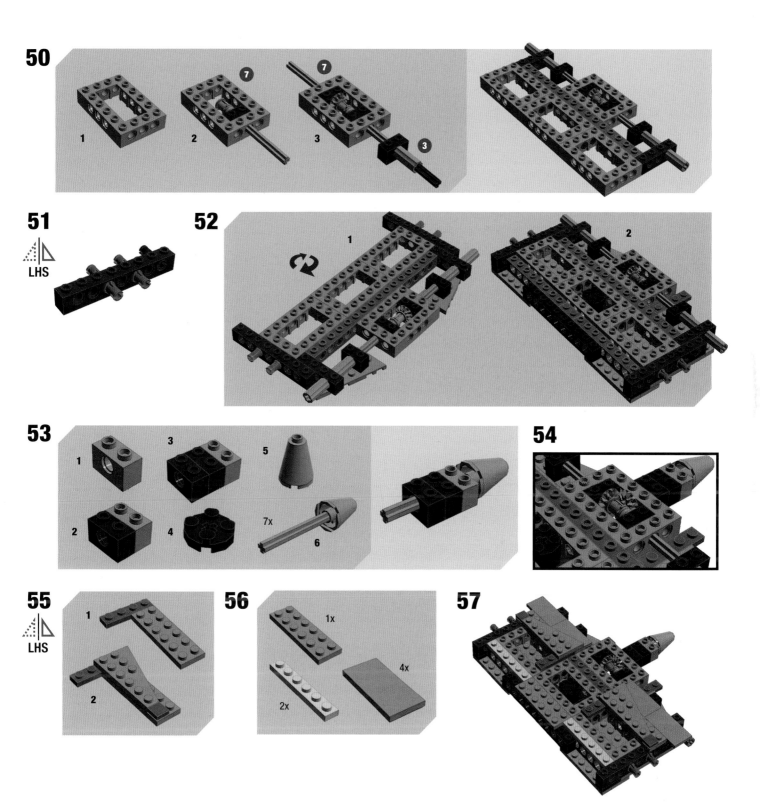

**51**

LHS

**52**

1

2

**53**

1
2
3
4
5
6
7x

**54**

**55**

LHS

1
2

**56**

1x
2x
4x

**57**

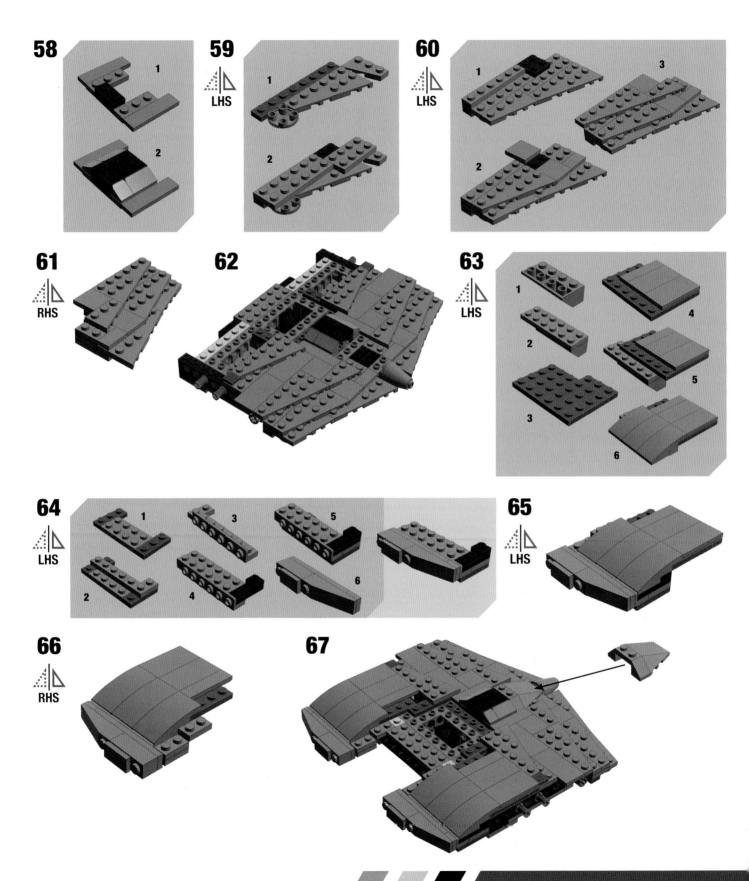

58

59 LHS

60 LHS

61 RHS

62

63 LHS

64 LHS

65 LHS

66 RHS

67

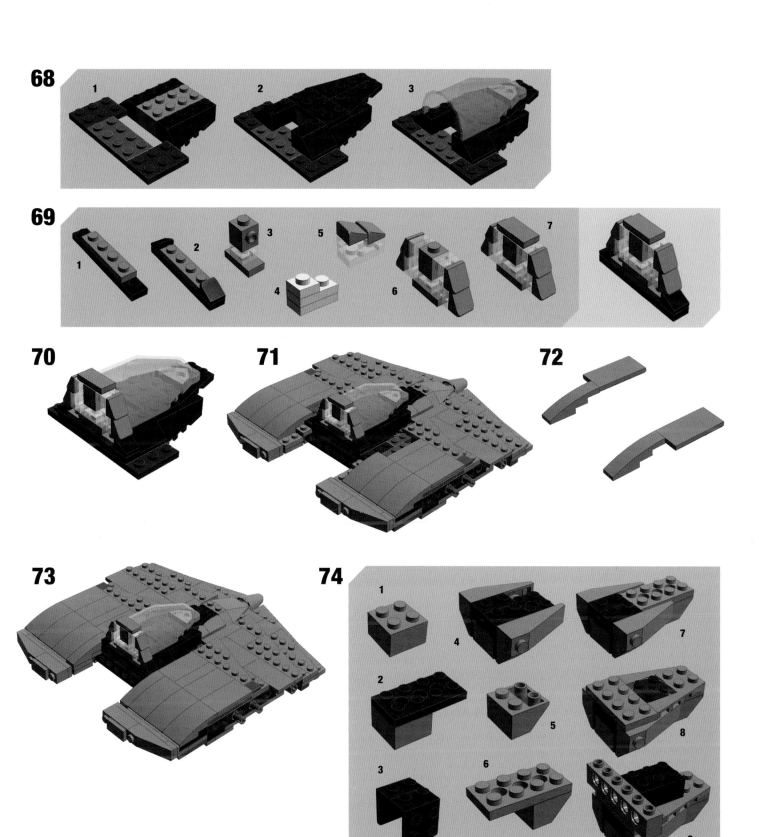

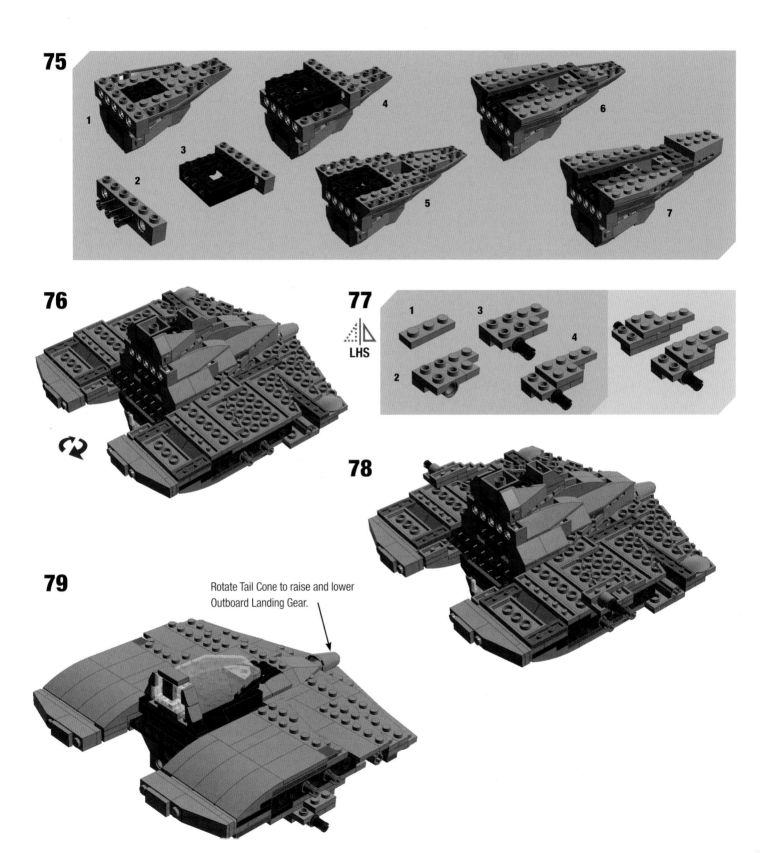

**75**

1

2

3

4

5

6

7

**76**

**77**

LHS

1

2

3

4

**78**

**79**

Rotate Tail Cone to raise and lower
Outboard Landing Gear.

# MODULE M

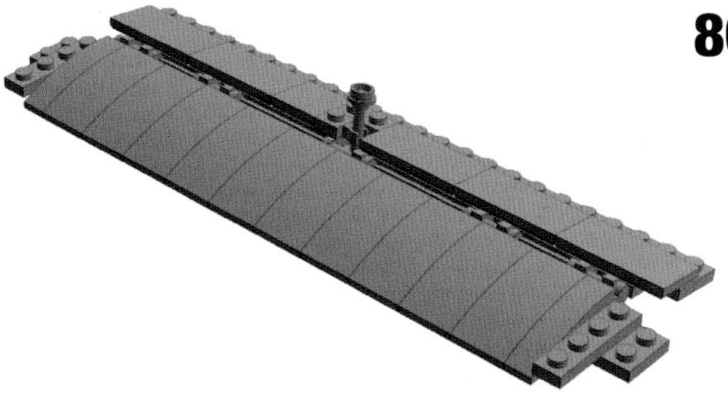

**80**

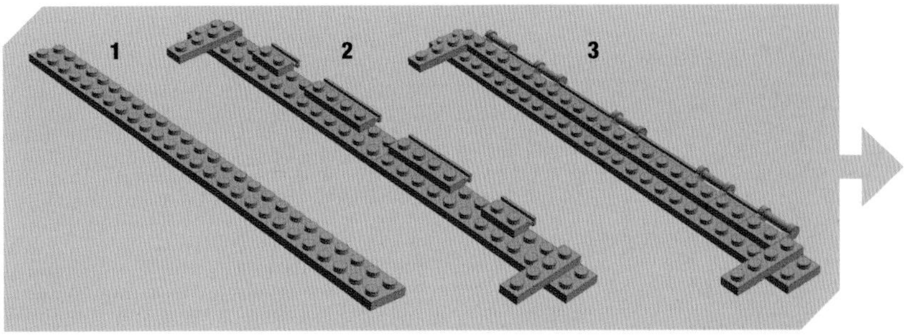

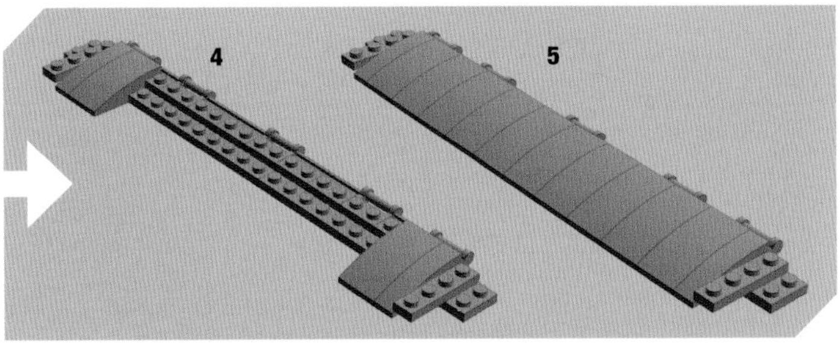

**81**

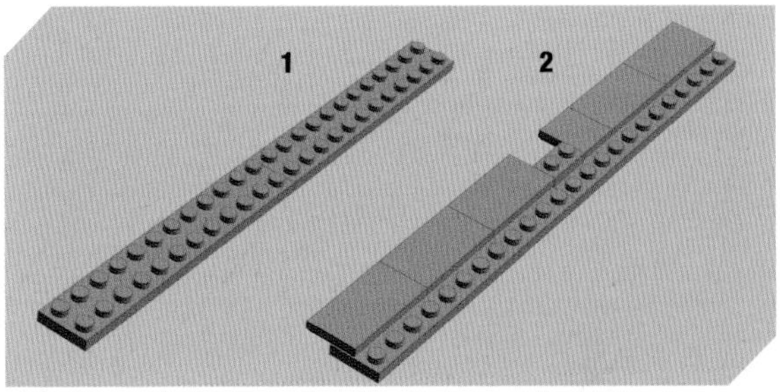

**82**

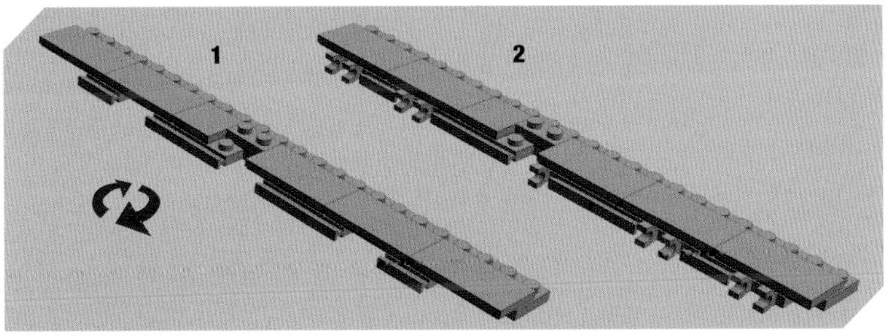

**83**

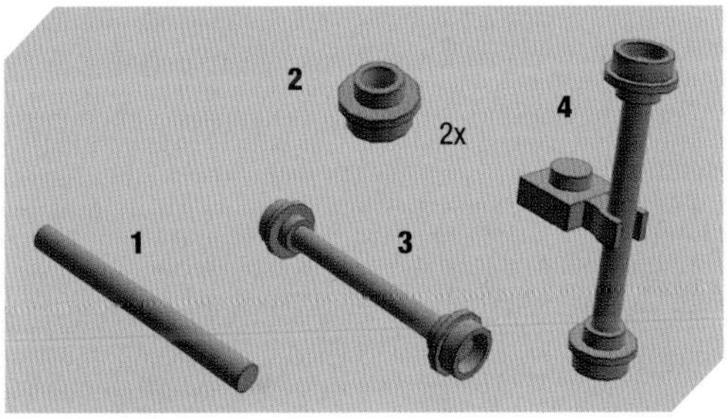

**84**

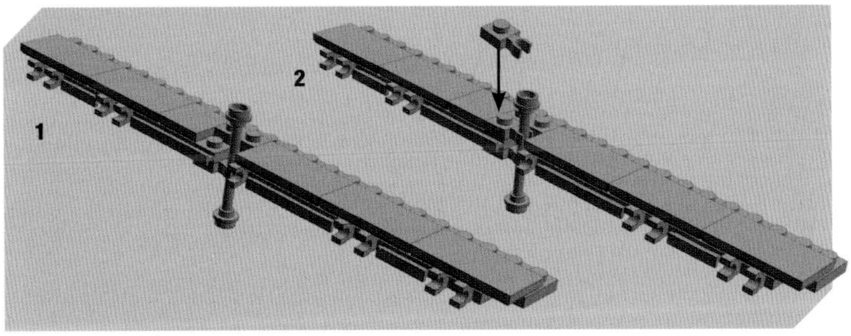

**85**

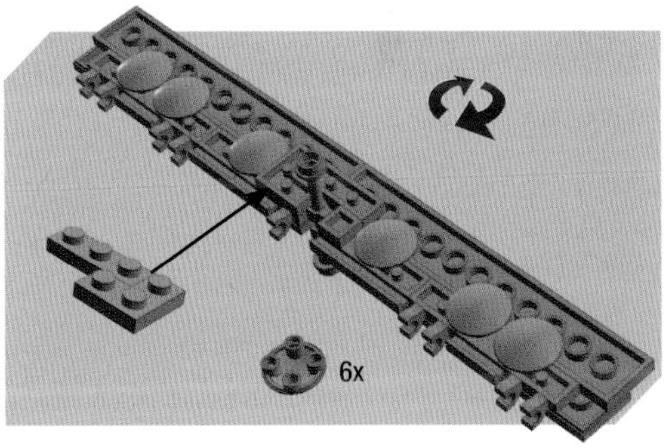

**86**

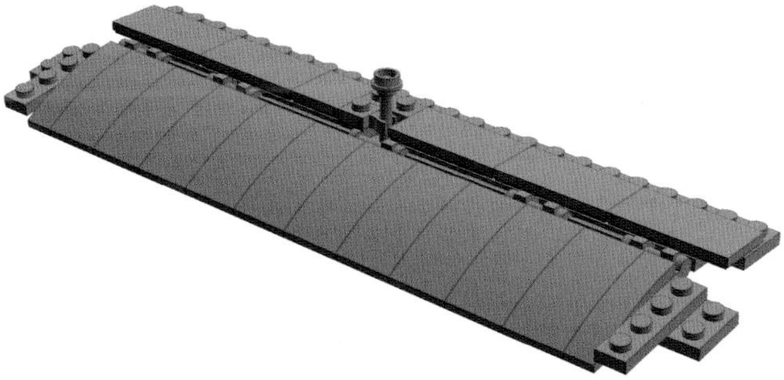

**87**

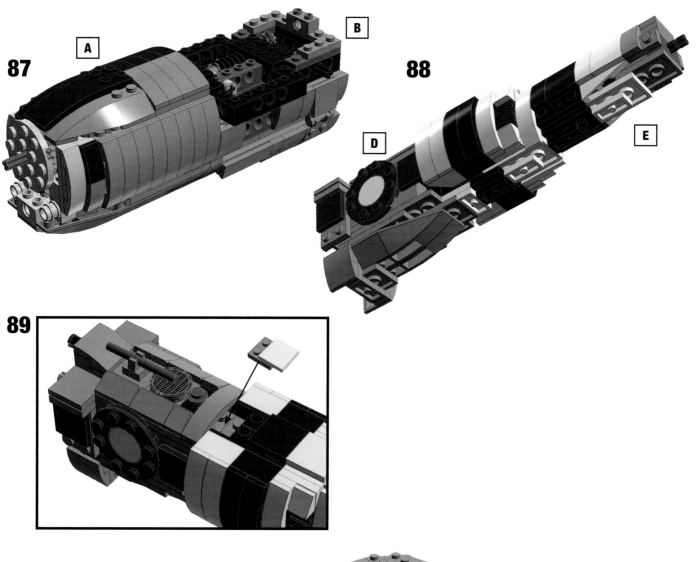

**88**

**89**

**90**

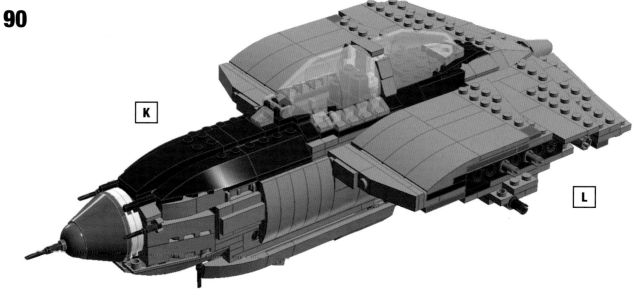

**91**

**92**

L

F

**93**

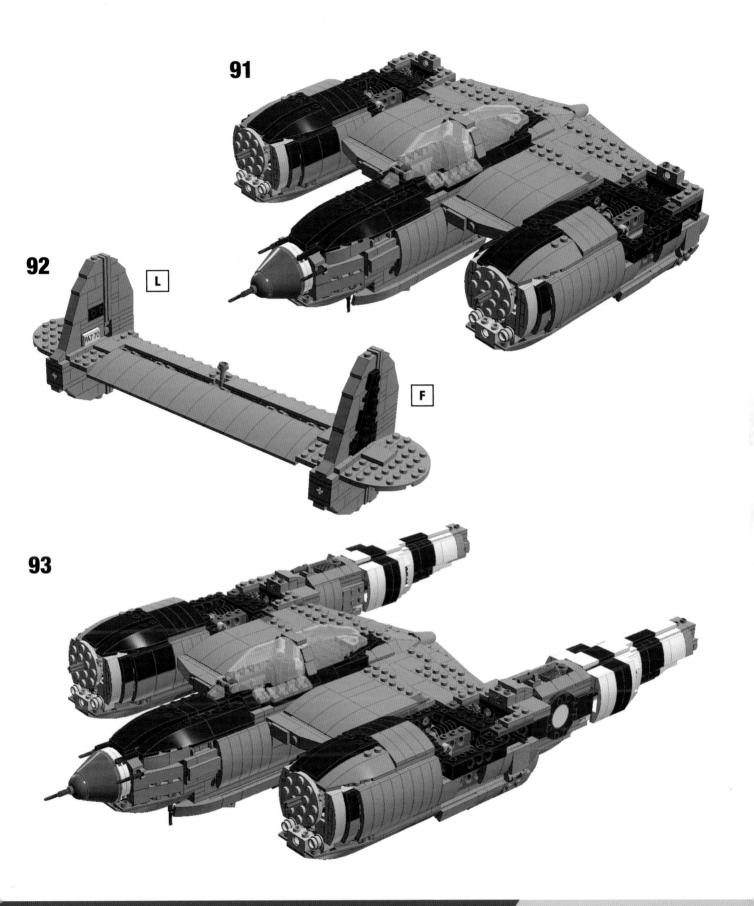

**94**

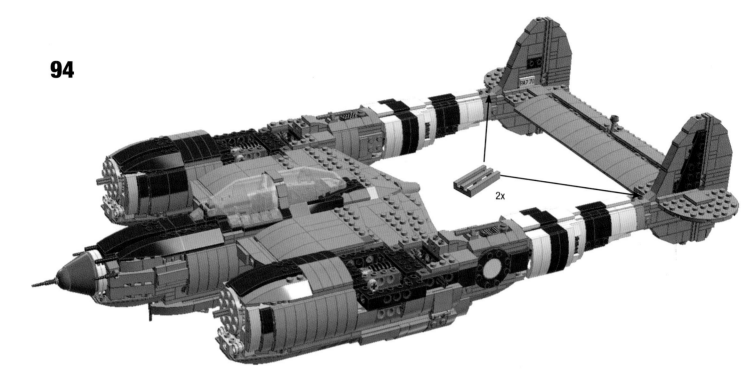

2x

**95**

G

H

I

J

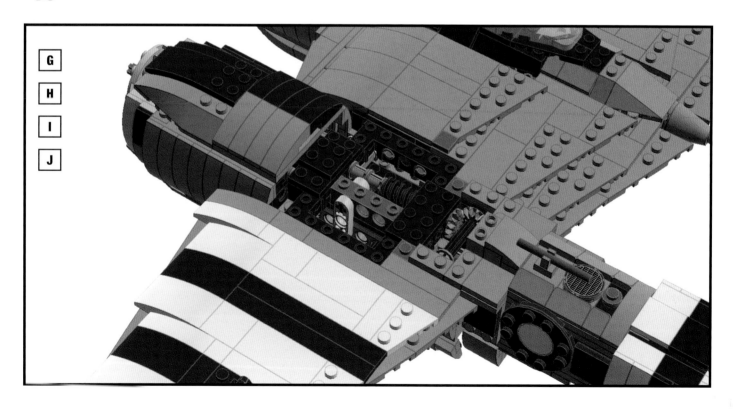

**96**

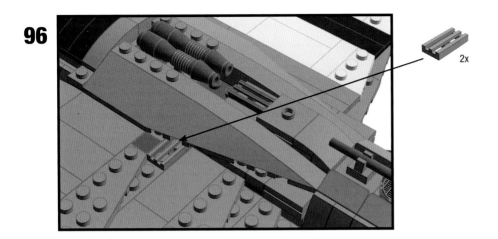

2x

**97**

C

V-1710 Engine
Step 25 Propeller
Step 27 Propeller Nose

# ALLISON ENGINE COMPANY
# V-1710 V-12 ENGINE

**scale: 1:21**

Of the engine models in this book, the Allison V-1710 V-12 aero engine is the only one that is a mechanical model. Unfortunately, due to space restrictions, the model has two V-6s, but they correspond well to the engine size of the V-1710 as used in the Lockheed P-38 Lightning, and they illustrate the technical concept of a piston V engine.

Manufacturability tends to limit wild technical features, and the Allison shows why: it could be adapted to drive long shafts and gearboxes and even could have the entire rotation direction reversed. This was critical for installation in twin-engine aircraft such as the P-38, permitting one clockwise and one counterclockwise functioning engine to balance out the engine torque. All variants of the engine could be assembled on the same production line, improving cost and manufacturing efficiency.

The engine ran on low-octane fuel. Early in the war, this limited total engine power and performance at high altitude. Two notable applications—the early P-51 Mustang and the P-38 Lightning—were limited in their ability to operate under these conditions (an issue in Europe), and the remedy for the later P-51s was switching to the Rolls-Royce Merlin V-12. The number of surviving engines and aircraft is due in part to the reliable nature of the V-1710.

Like the P-38 aircraft, the end of the war brought swift obsolesce to the engine with the arrival of the turbojet. Many surplus engines found homes in drag racers and land-speed-record racers.

| | |
|---|---|
| **COUNTRY OF ORIGIN:** | United States |
| **MANUFACTURER:** | Allison Engine Company |
| **PRODUCTION:** | 1930–1948 |
| **NUMBER MADE:** | 69,305 |
| **TYPE:** | 12-cylinder supercharged liquid-cooled 60° 'Vee' piston aircraft engine |
| **DISPLACEMENT:** | 1,710 cid (28L) |
| **DRY WEIGHT:** | 1,395 lb (633 kg) |
| **POWER OUTPUT:** | 1,500 hp (1,119 kW) @ 3,000 rpm |
| **VARIANTS:** | Allison V-3420 |
| **MAJOR APPLICATIONS:** | Lockheed P-38 Lightning<br>North American A-36, P-51, F-82<br>Boeing XB-38, Flying Fortress<br>Curtiss P-40, XP-60A, YR-37<br>Douglass DC-8, XB-42<br>Bell FM-1, FL Airabonita, P-39, P 63 |

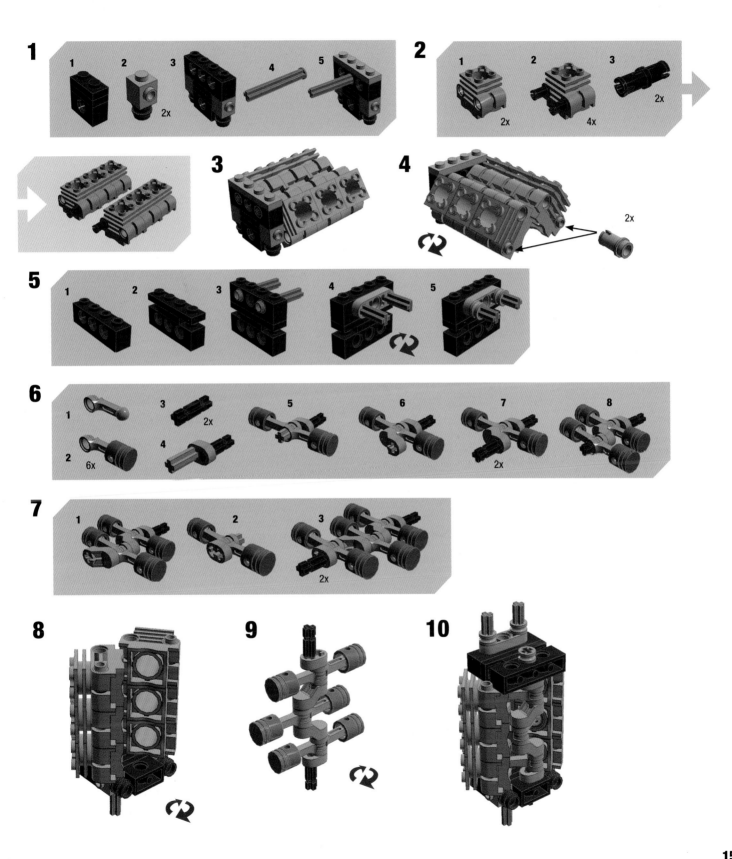

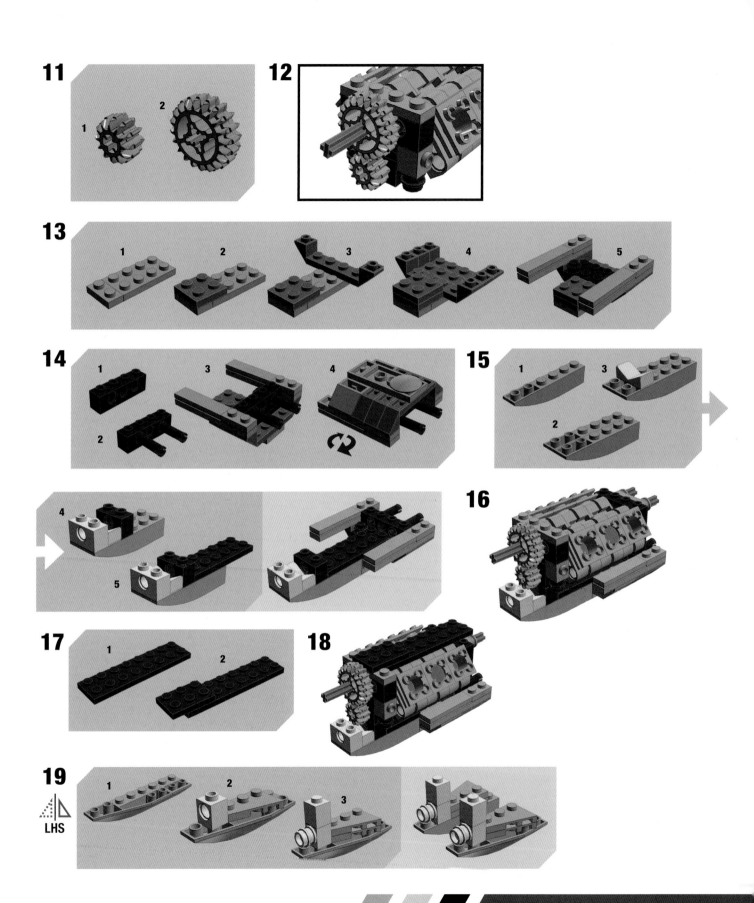

**20**

**21**

1

3

2

**22**

1

2

3

**23**

**24**

1

2

3

4

3x

**25**

**26**

1

2

3

4

5

6

**27**

1

2

4

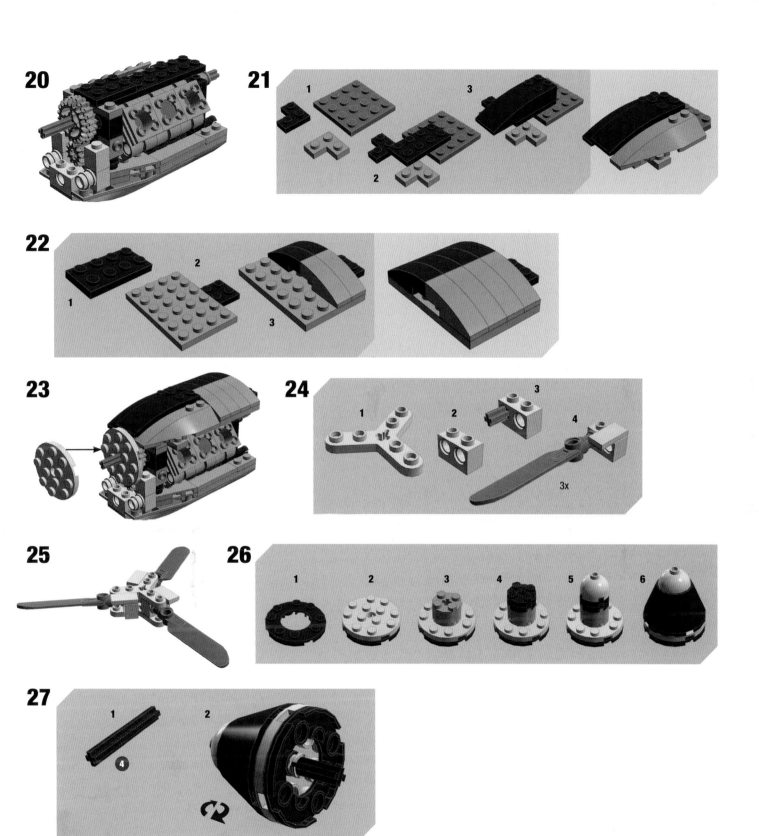

**28**

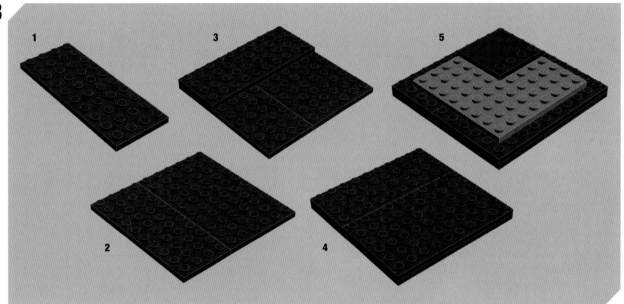

**29**

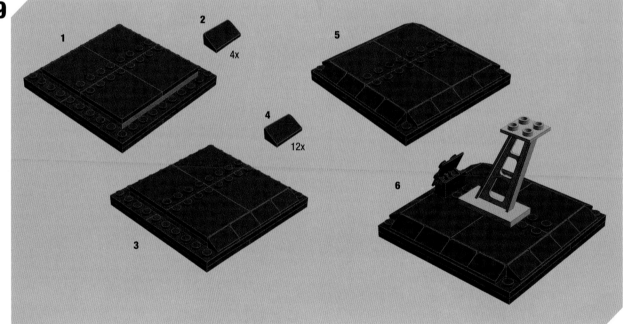

**30**

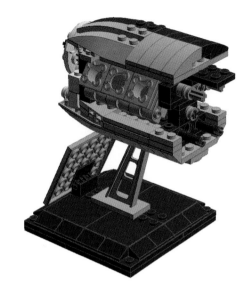 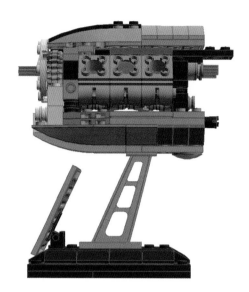

**31**

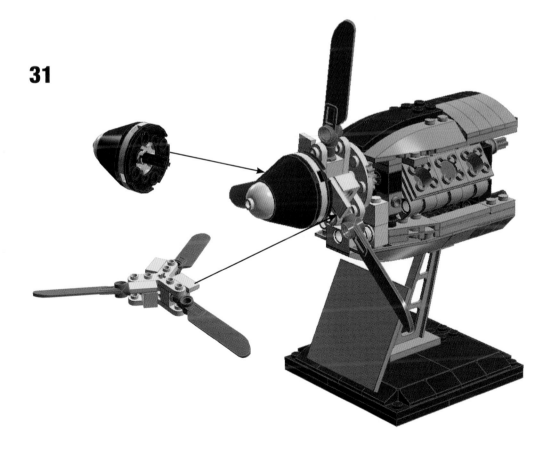

# BUILD COMPONENTS

## PART SUBSTITUTIONS

You likely do not have all the parts needed to complete the builds in this book in your collection already. And if you can't find the parts from LEGO® or a third-party vendor, remember, LEGO is a pretty adaptable building medium—there is almost always another way to build an assembly of parts other than the one shown. Use your imagination and try with the parts you do have. This is what expert MOC builders do every time they design their own models. It is the essence of their creativity.

## COLORS

One of the most fun things about LEGO is its vibrancy and range of colors. Models in this book are generally represented in one of the expected color and pattern representations typical for that aircraft. The experienced builder should feel free to deviate a little (or a lot!) from the color use represented here. Unfortunately, not every part is available in each of the LEGO colors, and it is often hinges, wedge plates, headlight bricks, and other specialist bricks that may limit the option to deviate from the build as exactly shown in the instructions. But remember, with only a little part substitution, many more colors may be available, including perhaps your favorites!

## LEGO COLOR CODES:

 1
White

28
Dark Green

141
Earth Green

2
Old Gray

 40
Transparent

154
New Dark Red

5
Brick Yellow

 41
Transparent Red

192
Reddish Brown

21
Bright Red

 47
Transparent Flouresant
Red Orange

194
Medium Stone Gray

23
Bright Blue

111
Transparent Brown

199
Dark Stone Gray

24
Dark Yellow

138
Sand Yellow

315
Silver Metallic

 26
Black

140
Earth Blue

# FOKKER-FLUGZEUGWERKE
# FOKKER DR.1

| PART | COLOR | QUANTITY | PART | COLOR | QUANTITY | PART | COLOR | QUANTITY | PART | COLOR | QUANTITY | PART | COLOR | QUANTITY |
|---|---|---|---|---|---|---|---|---|---|---|---|---|---|---|
| 3021- | 1 | 2 | 3070b- | 21 | 2 | 4733- | 26 | 1 | 32028- | 21 | 6 | 87087- | 21 | 1 |
|  | 21 | 1 | 3623- | 21 | 4 | 4740- | 40 | 1 | 42446- | 199 | 2 | 87580- | 21 | 2 |
| 3023- | 21 | 1 | 3710- | 21 | 1 | 6141- | 26 | 1 | 43722- | 21 | 2 | 87994- | 194 | 2 |
| 3024- | 1 | 2 | 3795- | 21 | 1 |  | 194 | 4 | 43723- | 21 | 2 |  |  |  |
|  | 21 | 2 | 4070- | 21 | 3 | 6541- | 21 | 1 | 50746- | 1 | 3 |  |  |  |
| 3068b- | 21 | 2 | *4085d-* | 21 | 6 | 30162- | 199 | 1 | 63868- | 1 | 1 |  |  |  |
| 3069b- | 21 | 1 |  | 194 | 2 | 30374- | 26 | 1 | 85861- | 1 | 2 |  |  |  |

Numbers in italic indicate alternate part numbers listed in the Parts Index (page 185).

# SOPWITH AVIATION COMPANY
# SOPWITH CAMEL

| PART | COLOR | QUANTITY | PART | COLOR | QUANTITY | PART | COLOR | QUANTITY | PART | COLOR | QUANTITY | PART | COLOR | QUANTITY |
|---|---|---|---|---|---|---|---|---|---|---|---|---|---|---|
| 2431- | 194 | 2 | 3024- | 1 | 1 | 4740- | 40 | 1 | 30162- | 199 | 1 | 63868- | 1 | 1 |
| 2654- | 23 | 4 |  | 194 | 1 | 6141- | 23 | 2 | 30374- | 1 | 1 | 85861- | 1 | 3 |
| 3021- | 194 | 1 | 3623- | 141 | 1 | 6541- | 199 | 1 | 30377- | 5 | 2 | 87087- | 141 | 2 |
| 3023- | 141 | 1 | 3710- | 194 | 2 | 6636- | 192 | 2 | 42446- | 199 | 2 | 87580- | 192 | 2 |
|  |  |  | 4070- | 192 | 1 | 26047- | 26 | 4 | 50746- | 21 | 2 |  |  |  |
|  |  |  |  |  |  |  |  |  |  | 23 | 1 |  |  |  |

# DE HAVILLAND
# DH.88 COMET

| PART | COLOR | QUANTITY | PART | COLOR | QUANTITY |
|---|---|---|---|---|---|
| 2654- | 21 | 2 | 4740- | 40 | 2 |
| 3021- | 21 | 1 | 6141- | 194 | 2 |
| 3023- | 21 | 2 | 11477- | 21 | 1 |
| 3024- | 21 | 7 | 14769- | 21 | 2 |
| 3069b- | 21 | 1 | 24299- | 21 | 1 |
| 3070b- | 21 | 1 | 24307- | 21 | 1 |
| 3623- | 1 | 2 | 41769- | 21 | 2 |
|  | 21 | 3 | 41770- | 21 | 2 |
| 3666- | 21 | 1 | 43722- | 21 | 1 |
| 3710- | 21 | 1 | 43723- | 21 | 1 |
| 4070- | 21 | 2 | 47905- | 21 | 2 |
| 4081- | 21 | 1 | 50746- | 1 | 1 |
| 4589- | 21 | 3 |  | 21 | 2 |
|  |  |  |  | 40 | 1 |

# P-51D MUSTANG

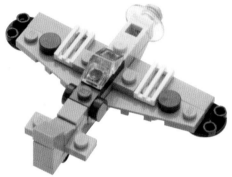

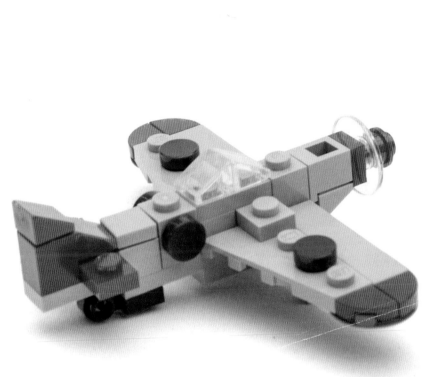

| PART | COLOR | QUANTITY | PART | COLOR | QUANTITY | PART | COLOR | QUANTITY | PART | COLOR | QUANTITY | PART | COLOR | QUANTITY |
|---|---|---|---|---|---|---|---|---|---|---|---|---|---|---|
| 2431- | 194 | 2 | 3024- | 21 | 1 | 4081- | 26 | 1 | 41770- | 194 | 1 | 85861- | 26 | 2 |
| 2654- | 199 | 2 |  | 194 | 2 | 4740- | 40 | 1 | 42446- | 199 | 2 | 87087- | 194 | 1 |
| 3005- | 21 | 1 | 3070b- | 194 | 1 | 6141- | 21 | 1 | 47905- | 194 | 1 | 98138- | 140 | 4 |
| 3021- | 194 | 1 | 3623- | 21 | 1 | 25269- | 21 | 4 | 50746- | 21 | 2 |  |  |  |
| 3023- | 194 | 3 |  | 194 | 3 | 30374- | 26 | 1 |  | 40 | 2 |  |  |  |
|  |  |  | 4070- | 194 | 1 | 41769- | 194 | 1 |  | 194 | 1 |  |  |  |

| PART | COLOR | QUANTITY | PART | COLOR | QUANTITY | PART | COLOR | QUANTITY | PART | COLOR | QUANTITY | PART | COLOR | QUANTITY |
|---|---|---|---|---|---|---|---|---|---|---|---|---|---|---|
| 2412- | 1 | 2 | 3023- | 26 | 1 | 4070- | 24 | 1 | 41769- | 194 | 1 | 85861- | 26 | 2 |
| 2431- | 194 | 2 |  | 194 | 2 | 4081- | 26 | 1 | 41770- | 194 | 1 | 87087- | 24 | 1 |
| 2654- | 26 | 2 | 3024- | 24 | 1 | 4740- | 40 | 1 | 42446- | 199 | 2 | 98138- | 140 | 4 |
| 3005- | 194 | 1 |  | 194 | 2 | 6141- | 24 | 1 | 47905- | 26 | 1 |  |  |  |
| 3021- | 194 | 1 | 3070b- | 194 | 1 | 25269- | 194 | 4 | 50746- | 24 | 1 |  |  |  |
|  |  |  | 3623- | 194 | 4 | 30374- | 26 | 1 |  | 40 | 2 |  |  |  |

# MIKOYAN
# MiG-29

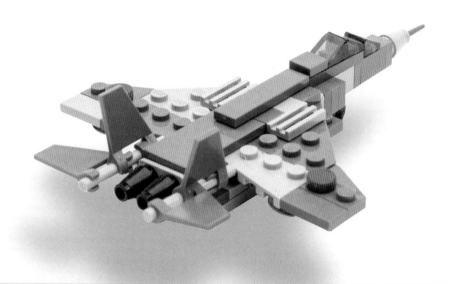

| PART | COLOR | QUANTITY | PART | COLOR | QUANTITY | PART | COLOR | QUANTITY | PART | COLOR | QUANTITY | PART | COLOR | QUANTITY |
|------|-------|----------|------|-------|----------|------|-------|----------|------|-------|----------|------|-------|----------|
| **2412-** | 194 | 2 | **3069b-** | 194 | 1 | **4589-** | 26 | 2 | **30503-** | 194 | 1 | **48729-** | 26 | 1 |
| **2420-** | 199 | 4 | | 199 | 3 | | 194 | 1 | | 199 | 1 | **50746-** | 111 | 3 |
| **2431-** | 199 | 1 | **3070b-** | 199 | 1 | *6019-* | 199 | 2 | **41769-** | 199 | 1 | **55298-** | 199 | 1 |
| **2654-** | 199 | 2 | **3623-** | 199 | 1 | **6141-** | 26 | 4 | **41770-** | 194 | 1 | **87079-** | 199 | 1 |
| **3020-** | 199 | 1 | **3710-** | 194 | 2 | **24299-** | 199 | 1 | **42446-** | 199 | 2 | **87087-** | 199 | 1 |
| **3023-** | 199 | 2 | **3794-** | 194 | 3 | **24307-** | 199 | 1 | **44676-** | 199 | 4 | **98138-** | 21 | 2 |
| **3024-** | 194 | 4 | | 199 | 5 | **30374-** | 194 | 2 | **47905-** | 194 | 1 | **99780-** | 194 | 2 |
| | 199 | 3 | | | | | | | | | | | | |

Numbers in italic indicate alternate part numbers listed in the Parts Index (page 185).

# GRUMMAN
# F-14 TOMCAT

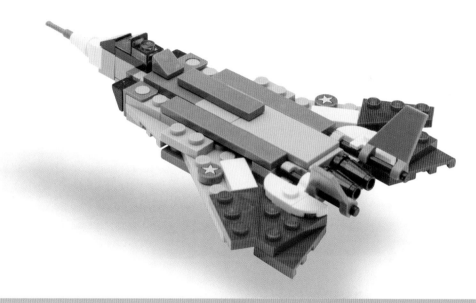

| PART | COLOR | QUANTITY | PART | COLOR | QUANTITY | PART | COLOR | QUANTITY | PART | COLOR | QUANTITY | PART | COLOR | QUANTITY |
|---|---|---|---|---|---|---|---|---|---|---|---|---|---|---|
| **2420-** | 194 | 4 | **3024-** | 1 | 2 | **4070-** | 194 | 1 | **30374-** | 26 | 2 | **50746-** | 26 | 3 |
| | 199 | 2 | | 111 | 1 | *4589-* | 1 | 1 | **42446-** | 199 | 4 | | 111 | 1 |
| **2431-** | 199 | 1 | | 194 | 4 | | 26 | 2 | **43722-** | 21 | 2 | | 199 | 1 |
| **2450-** | 21 | 2 | **3069b-** | 1 | 2 | *6019-* | 1 | 2 | | 194 | 1 | **54383-** | 194 | 1 |
| **3020-** | 194 | 1 | **3070b-** | 111 | 1 | | 194 | 2 | **43723-** | 21 | 2 | **54384-** | 194 | 1 |
| | 199 | 1 | | 199 | 2 | **6141-** | 26 | 4 | | 194 | 1 | **55298-** | 199 | 1 |
| **3022-** | 199 | 2 | **3176-** | 199 | 2 | | 194 | 3 | **44676-** | 199 | 2 | **87079-** | 194 | 1 |
| **3023-** | 26 | 1 | **3666-** | 194 | 2 | **6636-** | 199 | 2 | **47905-** | 194 | 1 | **87580-** | 199 | 1 |
| | 194 | 1 | **3710-** | 194 | 1 | **24299-** | 199 | 2 | **48729-** | 26 | 1 | **98138-** | 140 | 2 |
| | 199 | 2 | **3794-** | 194 | 3 | **24307-** | 199 | 2 | | | | **99780-** | 194 | 2 |
| | | | | 199 | 2 | **25269-** | 1 | 4 | | | | | | |

Numbers in italic indicate alternate part numbers listed in the Parts Index (page 185).

# NORTHROP-GRUMMAN
# B-2 SPIRIT

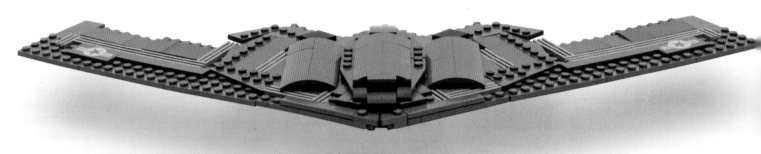

| PART | COLOR | QUANTITY | PART | COLOR | QUANTITY | PART | COLOR | QUANTITY | PART | COLOR | QUANTITY | PART | COLOR | QUANTITY |
|---|---|---|---|---|---|---|---|---|---|---|---|---|---|---|
| 2412- | 194 | 28 | 3023- | 1 | 1 | 3070b- | 26 | 2 | 4162- | 199 | 2 | 43722- | 199 | 4 |
| 2420- | 24 | 1 | | 21 | 2 | | 199 | 7 | 4282- | 199 | 2 | 43723- | 199 | 4 |
| | 199 | 12 | | 24 | 2 | 3176- | 199 | 1 | 4510- | 199 | 2 | 48336- | 199 | 4 |
| 2431- | 199 | 10 | | 26 | 3 | 3460- | 199 | 2 | 6141- | 24 | 2 | 54383- | 199 | 2 |
| 2444- | 26 | 8 | | 28 | 1 | 3623- | 194 | 2 | 6636- | 199 | 2 | 54384- | 199 | 2 |
| 2654- | 199 | 8 | | 199 | 5 | | 199 | 4 | 11477- | 26 | 2 | 60470- | 194 | 4 |
| 2780- | 26 | 4 | 3024- | 199 | 2 | 3666- | 199 | 2 | 14719- | 194 | 1 | 61678- | 199 | 2 |
| 3020- | 199 | 4 | 3031- | 199 | 2 | 3709- | 199 | 1 | 15068- | 26 | 1 | 63864- | 199 | 2 |
| 3021- | 5 | 1 | 3032- | 199 | 6 | 3710- | 1 | 1 | | 199 | 24 | 73983- | 26 | 2 |
| | 23 | 1 | 3034- | 21 | 1 | | 199 | 4 | 24299- | 199 | 1 | | 199 | 2 |
| | 28 | 1 | 3035- | 199 | 2 | 3794- | 194 | 2 | 24307- | 199 | 1 | 87079- | 21 | 1 |
| | 199 | 4 | 3068b- | 26 | 4 | 3795- | 26 | 2 | 30136- | 194 | 1 | | 199 | 19 |
| 3022- | 199 | 7 | | 199 | 15 | | 199 | 12 | 32028- | 199 | 8 | 87580- | 1 | 3 |
| | | | 3069b- | 1 | 1 | 3958- | 199 | 1 | 41769- | 199 | 10 | | | |
| | | | | 199 | 7 | 4032- | 26 | 3 | 41770- | 199 | 10 | | | |

Numbers in italic indicate alternate part numbers listed in the Parts Index (page 185).
This model includes printed bricks available from The Big Brick (see page 191).

# ALBATROS D.VA

| PART | COLOR | QUANTITY |
|---|---|---|
| 2420- | 1 | 8 |
|  | 5 | 6 |
|  | 21 | 2 |
|  | 28 | 2 |
| 2431- | 5 | 4 |
|  | 194 | 4 |
| 2431px17- | 199 | 1 |
| 2444- | 5 | 1 |
|  | 21 | 2 |
|  | 194 | 6 |
| 2450- | 21 | 2 |
| *2555-* | 21 | 4 |
|  | 194 | 7 |
| 2654- | 21 | 8 |
|  | 194 | 6 |
| 2780- | 26 | 12 |
| 2815- | 26 | 2 |
| 2921- | 21 | 2 |
| 2952- | 192 | 1 |
| 3005- | 5 | 4 |
|  | 21 | 1 |
|  | 26 | 2 |
| 3020- | 5 | 4 |
|  | 21 | 4 |
| 3021- | 5 | 1 |
|  | 21 | 5 |
|  | 26 | 1 |
|  | 194 | 4 |
| 3022- | 5 | 2 |
|  | 21 | 1 |
|  | 23 | 1 |
|  | 194 | 2 |
|  | 199 | 1 |
| 3023- | 5 | 17 |
|  | 21 | 12 |
|  | 26 | 2 |
|  | 28 | 1 |
|  | 194 | 6 |
| 3024- | 1 | 8 |
|  | 5 | 8 |
|  | 21 | 13 |
|  | 26 | 10 |
|  | 194 | 6 |
| 3028- | 194 | 2 |
| 3029- | 21 | 2 |
| 3031- | 5 | 1 |
| 3040- | 21 | 2 |
| 3062- | 194 | 1 |
| 3068b- | 5 | 1 |
|  | 21 | 4 |
|  | 194 | 2 |
| 3069b- | 5 | 6 |
|  | 21 | 6 |
|  | 194 | 4 |
| 3070b- | 5 | 4 |
|  | 21 | 5 |
|  | 194 | 7 |
| 3460- | 5 | 2 |
| 3622- | 26 | 1 |
| 3623- | 5 | 6 |
|  | 21 | 3 |
|  | 26 | 1 |
| 3660- | 21 | 1 |
| 3665- | 21 | 1 |
| 3666- | 5 | 2 |
|  | 21 | 4 |
| 3700- | 5 | 1 |
|  | 21 | 1 |
|  | 26 | 1 |
|  | 194 | 1 |
|  | 199 | 2 |
| 3701- | 5 | 3 |
|  | 26 | 1 |
|  | 194 | 2 |
| 3709b- | 194 | 2 |
| 3710- | 5 | 6 |
|  | 21 | 1 |
|  | 194 | 5 |
| 3747b- | 21 | 1 |
| 3794- | 5 | 4 |
|  | 21 | 3 |
|  | 192 | 1 |
| 3795- | 21 | 3 |
| 4079- | 192 | 1 |
| 4081- | 21 | 1 |
| *4085d-* | 21 | 3 |
| 4162- | 21 | 4 |
|  | 194 | 2 |
| 4185- | 194 | 2 |
| 4287- | 21 | 2 |
| 4519- | 21 | 1 |
| *4589-* | 26 | 1 |
| 4599- | 26 | 3 |
|  | 194 | 1 |
| 4740- | 21 | 2 |
| *6019-* | 194 | 1 |
| 6141- | 21 | 1 |
|  | 23 | 2 |
|  | 194 | 1 |
| 6143- | 5 | 1 |
|  | 199 | 1 |
| 6179- | 21 | 4 |
|  | 194 | 4 |
| *6191-* | 194 | 2 |
| 6541- | 21 | 3 |
| *6587-* | 199 | 4 |
| 6590- | 194 | 1 |
| 6636- | 5 | 2 |
|  | 21 | 2 |
| 11211- | 194 | 2 |
| 11402e- | 26 | 1 |
| 11477- | 5 | 2 |
|  | 21 | 2 |
| 15068- | 5 | 4 |
|  | 21 | 3 |
| 15397- | 26 | 6 |
|  | 192 | 2 |
| 23443- | 26 | 14 |
| 24299- | 194 | 1 |
| 24307- | 194 | 1 |
| 26047- | 26 | 2 |
| 30137- | 199 | 1 |
| 30374- | 26 | 1 |
| 30414- | 5 | 4 |
| 30503- | 194 | 2 |
| 30565- | 21 | 2 |
| 32028- | 21 | 4 |
|  | 194 | 4 |
| 32064- | 5 | 1 |
|  | 199 | 2 |
| 32123- | 194 | 2 |
| 32184- | 26 | 2 |
| 41769- | 5 | 2 |
|  | 21 | 1 |
|  | 194 | 2 |
| 41770- | 5 | 2 |
|  | 21 | 1 |
|  | 194 | 2 |
| 43722- | 194 | 1 |
| 43723- | 194 | 1 |
| 44728- | 5 | 4 |
| 47905- | 194 | 1 |
| 48336- | 5 | 2 |
|  | 21 | 2 |
|  | 194 | 2 |
| 48729- | 26 | 10 |
| 50746- | 5 | 2 |
|  | 21 | 2 |
|  | 40 | 2 |
| 59443- | 21 | 2 |
| 60470- | 21 | 4 |
| *61678-* | 5 | 2 |
| 63864- | 5 | 4 |
|  | 21 | 3 |
| 73587- | 194 | 1 |
| 73983- | 5 | 8 |
| 85861- | 26 | 1 |
| 85984- | 5 | 1 |
|  | 21 | 2 |
| 87079- | 5 | 1 |
|  | 21 | 2 |
|  | 194 | 5 |
| 87087- | 5 | 2 |
|  | 21 | 7 |
|  | 26 | 1 |
| 87994- | 26 | 4 |
| 98138- | 21 | 1 |
| 99781- | 194 | 1 |

Numbers in italic indicate alternate part numbers listed in the Parts Index (page 185).

# SUPERMARINE
# SPITFIRE Mk VB

| PART | COLOR | QUANTITY | PART | COLOR | QUANTITY | PART | COLOR | QUANTITY | PART | COLOR | QUANTITY | PART | COLOR | QUANTITY |
|---|---|---|---|---|---|---|---|---|---|---|---|---|---|---|
| 553c- | 1 | 1 | 3023- | 1 | 10 | 3623- | 1 | 12 | 4589- | 1 | 2 | 43093- | 23 | 2 |
| 2412- | 24 | 1 | | 26 | 7 | | 138 | 2 | | 199 | 1 | 43722- | 1 | 3 |
| | 194 | 4 | | 40 | 2 | | 140 | 2 | 6019- | 199 | 2 | | 141 | 1 |
| 2420- | 1 | 6 | | 141 | 7 | | 141 | 2 | 6070- | 40 | 1 | | 192 | 2 |
| | 138 | 2 | | 192 | 6 | | 192 | 1 | 6091- | 26 | 1 | 43723- | 1 | 3 |
| | 192 | 4 | | 194 | 3 | | 194 | 2 | | 141 | 4 | | 141 | 1 |
| | 194 | 4 | | 199 | 3 | 3660- | 1 | 1 | | 192 | 2 | | 192 | 2 |
| 2431- | 141 | 3 | 3024- | 1 | 6 | 3666- | 1 | 1 | 6141- | 1 | 1 | 44728- | 26 | 2 |
| | 192 | 6 | | 21 | 2 | | 138 | 3 | | 21 | 4 | | 199 | 4 |
| | 199 | 1 | | 26 | 4 | | 141 | 2 | | 26 | 4 | 47397- | 1 | 1 |
| 2431px17- | 199 | 1 | | 138 | 1 | | 192 | 2 | | 194 | 2 | 47398- | 1 | 1 |
| 2436b- | 194 | 4 | | 141 | 6 | | 199 | 2 | 6143- | 26 | 1 | 47905- | 192 | 1 |
| 2444- | 194 | 8 | | 192 | 3 | 3700- | 192 | 2 | 6246a- | 199 | 1 | | 199 | 1 |
| 2555- | 199 | 2 | | 194 | 10 | | 199 | 4 | 6538- | 26 | 1 | 48336- | 199 | 9 |
| 2654- | 1 | 5 | | 199 | 2 | 3701- | 26 | 2 | 6541- | 1 | 1 | 50746- | 1 | 2 |
| 2780- | 26 | 15 | 3031- | 1 | 1 | 3709b- | 1 | 2 | | 199 | 3 | | 21 | 1 |
| 2921- | 199 | 2 | | 192 | 3 | 3710- | 1 | 5 | 6562- | 5 | 1 | | 26 | 12 |
| 3001- | 199 | 1 | | 194 | 1 | | 138 | 3 | 6587- | 199 | 2 | | 40 | 10 |
| 3003- | 21 | 15 | 3034- | 1 | 2 | | 141 | 4 | 11215- | 26 | 1 | | 141 | 10 |
| 3004- | 1 | 2 | 3062- | 1 | 2 | | 192 | 7 | 11477- | 141 | 12 | | 192 | 2 |
| 3005- | 192 | 1 | 3068b- | 1 | 2 | 3794- | 1 | 1 | | 192 | 12 | 52107- | 26 | 1 |
| 3009- | 138 | 2 | | 138 | 6 | | 26 | 1 | 11833- | 140 | 4 | 56902- | 194 | 2 |
| 3020- | 1 | 5 | | 192 | 3 | | 138 | 3 | 14769- | 21 | 2 | 60470- | 26 | 4 |
| | 26 | 2 | | 199 | 1 | | 192 | 7 | 15068- | 141 | 1 | 61254- | 26 | 2 |
| | 138 | 2 | 3069b- | 1 | 2 | | 194 | 1 | 15790- | 26 | 1 | 63864- | 199 | 2 |
| | 141 | 2 | | 138 | 3 | | 199 | 1 | 18674- | 1 | 2 | 63868- | 199 | 4 |
| | 192 | 2 | | 140 | 2 | 3795- | 194 | 1 | 18677- | 194 | 2 | 73587- | 194 Base | 1 |
| | 194 | 1 | | 192 | 9 | 3894- | 1 | 2 | 20482- | 26 | 1 | 85861- | 26 | 2 |
| | 199 | 3 | | 199 | 2 | | 199 | 2 | 30136- | 194 | 1 | 85984- | 138 | 8 |
| 3021- | 1 | 3 | 3070b- | 24 | 1 | 4032- | 194 | 1 | 30165- | 199 | 2 | | 192 | 6 |
| | 141 | 2 | | 141 | 2 | | 199 | 2 | 30414- | 194 | 2 | 87087- | 1 | 2 |
| | 192 | 3 | | 192 | 7 | 4070- | 1 | 2 | 32017- | 1 | 2 | | 141 | 4 |
| 3022- | 1 | 5 | | 199 | 1 | | 199 | 4 | 32028- | 138 | 15 | | 194 | 2 |
| | 21 | 1 | 3460- | 192 | 2 | 4079- | 192 | 1 | 32064- | 26 | 3 | 87580- | 199 | 1 |
| | 26 | 4 | | 199 | 4 | 4081- | 1 | 1 | 41769- | 141 | 4 | 87994- | 194 | 2 |
| | 194 | 1 | | | | 4085d- | 192 | 3 | | 192 | 3 | 92947- | 194 | 1 |
| | 199 | 1 | | | | 4274- | 194 | 6 | 41770- | 141 | 4 | 98138- | 21 | 2 |
| | | | | | | 4207- | 1 | 2 | | 192 | 3 | 99781- | 26 | 1 |
| | | | | | | | | | 42003- | 194 | 2 | | 194 | 2 |

Numbers in italic indicate alternate part numbers listed in the Parts Index (page 185).

## ROLLS-ROYCE LIMITED
# MERLIN 61 V-12 ENGINE

| PART | COLOR | QUANTITY | PART | COLOR | QUANTITY | PART | COLOR | QUANTITY | PART | COLOR | QUANTITY | PART | COLOR | QUANTITY |
|---|---|---|---|---|---|---|---|---|---|---|---|---|---|---|
| 553c- | 1 | 1 | 3023- | 1 | 1 | 3700- | 199 | 3 | 6141- | 26 | 4 | 30136- | 194 | 1 |
| 2412- | 194 | 4 | | 26 | 1 | 3794- | 26 | 1 | | 194 | 2 | 32062- | 21 | 1 |
| 2654- | 1 | 1 | | 199 | 1 | 3795- | 194 | 1 | 6179- | 26 | 2 | 32064- | 26 | 2 |
| 2780- | 26 | 1 | 3024- | 26 | 1 | 4070- | 1 | 2 | 6538- | 26 | 1 | 48336- | 199 | 4 |
| 3004- | 1 | 1 | 3068b- | 2 | 1 | | 199 | 4 | 6562- | 5 | 1 | 50746- | 26 | 8 |
| 3022- | 26 | 2 | 3070b- | 24 | 1 | 4476b- | 194 | 1 | *6587*- | 199 | 1 | 60470- | 26 | 4 |
| | 194 | 1 | 3660- | 1 | 1 | 6091- | 26 | 1 | 15790- | 26 | 1 | | | |

Numbers in italic indicate alternate part numbers listed in the Parts Index (page 185).

# MITSUBISHI
# A6M ZERO

| PART | COLOR | QUANTITY | PART | COLOR | QUANTITY | PART | COLOR | QUANTITY | PART | COLOR | QUANTITY | PART | COLOR | QUANTITY |
|---|---|---|---|---|---|---|---|---|---|---|---|---|---|---|
| 2412- | 21 | 1 | | 199 | 5 | 3794- | 1 | 14 | 6636- | 1 | 2 | | 199 | 2 |
| 2420- | 1 | 8 | 3024- | 1 | 13 | | 26 | 1 | 11211- | 1 | 2 | 49668- | 1 | 2 |
| | 26 | 7 | | 21 | 2 | | 199 | 1 | 11215- | 26 | 1 | 50746- | 1 | 8 |
| | 199 | 4 | | 26 | 7 | 3795- | 1 | 1 | 11477- | 1 | 11 | | 26 | 4 |
| 2431- | 1 | 3 | | 194 | 2 | 3832- | 1 | 2 | 15068- | 1 | 16 | | 40 | 16 |
| | 21 | 2 | | 199 | 18 | 3894- | 1 | 4 | 15712- | 26 | 14 | 52107- | 26 | 1 |
| 2431px17- | 199 | 1 | 3031- | 1 | 5 | 3942c- | 1 | 1 | 17485- | 194 | 2 | 56902- | 194 | 2 |
| *2436b-* | 1 | 4 | | 199 | 1 | 4032- | 1 | 2 | 18677- | 194 | 2 | 60474- | 21 | 4 |
| 2444- | 1 | 4 | 3040- | 1 | 3 | | 26 | 1 | 20482- | 26 | 1 | 61254- | 26 | 2 |
| | 194 | 4 | 3068b- | 1 | 5 | | 194 | 2 | 24201- | 194 | 1 | 63864- | 1 | 11 |
| *2555-* | 1 | 2 | | 199 | 1 | | 199 | 2 | *24316-* | 199 | 1 | 63868- | 1 | 2 |
| 2654- | 1 | 6 | 3069b- | 1 | 22 | 4079- | 192 | 1 | 24947- | 1 | 1 | 63985- | 1 | 1 |
| | 21 | 2 | | 21 | 2 | 4081- | 1 | 2 | 30165- | 199 | 2 | 64727- | 194 | 2 |
| | 40 | 1 | | 26 | 3 | *4085d-* | 1 | 3 | 30374- | 1 | 1 | 73587- | 194 | 1 |
| | 194 | 1 | | 40 | 2 | 4162- | 1 | 2 | 30377- | 194 | 3 | 85861- | 1 | 3 |
| 2780- | 26 | 14 | 3070b- | 1 | 7 | 4274- | 23 | 2 | 30414- | 194 | 2 | | 26 | 4 |
| 2819- | 194 | 3 | | 24 | 3 | | 194 | 8 | | 199 | 2 | 85984- | 1 | 8 |
| 2921- | 1 | 1 | | 199 | 1 | *4589b-* | 1 | 1 | 32017- | 1 | 2 | 87079- | 1 | 5 |
| 3003- | 26 | 1 | 3460- | 1 | 3 | *6019-* | 1 | 4 | 32028- | 1 | 18 | 87087- | 1 | 2 |
| 3004- | 1 | 1 | | 199 | 2 | | 194 | 1 | 32064- | 1 | 1 | | 194 | 2 |
| 3005- | 1 | 2 | 3623- | 1 | 19 | 6070- | 40 | 1 | | 26 | 1 | 87580- | 21 | 1 |
| | 194 | 2 | | 26 | 7 | 6091- | 1 | 2 | 32125- | 194 | 1 | 87994- | 26 | 2 |
| 3020- | 1 | 5 | | 199 | 2 | 6141- | 1 | 1 | 41769- | 1 | 9 | 92947- | 194 | 2 |
| | 194 | 2 | 3666- | 1 | 7 | | 21 | 4 | 41770- | 1 | 9 | 93550- | 315 | 1 |
| | 199 | 3 | | 194 | 2 | | 24 | 4 | 42003- | 194 | 2 | 99781- | 1 | 4 |
| 3021- | 1 | 8 | 3700- | 1 | 2 | | 26 | 2 | 43093- | 23 | 2 | | 194 | 1 |
| 3022- | 1 | 4 | | 199 | 4 | | 194 | 1 | 43722- | 1 | 5 | | | |
| | 194 | 2 | 3701- | 26 | 2 | | 315 | 14 | 43723- | 1 | 5 | | | |
| 3023- | 1 | 20 | 3709b- | 1 | 2 | 6143- | 26 | 1 | 44728- | 194 | 2 | | | |
| | 21 | 1 | 3710- | 1 | 7 | 6541- | 1 | 3 | 47397- | 1 | 1 | | | |
| | 26 | 4 | | 26 | 3 | | 26 | 2 | 47398- | 1 | 1 | | | |
| | 40 | 10 | | 194 | 8 | *6587-* | 199 | 2 | 47905- | 1 | 1 | | | |
| | 194 | 2 | | 199 | 2 | 6590- | 21 | 1 | 48336- | 1 | 3 | | | |

Numbers in italic indicate alternate part numbers listed in the Parts Index (page 185).

# NAKAJIMA AIRCRAFT COMPANY
# NK1C SAKAE-12

| PART | COLOR | QUANTITY | PART | COLOR | QUANTITY | PART | COLOR | QUANTITY | PART | COLOR | QUANTITY | PART | COLOR | QUANTITY |
|------|-------|----------|------|-------|----------|------|-------|----------|------|-------|----------|------|-------|----------|
| 2420- | 26 | 7 | 3069b- | 26 | 3 | 4476b- | 2 | 1 | 6541- | 26 | 2 | 30377- | 194 | 3 |
| 2654- | 194 | 1 | 3070b- | 24 | 3 | *6019-* | 194 | 1 | *6587-* | 199 | 1 | 32125- | 194 | 1 |
| 2819- | 194 | 3 | 3623- | 26 | 7 | 6141- | 194 | 1 | 6590- | 21 | 1 | 63985- | 1 | 1 |
| 3024- | 26 | 3 | 3710- | 26 | 4 | | 315 | 14 | 15712- | 26 | 14 | 85861- | 26 | 5 |
| | 194 | 2 | 4032- | 26 | 1 | 6180- | 26 | 2 | *24316-* | 199 | 1 | 87580- | 26 | 1 |

Numbers in italic indicate alternate part numbers listed in the Parts Index (page 185).

# DASSAULT
# MIRAGE IIIO

| PART | COLOR | QUANTITY | PART | COLOR | QUANTITY | PART | COLOR | QUANTITY | PART | COLOR | QUANTITY | PART | COLOR | QUANTITY |
|---|---|---|---|---|---|---|---|---|---|---|---|---|---|---|
| 2412- | 24 | 2 | 3069b- | 26 | 2 | 4162- | 26 | 2 | 30033- | 26 | 1 | 50746- | 26 | 1 |
| | 26 | 2 | | 141 | 1 | 4274- | 194 | 2 | 30136- | 194 | 1 | | 141 | 1 |
| | 194 | 1 | | 199 | 7 | 4286- | 141 | 1 | 30355- | 194 | 1 | | 199 | 5 |
| 2420- | 26 | 6 | 3070b- | 21 | 1 | | 199 | 2 | 30356- | 194 | 1 | 54383- | 194 | 1 |
| | 194 | 4 | | 141 | 4 | 4287- | 194 | 2 | 30374- | 26 | 1 | | 199 | 1 |
| | 199 | 4 | | 199 | 2 | 4349- | 1 | 2 | 30414- | 26 | 2 | 54384- | 194 | 1 |
| 2431- | 141 | 4 | 3460- | 199 | 2 | 4588- | 1 | 4 | | 194 | 2 | | 199 | 1 |
| | 199 | 4 | 3623- | 141 | 3 | 4589b- | 26 | 4 | | 199 | 2 | 55982- | 26 | 2 |
| 2436b- | 26 | 3 | | 194 | 12 | | 182 | 1 | 32000- | 194 | 1 | 58176- | 1 | 2 |
| 2444- | 194 | 6 | | 199 | 4 | | 194 | 2 | 32006- | 194 | 1 | 60470- | 26 | 4 |
| 2449- | 141 | 1 | 3666- | 26 | 3 | 6019- | 194 | 1 | 32028- | 194 | 2 | 60478- | 194 | 1 |
| 2555- | 26 | 2 | | 141 | 2 | | 199 | 8 | | 199 | 2 | 61409- | 141 | 1 |
| 2654- | 194 | 5 | 3700- | 194 | 1 | 6081- | 141 | 2 | 32062- | 26 | 2 | | 199 | 1 |
| 2780- | 26 | 7 | 3701- | 26 | 2 | | 199 | 2 | 32064- | 26 | 1 | 61678- | 194 | 1 |
| 2921- | 26 | 1 | | 194 | 2 | 6091- | 141 | 6 | 32123- | 194 | 2 | 63864- | 141 | 9 |
| 3004- | 199 | 1 | 3702- | 194 | 1 | | 199 | 4 | 32770- | 194 | 4 | | 194 | 2 |
| 3005- | 26 | 1 | 3705- | 26 | 1 | 6141- | 1 | 2 | 41677- | 199 | 2 | | 199 | 4 |
| 3020- | 26 | 6 | 3708- | 26 | 1 | | 21 | 2 | 41769- | 141 | 4 | 73587- | 194 | 2 |
| | 141 | 2 | 3710- | 24 | 2 | | 24 | 4 | | 194 | 2 | 73983- | 194 | 4 |
| | 194 | 8 | | 26 | 13 | | 26 | 4 | | 199 | 4 | | 199 | 4 |
| 3021- | 141 | 4 | | 141 | 4 | | 199 | 3 | 41770- | 141 | 4 | 85970- | 199 | 1 |
| | 194 | 5 | | 194 | 11 | 6233- | 26 | 1 | | 194 | 2 | 87079- | 26 | 1 |
| | 199 | 4 | | 199 | 6 | 6558- | 26 | 2 | | 199 | 4 | | 199 | 2 |
| 3022- | 26 | 5 | 3747b- | 26 | 1 | 6587- | 199 | 1 | 42610- | 194 | 3 | 87087- | 26 | 4 |
| 3023- | 21 | 3 | 3794- | 194 | 7 | 6589- | 194 | 3 | 43093- | 23 | 5 | | 141 | 1 |
| | 26 | 3 | | 199 | 19 | 6632- | 194 | 2 | | 26 | 1 | | 194 | 4 |
| | 140 | 1 | 3795- | 194 | 2 | 6636- | 24 | 2 | 43719- | 199 | 1 | 87580- | 194 | 4 |
| | 141 | 5 | 3894- | 194 | 2 | 11477- | 141 | 4 | 43722- | 141 | 4 | 92279- | 111 | 1 |
| | 194 | 4 | 3942c- | 26 | 1 | | 199 | 3 | | 194 | 1 | 92409- | 26 | 3 |
| | 199 | 8 | 4032- | 23 | 2 | 14719- | 194 | 2 | | 199 | 2 | 92947- | 26 | 3 |
| 3024- | 24 | 2 | | 26 | 8 | 15068- | 141 | 4 | 43723- | 141 | 4 | | 182 | 1 |
| | 26 | 2 | | 194 | 1 | | 194 | 2 | | 194 | 1 | | 194 | 3 |
| | 141 | 4 | 4070- | 26 | 3 | | 199 | 6 | | 199 | 2 | 93606- | 141 | 2 |
| | 199 | 2 | | 194 | 2 | 18674- | 23 | 2 | 44728- | 26 | 1 | 98138- | 1 | 2 |
| 3031- | 194 | 1 | 4081- | 199 | 2 | 18677- | 194 | 6 | | 194 | 4 | 98282- | 26 | 2 |
| 3062- | 1 | 4 | 4085d- | 194 | 3 | 24299- | 199 | 2 | 47905- | 199 | 1 | 99780- | 26 | 2 |
| 3068b- | 141 | 4 | | 199 | 2 | 24307- | 199 | 2 | 48336- | 199 | 4 | | 199 | 4 |

Numbers in italic indicate alternate part numbers listed in the Parts Index (page 185).

# SNECMA
# ATAR 09C JET ENGINE

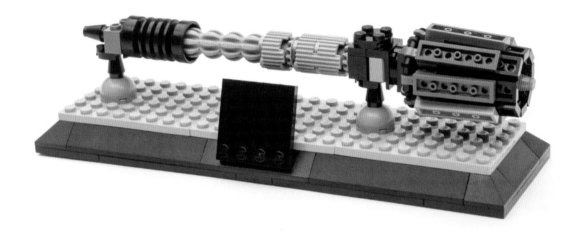

| PART | COLOR | QUANTITY | | PART | COLOR | QUANTITY | | PART | COLOR | QUANTITY | | PART | COLOR | QUANTITY | | PART | COLOR | QUANTITY |
|---|---|---|---|---|---|---|---|---|---|---|---|---|---|---|---|---|---|---|
| **553c-** | 26 | 2 | | **3045-** | 26 | 4 | | **3937-** | 26 | 1 | | **6179-** | 26 | 1 | | **32123-** | 194 | 1 |
| **3022-** | 26 | 1 | | **3700-** | 194 | 1 | | **4032-** | 26 | 5 | | *6587-* | 199 | 1 | | **32770-** | 194 | 4 |
| **3023-** | 26 | 2 | | **3708-** | 26 | 1 | | **4445-** | 26 | 4 | | **6589-** | 194 | 3 | | **44728-** | 26 | 1 |
| **3028-** | 194 | 2 | | **3710-** | 26 | 8 | | *4589b-* | 26 | 3 | | **23949-** | 26 | 2 | | **55982-** | 26 | 2 |
| **3034-** | 26 | 5 | | | 141 | 2 | | | 182 | 1 | | **30033-** | 26 | 1 | | **92947-** | 26 | 2 |
| **3035-** | 26 | 2 | | | 194 | 2 | | *6019-* | 199 | 8 | | **30136-** | 194 | 1 | | | 182 | 1 |
| **3037-** | 26 | 2 | | | 199 | 4 | | **6134-** | 26 | 1 | | **32064-** | 26 | 1 | | | 194 | 3 |

Numbers in italic indicate alternate part numbers listed in the Parts Index (page 185).

# F-35 LIGHTNING II

| PART | COLOR | QUANTITY | PART | COLOR | QUANTITY | PART | COLOR | QUANTITY | PART | COLOR | QUANTITY | PART | COLOR | QUANTITY |
|---|---|---|---|---|---|---|---|---|---|---|---|---|---|---|
| 2412- | 194 | 2 | 3024- | 21 | 1 | 3737- | 26 | 1 | 6632- | 194 | 1 | 32126- | 194 | 2 |
| 2420- | 192 | 2 | | 26 | 2 | 3794- | 26 | 2 | 6636- | 1 | 2 | 32770- | 194 | 4 |
| | 194 | 2 | | 194 | 1 | | 194 | 1 | | 199 | 4 | 32523- | 199 | 2 |
| | 199 | 1 | | 199 | 8 | | 199 | 1 | 11211- | 194 | 2 | 41747- | 199 | 1 |
| 2431- | 199 | 6 | 3032- | 199 | 2 | 3832- | 199 | 2 | 11477- | 194 | 4 | 41748- | 199 | 1 |
| 2444- | 194 | 6 | 3039- | 194 | 2 | 4032- | 26 | 5 | | 199 | 2 | 41763- | 194 | 3 |
| | 199 | 2 | 3068b- | 5 | 1 | | 194 | 1 | 15068- | 194 | 4 | 41764- | 194 | 2 |
| 2450- | 199 | 8 | | 199 | 2 | 4070- | 194 | 1 | | 199 | 8 | 41765- | 194 | 2 |
| *2555-* | 199 | 4 | 3069b- | 199 | 10 | 4162- | 199 | 2 | 17485- | 194 | 1 | 41769- | 199 | 3 |
| 2654- | 194 | 9 | 3070b- | 41 | 1 | 4274- | 194 | 2 | 18677- | 194 | 5 | 41770- | 199 | 3 |
| | 199 | 6 | | 199 | 7 | 4519- | 194 | 2 | 24299- | 199 | 3 | 42060- | 199 | 1 |
| 2780- | 26 | 16 | 3176- | 194 | 2 | *4589b-* | 182 | 1 | 24307- | 199 | 3 | 42061- | 199 | 1 |
| 3020- | 1 | 2 | 3460- | 26 | 2 | | 194 | 1 | 30033- | 26 | 1 | 42610- | 194 | 3 |
| | 26 | 2 | | 194 | 2 | 4733- | 194 | 1 | 30136- | 26 | 1 | 43093- | 23 | 1 |
| | 194 | 3 | | 199 | 2 | 4854- | 194 | 1 | 30374- | 194 | 3 | | 26 | 1 |
| | 199 | 3 | 3623- | 194 | 3 | 4865- | 26 | 2 | 30414- | 194 | 2 | 43122- | 26 | 1 |
| 3021- | 5 | 1 | | 199 | 5 | 4871- | 194 | 1 | 30503- | 194 | 4 | 43722- | 194 | 1 |
| | 26 | 3 | 3660- | 194 | 2 | *6019-* | 194 | 2 | 30504- | 194 | 2 | | 199 | 1 |
| | 194 | 1 | 3665- | 194 | 10 | | 199 | 8 | 30526- | 26 | 1 | 43723- | 194 | 1 |
| | 199 | 2 | 3666- | 1 | 4 | 6106- | 2 | 2 | 32000- | 26 | 2 | | 199 | 1 |
| 3022- | 1 | 1 | 3700- | 26 | 1 | 6141- | 21 | 2 | | 199 | 4 | 44728- | 26 | 2 |
| | 26 | 2 | | 194 | 2 | | 40 | 2 | 32002- | 199 | 2 | 45677- | 199 | 1 |
| | 194 | 2 | 3701- | 26 | 4 | | 194 | 6 | 32006- | 194 | 1 | 47905- | 194 | 3 |
| | 199 | 3 | | 199 | 1 | 6231- | 199 | 2 | 32013- | 194 | 2 | 48336- | 194 | 2 |
| 3023- | 5 | 1 | 3709b- | 26 | 2 | 6536- | 194 | 2 | 32028- | 194 | 6 | | 199 | 13 |
| | 21 | 6 | 3710- | 1 | 5 | 6541- | 194 | 2 | | 199 | 9 | 49668- | 26 | 8 |
| | 26 | 9 | | 26 | 1 | | 199 | 2 | 32064- | 1 | 1 | 50746- | 194 | 5 |
| | 194 | 5 | | 194 | 6 | 6562- | 194 | 1 | | 26 | 1 | | 199 | 5 |
| | 199 | 16 | | 199 | 5 | 6589- | 194 | 2 | 32123- | 194 | 1 | 51739- | 194 | 2 |

Numbers in italic indicate alternate part numbers listed in the Parts Index (page 185).
This model includes printed bricks available from The Big Brick (see page 191).

| PART | COLOR | QUANTITY |
|---|---|---|
| 54383- | 194 | 1 |
| | 199 | 1 |
| 54384- | 194 | 1 |
| | 199 | 1 |
| 55982- | 194 | 2 |
| 60470- | 26 | 2 |
| | 194 | 11 |
| *61678-* | 199 | 3 |
| 63864- | 199 | 2 |
| 63868- | 199 | 4 |
| 72454- | 199 | 1 |
| 73587- | 194 | 1 |
| 85984- | 1 | 2 |
| | 26 | 2 |
| | 194 | 6 |
| | 199 | 4 |
| 87087- | 26 | 2 |
| | 194 | 5 |
| | 199 | 4 |
| 92279- | 111 | 1 |
| 92280- | 26 | 1 |
| 92409- | 26 | 3 |
| 92947- | 26 | 1 |
| | 182 | 1 |
| 93273- | 199 | 4 |
| 93606- | 199 | 2 |
| 99780- | 194 | 4 |
| 99781- | 194 | 2 |

**ADDITIONAL PARTS FOR F-35A**

| PART | COLOR | QUANTITY |
|---|---|---|
| 2654- | 21 | 1 |
| 3021- | 194 | 3 |
| 3022- | 21 | 1 |
| 3023- | 1 | 1 |
| | 21 | 1 |
| | 24 | 1 |
| 3031- | 1 | 1 |
| 3068b- | 199 | 1 |
| 3460- | 199 | 2 |
| 3623- | 194 | 2 |
| 3794- | 199 | 1 |
| 4032- | 21 | 1 |
| 6141- | 194 | 2 |
| 41769- | 199 | 1 |
| 41770- | 199 | 1 |
| 93273- | 199 | 5 |

**ADDITIONAL PARTS FOR F-35C**

| PART | COLOR | QUANTITY | PART | COLOR | QUANTITY |
|---|---|---|---|---|---|
| 2450- | 194 | 2 | 3710- | 21 | 2 |
| 2654- | 21 | | 3794- | 199 | 1 |
| 3005- | 194 | 2 | 4032- | 21 | 1 |
| 3021- | 1999 | 9 | 4287- | 194 | 2 |
| 3022- | 21 | 1 | 6106- | 194 | 4 |
| 3023- | 1 | 1 | 6141- | 194 | 2 |
| | 24 | 1 | 41769- | 199 | 1 |
| | 194 | 2 | 41770- | 199 | 1 |
| | 199 | | 48336- | 199 | 1 |
| 3031- | 1 | 1 | 49668- | 194 | 6 |
| 3069b- | 199 | 3 | 60470- | 194 | 1 |
| 3460- | 199 | 2 | 63864- | 199 | 2 |
| 3623- | 194 | 4 | 87079- | 199 | 2 |
| | 199 | 2 | 98138- | 194 | 2 |
| 3666- | 199 | 2 | 93273- | 199 | 5 |

## LOCKHEED
# SR-71 BLACKBIRD

| PART | COLOR | QUANTITY | PART | COLOR | QUANTITY | PART | COLOR | QUANTITY | PART | COLOR | QUANTITY | PART | COLOR | QUANTITY |
|---|---|---|---|---|---|---|---|---|---|---|---|---|---|---|
| 2412- | 26 | 2 | 3020- | 23 | 1 | 3034- | 26 | 3 | | 26 | 8 | 3938- | 26 | 2 |
| 2420- | 1 | 4 | | 24 | 1 | 3035- | 26 | 1 | 3665- | 26 | 2 | 3942c- | 26 | 3 |
| | 21 | 7 | | 26 | 6 | | 199 | 3 | 3666- | 1 | 2 | 4032- | 21 | 1 |
| | 23 | 2 | | 194 | 2 | 3038- | 26 | 2 | | 26 | 8 | | 26 | 3 |
| | 26 | 6 | 3021- | 1 | 1 | 3039pb/px | variety* | 6 | | 199 | 7 | 4070- | 26 | 28 |
| | 194 | 2 | | 26 | 1 | 3040- | 26 | 10 | 3700- | 21 | 1 | | 154 | 2 |
| | 199 | 6 | | 194 | 1 | 3068b- | 26 | 4 | | 23 | 1 | 4161- | 26 | 6 |
| 2431px17 | 199 | 1 | 3022- | 21 | 2 | 3069b- | 26 | 12 | | 26 | 12 | 4162- | 1 | 2 |
| 2450- | 21 | 2 | | 23 | 1 | 3069bps2- | 26 | 4 | 3701- | 26 | 8 | 4286- | 26 | 12 |
| 2555- | 26 | 6 | | 24 | 1 | 3069bpb277- | 26 | 2 | | 199 | 2 | | 199 | 8 |
| 2569- | 47 | 2 (Opt) | | 26 | 1 | 3070b- | 21 | 6 | 3705- | 26 | 3 | 4287- | 26 | 12 |
| 2654- | 26 | 15 | | 199 | 4 | | 26 | 4 | 3710- | 21 | 1 | 4445- | 26 | 4 |
| 2780- | 26 | 33 | 3023- | 21 | 7 | 3297- | 26 | 12 | | 26 | 41 | 4477- | 26 | 2 |
| 2877- | 26 | 48 | | 23 | 3 | 3298- | 26 | 4 | | 194 | 1 | 4589b- | 26 | 3 |
| 2921- | 26 | 2 | | 24 | 1 | 3299- | 26 | 2 | | 199 | 3 | | 47 | 2 |
| 3004- | 26 | 2 | | 26 | 40 | 3330- | 26 | 1 | 3738- | 26 | 1 | 4742- | 26 | 2 |
| 3005- | 26 | 8 | | 194 | 4 | 3460- | 26 | 6 | 3747b- | 26 | 34 | 6091- | 26 | 2 |
| 3010- | 26 | 6 | | 199 | 4 | | 194 | 4 | 3794- | 1 | 2 | 6141- | 21 | 6 |
| | | | 3024- | 21 | 6 | 3623- | 21 | 6 | | 26 | 6 | | 24 | 2 |
| | | | | 26 | 64 | | 26 | 20 | 3795- | 21 | 1 | | 26 | 6 |
| | | | 3031- | 24 | 1 | | 194 | 1 | | 199 | 2 | 6143- | 21 | 1 |
| | | | | 199 | 1 | 3660- | 21 | 7 | 3937- | 194 | 2 | | 47 | 2 |

Numbers in italic indicate alternate part numbers listed in the Parts Index (page 185).
This model includes printed bricks available from The Big Brick (see page 191).
* see page 111

| PART | COLOR | QUANTITY | PART | COLOR | QUANTITY | PART | COLOR | QUANTITY | PART | COLOR | QUANTITY | PART | COLOR | QUANTITY |
|------|-------|----------|------|-------|----------|------|-------|----------|------|-------|----------|------|-------|----------|
| 6222- | 26 | 12 | 24299- | 21 | 2 | 41531- | 26 | 2 | | 40 | 2 | 87994- | 26 | 2 |
| 6259- | 26 | 8 | | 26 | 4 | 41747- | 26 | 1 | 50950- | 26 | 4 | 91988 | 26 | 1 |
| 6586- | 26 | 4 | 24307- | 21 | 2 | 41748- | 26 | 1 | 50955- | 26 | 1 | 92279- | 111 | 2 |
| 6538- | 26 | 1 | | 26 | 4 | 41763- | 26 | 2 | 50956- | 26 | 1 | 92947- | 1 | 2 |
| 6541- | 21 | 2 | 26047- | 26 | 2 | 41764- | 26 | 1 | 52107- | 26 | 4 | 99780- | 21 | 2 |
| | 26 | 45 | 30249- | 26 | 2 | 41765- | 26 | 1 | 54383- | 26 | 4 | | 26 | 9 |
| 6558- | 23 | 1 | 30414- | 26 | 2 | 41769- | 26 | 5 | 54384- | 26 | 4 | 99781- | 26 | 3 |
| | 26 | 16 | 32000- | 26 | 11 | 41770- | 26 | 5 | 60470- | 26 | 4 | | | |
| 6562- | 5 | 1 | 32013- | 26 | 5 | 42610- | 194 | 5 | 60474- | 26 | 6 | | | |
| 6587- | 199 | 8 | 32017- | 21 | 4 | 42611- | 26 | 5 | 60481- | 26 | 4 | | | |
| 6590- | 194 | 5 | | 26 | 2 | 43093- | 23 | 12 | 61678- | 26 | 4 | | | |
| 6632- | 26 | 4 | 32028- | 26 | 1 | | 26 | 8 | 63864- | 26 | 2 | | | |
| 6636- | 26 | 2 | 32039- | 26 | 3 | 43713- | 26 | 1 | 63868- | 26 | 4 | | | |
| 11214- | 199 | 2 | 32062- | 26 | 2 | 43722- | 26 | 3 | 63985- | 26 | 1 | | | |
| 11458- | 26 | 4 | 32064- | 21 | 1 | 43723- | 26 | 3 | 73587- | 194 | 1 | | | |
| 11477- | 26 | 2 | 32123- | 194 | 4 | 45301- | 26 | 1 | 85984- | 24 | 1 | | | |
| 15068- | 26 | 7 | 32184- | 26 | 6 | 47905- | 26 | 6 | | 26 | 71 | | | |
| 15100- | 26 | 6 | 32209- | 199 | 2 | 48336- | 26 | 3 | 87079- | 26 | 8 | | | |
| 18677- | 26 | 10 | 32449- | 21 | 2 | 49668- | 26 | 4 | 87087- | 26 | 6 | | | |
| 22889- | 26 | 1 | 32531- | 26 | 1 | 50746- | 26 | 14 | | 199 | 2 | | | |

LOCKHEED
# P-38 LIGHTNING

| PART | COLOR | QUANTITY | PART | COLOR | QUANTITY | PART | COLOR | QUANTITY | PART | COLOR | QUANTITY | PART | COLOR | QUANTITY |
|---|---|---|---|---|---|---|---|---|---|---|---|---|---|---|
| 553c- | 24 | 2 | 3004- | 1 | 4 | 3024- | 1 | 10 | 3070bp07- | 194 | 2 | 3705- | 26 | 5 |
|  | 199 | 1 |  | 26 | 8 |  | 21 | 6 | 3460- | 26 | 1 | 3706- | 26 | 3 |
| 2357- | 199 | 6 |  | 194 | 4 |  | 24 | 3 |  | 194 | 2 | 3707- | 26 | 3 |
| 2412- | 26 | 8 | 3005- | 24 | 4 |  | 26 | 7 |  | 199 | 6 | 3709b- | 26 | 1 |
|  | 194 | 6 |  | 194 | 8 |  | 40 | 6 | 3622- | 194 | 6 |  | 194 | 1 |
|  | 199 | 2 | 3009- | 194 | 2 |  | 194 | 33 | 3623- | 1 | 4 | 3710- | 1 | 8 |
| 2420- | 1 | 8 | 3010- | 194 | 6 |  | 199 | 4 |  | 21 | 5 |  | 21 | 2 |
|  | 24 | 8 | 3020- | 1 | 8 | 3030- | 194 | 1 |  | 23 | 4 |  | 23 | 2 |
|  | 26 | 7 |  | 21 | 2 | 3031- | 26 | 2 |  | 26 | 5 |  | 24 | 3 |
|  | 194 | 18 |  | 24 | 4 |  | 194 | 4 |  | 194 | 28 |  | 26 | 26 |
|  | 199 | 2 |  | 26 | 22 |  | 199 | 2 |  | 199 | 9 |  | 194 | 31 |
| 2431- | 1 | 3 |  | 192 | 1 | 3032- | 23 | 2 | 3647- | 194 | 3 |  | 199 | 10 |
|  | 194 | 16 |  | 194 | 21 |  | 194 | 4 | 3648- | 194 | 4 | 3737- | 26 | 2 |
| 2436b- | 26 | 6 |  | 199 | 2 | 3034- | 26 | 4 | 3660- | 194 | 15 | 3794- | 1 | 12 |
|  | 194 | 6 | 3021- | 1 | 4 |  | 194 | 8 | 3665- | 1 | 4 |  | 26 | 13 |
| 2444- | 1 | 2 |  | 21 | 8 | 3035- | 194 | 2 |  | 21 | 2 |  | 194 | 34 |
|  | 194 | 9 |  | 23 | 4 | 3037- | 26 | 2 |  | 194 | 12 | 3795- | 1 | 4 |
| 2445- | 26 | 2 |  | 26 | 12 | 3039- | 26 | 2 | 3666- | 1 | 4 |  | 21 | 3 |
|  | 194 | 5 |  | 28 | 4 | 3040- | 194 | 6 |  | 24 | 6 |  | 24 | 2 |
| 2540- | 199 | 1 |  | 194 | 18 | 3062- | 21 | 1 |  | 26 | 10 |  | 26 | 7 |
| 2555- | 26 | 2 |  | 199 | 4 |  | 24 | 2 |  | 192 | 1 |  | 194 | 14 |
|  | 194 | 2 | 3022- | 1 | 2 |  | 194 | 2 |  | 194 | 39 | 3832- | 1 | 4 |
| 2654- | 26 | 2 |  | 21 | 2 |  | 199 | 4 |  | 199 | 1 |  | 194 | 2 |
|  | 194 | 26 |  | 23 | 2 | 3068b- | 1 | 8 | 3700- | 21 | 2 | 3839- | 26 | 1 |
| 2730- | 26 | 1 |  | 26 | 10 |  | 26 | 3 |  | 24 | 2 | 3894- | 26 | 1 |
| 2780- | 26 | 55 |  | 140 | 4 |  | 140 | 8 |  | 26 | 11 |  | 194 | 2 |
| 2850- | 194 | 12 |  | 194 | 14 |  | 194 | 19 |  | 194 | 5 | 3937- | 194 | 2 |
| 2851- | 199 | 12 |  | 199 | 6 | 3069b- | 24 | 6 | 3701- | 21 | 2 | 3938- | 194 | 2 |
| 2852- | 194 | 12 | 3023- | 1 | 2 |  | 26 | 5 |  | 26 | 14 | 3942c- | 194 | 1 |
| 2853- | 194 | 4 |  | 21 | 6 |  | 194 | 21 |  | 192 | 1 | 3958- | 194 | 2 |
| 2854- | 194 | 4 |  | 23 | 6 | 3069bpb125- | 1 | 2 |  | 194 | 2 |  | 199 | 2 |
| 2877- | 26 | 1 |  | 24 | 2 | 3070b- | 1 | 8 |  | 199 | 8 | 4032- | 5 | 2 |
| 2921- | 194 | 4 |  | 26 | 25 |  | 26 | 3 | 3702- | 21 | 2 |  | 21 | 7 |
| 3001- | 194 | 2 |  | 28 | 2 |  | 194 | 4 |  | 199 | 2 | 4070- | 199 | 8 |
| 3002- | 26 | 1 |  | 40 | 4 |  | 199 | 2 | 3703- | 199 | 1 | 4085d- | 194 | 11 |
|  | 194 | 2 |  | 194 | 70 |  |  |  |  |  |  | 4095- | 194 | 1 |
| 3003- | 194 | 1 |  | 199 | 3 |  |  |  |  |  |  |  |  |  |

Numbers in italic indicate alternate part numbers listed in the Parts Index (page 185).
This model includes printed bricks available from The Big Brick (see page 191).

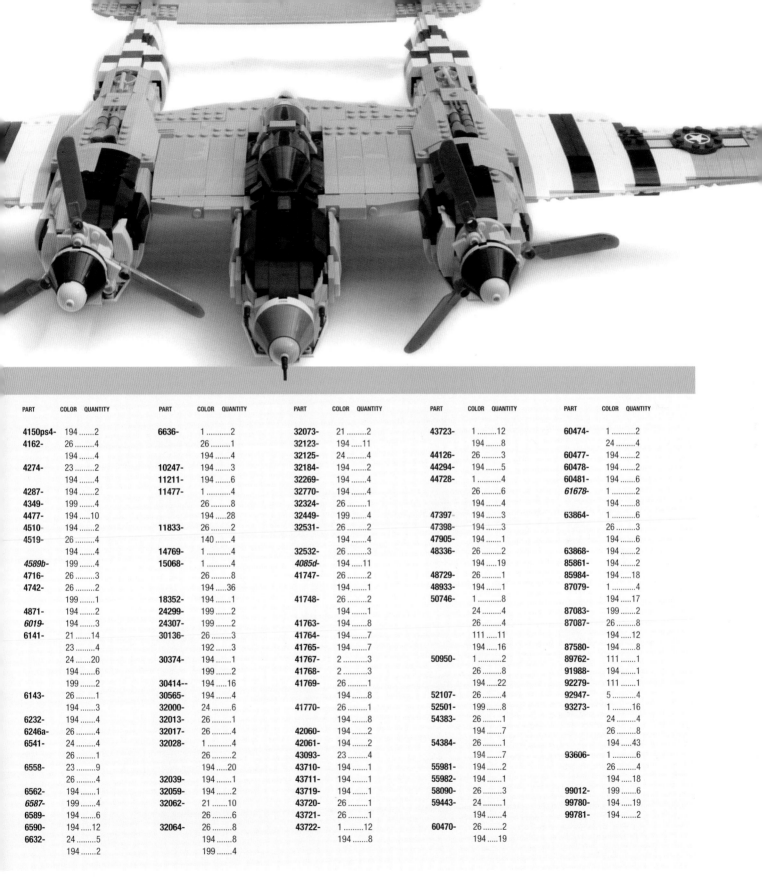

| PART | COLOR | QUANTITY | PART | COLOR | QUANTITY | PART | COLOR | QUANTITY | PART | COLOR | QUANTITY | PART | COLOR | QUANTITY |
|---|---|---|---|---|---|---|---|---|---|---|---|---|---|---|
| 4150ps4- | 194 | 2 | 6636- | 1 | 2 | 32073- | 21 | 2 | 43723- | 1 | 12 | 60474- | 1 | 2 |
| 4162- | 26 | 4 | | 26 | 1 | 32123- | 194 | 11 | | 194 | 8 | | 24 | 4 |
| | 194 | 4 | | 194 | 4 | 32125- | 24 | 4 | 44126- | 26 | 3 | 60477- | 194 | 2 |
| 4274- | 23 | 2 | 10247- | 194 | 3 | 32184- | 194 | 2 | 44294- | 194 | 5 | 60478- | 194 | 2 |
| | 194 | 4 | 11211- | 194 | 6 | 32269- | 194 | 4 | 44728- | 1 | 4 | 60481- | 194 | 6 |
| 4287- | 194 | 2 | 11477- | 1 | 4 | 32770- | 194 | 4 | | 26 | 6 | 61678- | 1 | 2 |
| 4349- | 199 | 4 | | 26 | 8 | 32324- | 26 | 1 | | 194 | 4 | | 194 | 8 |
| 4477- | 194 | 10 | | 194 | 28 | 32449- | 199 | 4 | 47397- | 194 | 3 | 63864- | 1 | 6 |
| 4510- | 194 | 2 | 11833- | 26 | 2 | 32531- | 26 | 2 | 47398- | 194 | 3 | | 26 | 3 |
| 4519- | 26 | 4 | | 140 | 4 | | 194 | 4 | 47905- | 194 | 1 | | 194 | 6 |
| | 194 | 4 | 14769- | 1 | 4 | 32532- | 26 | 3 | 48336- | 26 | 2 | 63868- | 194 | 2 |
| 4589b- | 199 | 4 | 15068- | 1 | 4 | 4085d- | 194 | 11 | | 194 | 19 | 85861- | 194 | 2 |
| 4716- | 26 | 3 | | 26 | 8 | 41747- | 26 | 2 | 48729- | 26 | 1 | 85984- | 194 | 18 |
| 4742- | 26 | 2 | | 194 | 36 | | 194 | 1 | 48933- | 194 | 1 | 87079- | 1 | 4 |
| | 199 | 1 | 18352- | 194 | 1 | 41748- | 26 | 2 | 50746- | 1 | 8 | | 194 | 17 |
| 4871- | 194 | 2 | 24299- | 199 | 2 | | 194 | 1 | | 24 | 4 | 87083- | 199 | 2 |
| 6019- | 194 | 3 | 24307- | 199 | 2 | 41763- | 194 | 8 | | 26 | 4 | 87087- | 26 | 8 |
| 6141- | 21 | 14 | 30136- | 26 | 3 | 41764- | 194 | 7 | | 111 | 11 | | 194 | 12 |
| | 23 | 4 | | 192 | 3 | 41765- | 194 | 7 | | 194 | 16 | 87580- | 194 | 8 |
| | 24 | 20 | 30374- | 194 | 1 | 41767- | 2 | 3 | 50950- | 1 | 2 | 89762- | 111 | 1 |
| | 194 | 6 | | 199 | 2 | 41768- | 2 | 3 | | 26 | 8 | 91988- | 194 | 1 |
| | 199 | 2 | 30414-- | 194 | 16 | 41769- | 26 | 1 | | 194 | 22 | 92279- | 111 | 1 |
| 6143- | 26 | 1 | 30565- | 194 | 4 | | 194 | 8 | 52107- | 26 | 4 | 92947- | 5 | 4 |
| | 194 | 3 | 32000- | 24 | 6 | 41770- | 26 | 1 | 52501- | 199 | 8 | 93273- | 1 | 16 |
| 6232- | 194 | 4 | 32013- | 26 | 1 | | 194 | 8 | 54383- | 26 | 1 | | 24 | 4 |
| 6246a- | 26 | 4 | 32017- | 26 | 4 | 42060- | 194 | 2 | | 194 | 7 | | 26 | 8 |
| 6541- | 24 | 4 | 32028- | 1 | 4 | 42061- | 194 | 2 | 54384- | 26 | 1 | | 194 | 43 |
| | 26 | 1 | | 26 | 2 | 43093- | 23 | 4 | | 194 | 7 | 93606- | 1 | 6 |
| 6558- | 23 | 9 | | 194 | 20 | 43710- | 194 | 1 | 55981- | 194 | 2 | | 26 | 4 |
| | 26 | 4 | 32039- | 194 | 1 | 43711- | 194 | 1 | 55982- | 194 | 1 | | 194 | 18 |
| 6562- | 194 | 1 | 32059- | 194 | 2 | 43719- | 194 | 1 | 58090- | 26 | 3 | 99012- | 199 | 6 |
| 6587- | 199 | 4 | 32062- | 21 | 10 | 43720- | 26 | 1 | 59443- | 24 | 1 | 99780- | 194 | 19 |
| 6589- | 194 | 6 | | 26 | 6 | 43721- | 26 | 1 | | 194 | 4 | 99781- | 194 | 2 |
| 6590- | 194 | 12 | 32064- | 26 | 8 | 43722- | 1 | 12 | 60470- | 26 | 2 | | | |
| 6632- | 24 | 5 | | 194 | 8 | | 194 | 8 | | 194 | 19 | | | |
| | 194 | 2 | | 199 | 4 | | | | | | | | | |

# V-1710
# V-12 ENGINE

| PART | COLOR | QUANTITY | PART | COLOR | QUANTITY | PART | COLOR | QUANTITY | PART | COLOR | QUANTITY | PART | COLOR | QUANTITY |
|------|-------|----------|------|-------|----------|------|-------|----------|------|-------|----------|------|-------|----------|
| 553c- | 24 | 1 | 3022- | 199 | 2 | 3710- | 26 | 1 | *6587-* | 199 | 2 | 41764- | 194 | 1 |
| 2420- | 26 | 1 | 3023- | 26 | 3 | | 194 | 1 | 6632- | 194 | 1 | 41765- | 194 | 1 |
| | 194 | 1 | | 194 | 3 | 3795- | 26 | 1 | 10202- | 194 | 1 | 43093- | 23 | 3 |
| 2431 | 194 | 2 | 3030- | 26 | 2 | 3937- | 26 | 1 | 11833- | 26 | 1 | 43722- | 194 | 2 |
| 2654- | 194 | 1 | 3031- | 199 | 1 | 4032- | 21 | 2 | 32000- | 24 | 3 | 43723- | 194 | 2 |
| 2780- | 26 | 8 | 3032- | 194 | 1 | 4274- | 194 | 2 | 32062- | 26 | 3 | 44126- | 26 | 1 |
| 2850- | 194 | 6 | 3033- | 26 | 2 | 4476b- | 2 | 1 | 32073- | 21 | 1 | 50746- | 24 | 2 |
| 2851- | 199 | 6 | 3034- | 26 | 1 | 4742- | 26 | 1 | 32123- | 194 | 3 | 50950- | 26 | 4 |
| 2852- | 194 | 6 | 3069b- | 24 | 3 | 6134- | 26 | 1 | 32125- | 24 | 2 | | 194 | 4 |
| 2853- | 194 | 2 | 3660- | 194 | 2 | 6141- | 21 | 6 | 32269- | 194 | 1 | 52501- | 199 | 3 |
| 2854- | 194 | 2 | 3666- | 194 | 2 | | 24 | 4 | 32770- | 194 | 1 | 60474- | 24 | 2 |
| 3005- | 24 | 2 | 3700- | 24 | 1 | 6143- | 194 | 1 | 41539- | 194 | 1 | 85984- | 26 | 16 |
| 3020- | 26 | 3 | | 26 | 2 | 6179- | 26 | 4 | 41747- | 26 | 1 | 87083- | 199 | 1 |
| | 194 | 1 | 3701- | 26 | 2 | 6541- | 24 | 2 | 41748- | 194 | 1 | 99012- | 199 | 3 |
| 3021- | 26 | 1 | 3705- | 21 | 1 | 6558- | 26 | 2 | 41763- | 194 | 2 | | | |

Numbers in italic indicate alternates part numbers listed in the Parts Index

# APPENDIX II
# PARTS INDEX

Not to scale.

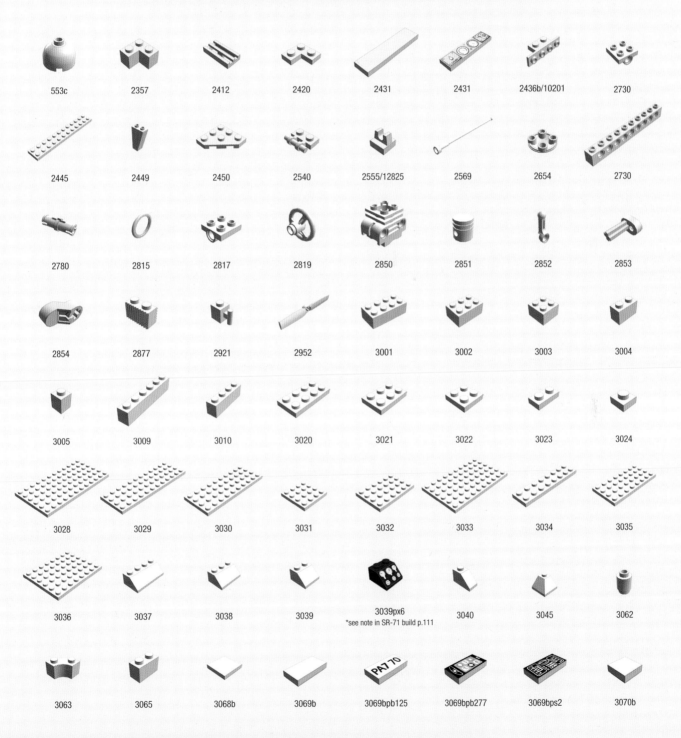

| | | | | | | | |
|---|---|---|---|---|---|---|---|
| 553c | 2357 | 2412 | 2420 | 2431 | 2431 | 2436b/10201 | 2730 |
| 2445 | 2449 | 2450 | 2540 | 2555/12825 | 2569 | 2654 | 2730 |
| 2780 | 2815 | 2817 | 2819 | 2850 | 2851 | 2852 | 2853 |
| 2854 | 2877 | 2921 | 2952 | 3001 | 3002 | 3003 | 3004 |
| 3005 | 3009 | 3010 | 3020 | 3021 | 3022 | 3023 | 3024 |
| 3028 | 3029 | 3030 | 3031 | 3032 | 3033 | 3034 | 3035 |
| 3036 | 3037 | 3038 | 3039 | 3039px6<br>*see note in SR-71 build p.111 | 3040 | 3045 | 3062 |
| 3063 | 3065 | 3068b | 3069b | 3069bpb125 | 3069bpb277 | 3069bps2 | 3070b |

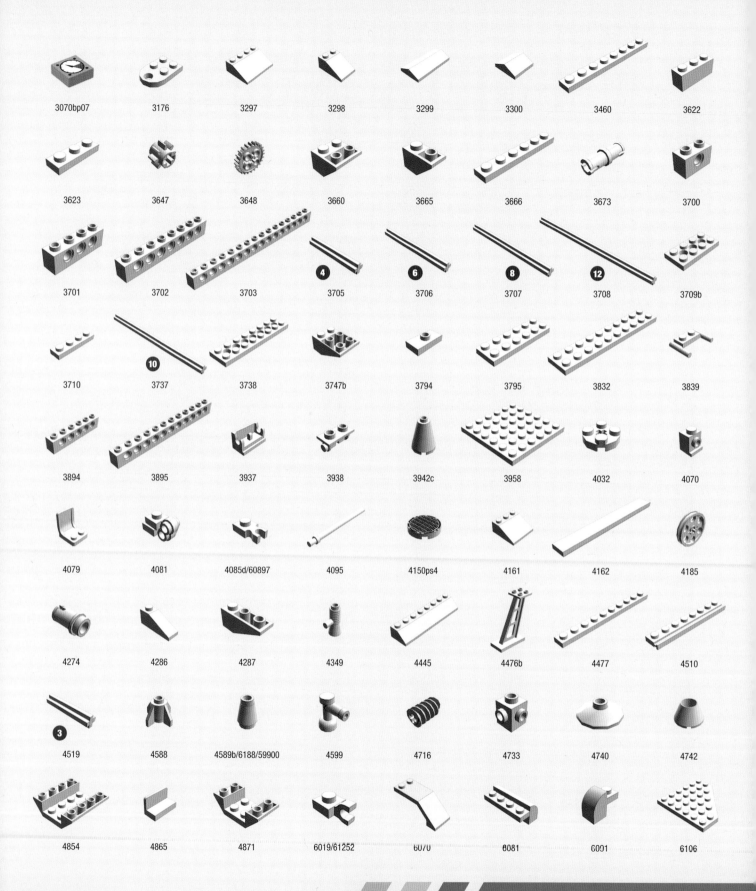

3070bp07

3176

3297

3298

3299

3300

3460

3622

3623

3647

3648

3660

3665

3666

3673

3700

3701

3702

3703

4 3705

6 3706

8 3707

12 3708

3709b

3710

10 3737

3738

3747b

3794

3795

3832

3839

3894

3895

3937

3938

3942c

3958

4032

4070

4079

4081

4085d/60897

4095

4150ps4

4161

4162

4185

4274

4286

4287

4349

4445

4476b

4477

4510

3 4519

4588

4589b/6188/59900

4599

4716

4733

4740

4742

4854

4865

4871

6019/61252

6070

6081

6091

6106

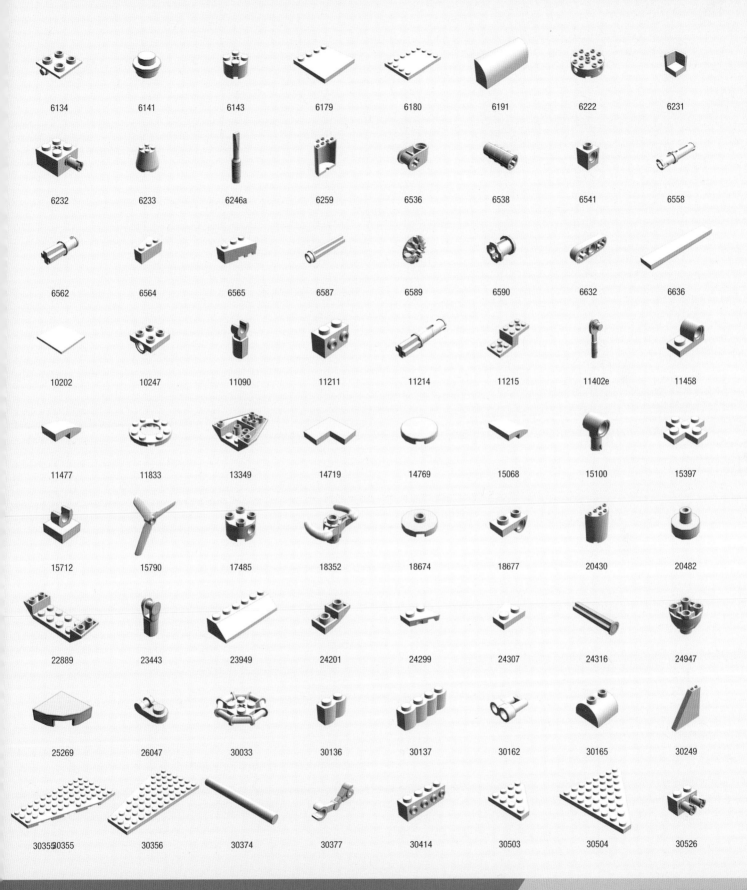

6134    6141    6143    6179    6180    6191    6222    6231

6232    6233    6246a    6259    6536    6538    6541    6558

6562    6564    6565    6587    6589    6590    6632    6636

10202    10247    11090    11211    11214    11215    11402e    11458

11477    11833    13349    14719    14769    15068    15100    15397

15712    15790    17485    18352    18674    18677    20430    20482

22889    23443    23949    24201    24299    24307    24316    24947

25269    26047    30033    30136    30137    30162    30165    30249

30355 30355    30356    30374    30377    30414    30503    30504    30526

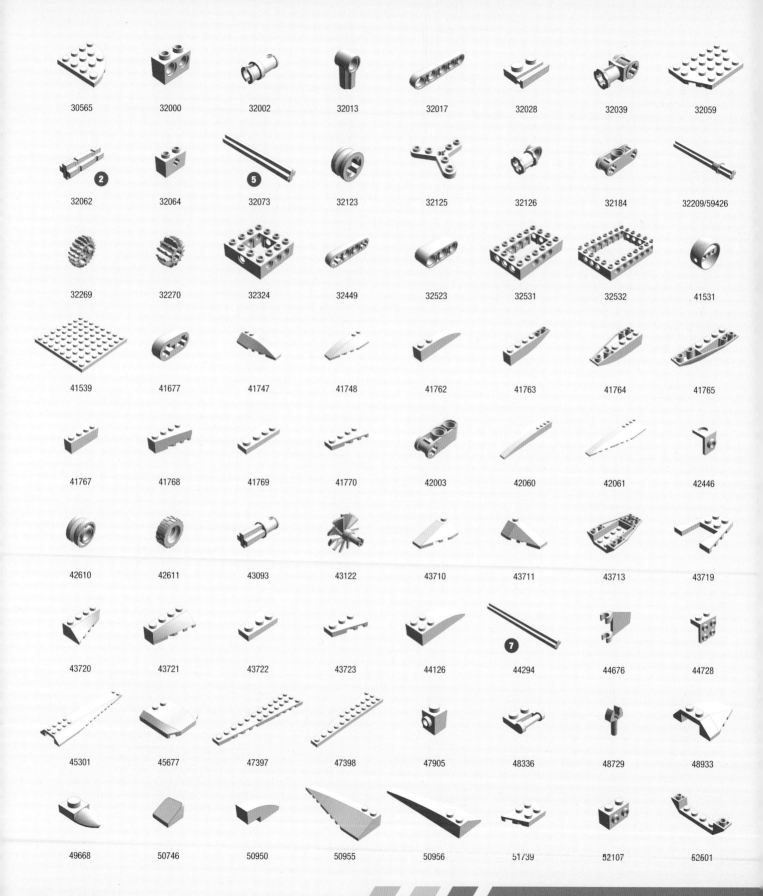

30565 32000 32002 32013 32017 32028 32039 32059

32062 32064 32073 32123 32125 32126 32184 32209/59426

32269 32270 32324 32449 32523 32531 32532 41531

41539 41677 41747 41748 41762 41763 41764 41765

41767 41768 41769 41770 42003 42060 42061 42446

42610 42611 43093 43122 43710 43711 43713 43719

43720 43721 43722 43723 44126 44294 44676 44728

45301 45677 47397 47398 47905 48336 48729 48933

49668 50746 50950 50955 50956 51739 52107 52601

54383  54384  55981  55982  56902  58090  58176  59443

60219  60470  60474  60477  60478  60481  61254  61409

61678/11153  61930c01  63864  63868  63965  64727  72454  73081

73587  73983  85080  85861  85970  85984  87079  87081

87083  87087  87580  87994  89762  91988  92279  92280

92409  92947  93273  93550  93606  98138  98282  99012

99207  99780  99781

# RESOURCES

## COMMUNITY

There is a great community around the world of children and adults who love LEGO®. There are LEGO clubs in almost every country where LEGO is sold. Aircraft is only one small building theme among hundreds, but for almost all of them you can find a like-minded group in some small corner of the internet. The internet and LEGO community also have image-sharing and other services that can be useful, no matter what your building subject matter is. The following websites may be a useful starting point:

Official LEGO website: www.lego.com

Bricklink (part purchase): www.bricklink.com/v2/mainpage

News and amazing creations of all types: www.brothers-brick.com

Extensive online LEGO community: www.eurobricks.com/forum

LEGO cars, aircraft, and other vehicles: www.thelegocarbolog.com

## HELP! I DON'T HAVE ANY TECHNIC®— HOW CAN I BUILD THE COMPLEX MODELS?

To this good question, I have two answers:

If your LEGO collection lacks any of the pieces required to build the model, never fear, there are ways and means of obtaining these parts. It does involve making purchases over the internet, and this is best done by a trusted adult. You can buy parts directly from the LEGO Company via the LEGO Shop@Home service—a place to purchase full LEGO sets, but also spare parts. This website is available across most of Europe, Asia, and the Americas. Alternatively, you can purchase online via a service called Bricklink. Bricklink is a web-service face for thousands of individual stores around the world. Most will be able to supply common parts, while some others will also be able to supply specialist and rare parts. The LEGO Company has no affiliation with the Bricklink service, so there are more risks associated with pricing, purchase, and shipping.

Except for the P-38 Lightning, there are very few Technic® parts used in any of the models, and those parts that are used are relatively common. If you are going to build the P-38 Lightning, though, you are probably going to be spending a lot of time on Bricklink, regardless.

## PRINTED BRICKS

Thanks to the team at The Big Brick online store, you are able to order the printed parts seen in this book. The decals are available for delivery worldwide. To add a little extra pizzazz to your aircraft, follow the link below:

http://www.thebigbrick.com/index.php/aircraft-parts-c-43

Printed parts are included in the following models:
- Northrop-Grumman B-2 Spirit (page 24)
- Lockheed-Martin F-35 Lightning II (page 86)
- Lockheed SR-71 Blackbird (page 106)
- Lockheed P-38 Lightning (page 130)

Additionally, The Big Brick has printed nameplates for each of the smaller Miniplanes, and the team is also able to provide custom brick-printing services.

## ABOUT THE AUTHOR

**PETER BLACKERT**, known within the Lego community as lego911, is one of the foremost builders of LEGO® scale-model transport. His first book, *How to Build Brick Cars,* showcased his artistic and engineering talents. In this follow-up book, Peter demonstrates this mechanical talent as he extends it in to the realm of aircraft.

Peter's full-time profession is at Ford Motor Company's Asia-Pacific Engineering Centres in Geelong and Melbourne, Australia. His focus is on Powertrain and Chassis Systems Engineering within the Advanced Vehicle Architecture team—skills that are transferred to the detailed engineering in many of his LEGO vehicles. Peter studied Systems Engineering at the University of Sydney and the Australian National University.